Three Years in Wonderland

Three Years in
WONDERLAND

The Disney Brothers, C. V. Wood, and the
Making of the Great American Theme Park

Todd James Pierce

University Press of Mississippi / Jackson

www.upress.state.ms.us

The University Press of Mississippi is a member
of the Association of American University Presses.

First printing 2016
∞
Library of Congress Cataloging-in-Publication Data available

ISBN 978-1-62846-241-8 (hardback)
ISBN 978-1-4968-0381-8 (ebook)

British Library Cataloging-in-Publication Data available

Everybody said, "What the hell's he want that damn amusement park for?" And I couldn't think of a good reason except—I don't know—I wanted it.

—**WALT DISNEY,** on the origins of Disneyland

We fought.

—**C. V. WOOD,** on his relationship with Walt Disney

Contents

Three Years in Wonderland

One

HOW THE STORY ENDS

Six months after Disneyland opened, the Disney brothers fired the park's first general manager. Their reasons likely included mismanagement and fraud, perhaps arson as well.

The first general manager of Disneyland was not an animator, nor was he a longtime studio employee. The first general manager was a tall, no-nonsense Texan named C. V. Wood, a man without any previous experience in the outdoor amusements industry. He was a conman, a jokester, a person who'd forged his own college degree. By most accounts, he was warm, personable, and exceptionally loyal. Insightful and brilliant, he was too smart for school. He was a man fascinated with Hollywood, determined to make his mark in Tinsel Town. In this regard, he was a success.

In his lifetime, Walt Disney only opened a single amusement park—Disneyland in Anaheim, California—but C. V. Wood opened many.

Shortly after leaving the Disney brothers, Wood—more often referred to as Woody—started a consulting firm, called Marco Engineering, that designed Disneyland-style theme parks for investment groups around the world. Woody started out small, working with only a few ex-Disneyland employees on a project called Pacific Ocean Park. One year later, he employed over a dozen men who once worked for Walt. By the end of the 1950s, he had hired nearly 100 studio artists, architects, engineers, and operations specialists—many of them money-whipped out of the Disney stables with higher salaries and generous benefits.

To the press, Woody once boasted that he would build "some 35 [Disneyland-style parks] throughout the country."[1] He opened outdoor extravaganzas in California, Colorado, and Massachusetts. He designed and oversaw the development of the first Six Flags park in Texas. In 1960, he completed a near-perfect replica of Disneyland a few miles from Manhattan, a park called Freedomland. It was the largest and most expensive fun center in the world.

In speaking to reporters, Woody openly called himself the "Master Planner of Disneyland." With clients, he minimized Walt's contributions to Disneyland, telling one that "Walt made wonderful movies and invented Mickey Mouse, but he didn't know anything about theme parks."[2] His promotional materials removed Walt from Disneyland, claiming that Disneyland was primarily built by "the team of C. V. Wood and Roy Disney."[3]

For this, Walt sued him.

If you read through both the first and second editions of *Disney A–Z*, a massive company encyclopedia, you'll find entries for Bill Evans, the man who landscaped Disneyland, and Admiral Joe Fowler, the man who oversaw much of the park's construction. You'll even find a few sentences on Van Arsdale France, the man who wrote the original employee training manual. But you'll find no entry for C. V. Wood. His name has been carefully scrubbed from almost all official Disney publications.[4]

But the fact remains that aside from Walt Disney, C. V. Wood was the single greatest contributor to the American theme park culture of the 1950s and 1960s. In some ways, his influence was more pervasive than that of Walt Disney. In his later years, Woody formed yet another company to create planned communities across the Southwest, towns that incorporated the extravagance and themed space of a Disneyland-style park. His most famous project, Lake Havasu City in Arizona, was a resort community built around a quaint English-style village. Spanning the nearby lake was the London Bridge—the *actual* London Bridge, which Woody shipped, stone by stone, to Arizona, where he reconstructed it over sand. The town, he figured, needed a tourist icon, much like a theme park needed a castle.

For Woody, the lesson of Disneyland was simple: he believed that Americans were drawn to spectacle, that they wanted to live in an environment that felt as large as a Hollywood movie. Woody and his designers changed America: they created theme parks; they built themed residential communities; men from his company later designed malls and reworked Las Vegas hotels into a series of cinematic showpieces. But the work of C. V. Wood is mostly forgotten.

Runners-up are rarely extolled for their vision and greatness.

When I first approached the Walt Disney Company to obtain information on C. V. Wood, I was told that the records on Woody's employment were beyond the public's reach, locked up in their legal department. One member of the Walt Disney Archives went so far as to explain that the files on C. V. Wood were not even available for *him* to review.[5]

Over the following eight years, as I researched material for this book, I developed a good working relationship with a few people at the Walt Disney Company. They provided me with a great deal of useful information—such as dates and notations from Walt Disney's personal datebook and contact information for retired employees who had worked for the company during the 1950s—but each time I broached the subject of C. V. Wood, I received the exact same response—including one such note from Dave Smith, founder of the company archives: "I regret that we cannot make copies of these items [available] for you."[6]

Some retired Disneyland employees also refused to comment on C. V. Wood. "I won't talk about that kind of stuff," the park's first accountant told me. "I find talking about those things untoward."[7]

For me, it soon became clear that the files on C. V. Wood were kept in the Disney legal department because, at some point—most likely, decades ago—company executives no longer wanted C. V. Wood included in its public history or in the history of Disneyland. There were also legal issues concerning C. V. Wood and Disney. But that only made me believe that the actual story of Disneyland was far more interesting than the version presented in old press materials—a story that spoke not only to Disneyland but to how that first cinematic theme park changed America.

That story, I soon learned, was largely focused on C. V. Wood.

Two

THE OTHER WALT DISNEY

Though C. V. Wood often described himself as a Texan, he didn't start his life in the Lone Star State. Woody was born on December 17, 1920, in the border town of Waynoka, Oklahoma. His family lived in a white brick house, centered on two acres of grassland, only a block from the train station where his father worked as a conductor and brakeman on the Santa Fe line from Waynoka to Amarillo, Texas. C. V. Jr. was most likely named after his father, Commodore Vanderbilt Wood,[1] though throughout his adult life he denied this connection to his family's interest in the railroad industry and felt that Commodore Vanderbilt sounded too working-class. As an adult, he was fond of telling business associates that he was "C-for-nothing V-for-nothing Wood."[2]

At the time of his birth, Woody was a large baby—so large that his family would later claim that he weighed 12 pounds. His mother, Eva Beaman Wood, had so wanted a girl that when she first heard her child was a boy, she began to weep, "It's a boy," to her sister even though she was still half-sedated with ether. "Oh, I don't want a boy," she cried. In his early years, his mother often dressed him in gender-neutral clothes, such as peg-top rompers. During his first year, his long hair lightened to a golden blond. More than once, his mother and his aunt put a little rouge on his cheeks and tried to pass him off as a girl, lamenting to each other, "Oh, wouldn't he have made the sweetest little girl?" But one day, when he was around three, as his mother and aunt were telling him how much they loved him, how handsome he was, Woody replied: "Yes, but you didn't want a boy. You wanted a girl. You want me to be a girl."[3]

It was only then that his mother and his aunt realized that their games of dress-up had affected him. Never again did they say one word to him about wanting a girl. But the experience left an impression on the young Wood, as following this realization, he began to forcibly embrace the strong masculine roles available to him. He wanted people to know he was a boy—and a tough boy at that.[4]

When he was young, C. V. Wood was never C. V., as his family was fond of nicknames. His father was rarely called by his given name, preferring to be called either Senior or Hunky[5]. As for the young C. V., his friends and teachers called him Junior, though later these same people would call him Woody and sometimes Woodsy. In public, his mother called him J. R., a derivative of Junior, but in private, she called him Sweet-Boy—a pet name that Woody's friends would tease him about for years.[6]

He spent his early years in Waynoka, which offered his family a good deal of culture and entertainment since it was one of the nation's largest rail hubs. At the age of five, Woody so loved the movies, westerns in particular, that he asked his parents to buy him a cowboy outfit like the one Tom Mix wore on screen. For Woody, however, the most important part of his outfit was not the cowhide vest or the empty gun holsters on his belt—it was the lariat.

For days, he attempted to teach himself to twirl the lariat like the cowboys he looked up to in movies, but he was unable to mimic their tricks. Each time he tried to spin the lasso into a loop, the rope struck the ground. Taking pity on him, his grandfather finally stood Woody on an old orange crate to give him extra height. He demonstrated how to hold the rope between his thumb and forefinger and then how to turn a flat loop, the most basic trick, in which the loop spun at a roper's side. Woody spent days practicing the flat loop, turning the rope first at his ankles, then his calves, then his knees—until he no longer needed the orange crate at all.

At the picture show, he paid special attention to the way the cowboys moved their lariats: passing the rope from hand to hand and making the loop so large they could step through it. Once he arrived home, he attempted to execute some of these maneuvers with mixed results. But with the help of ranch hands bringing cattle to town, he learned to twirl the rope with a showman's flair: he learned a trick called the merry-go-round, in which he moved the rope from side to side; he learned the wedding ring, a trick in which he encircled himself with the spinning rope; and he even learned the Texas Skip, in which he hopped through the loop—not dissimilar from an elaborate game of jump rope.

But before he started first grade, his father, Hunky Wood, received a promotion, causing his family to move to the slightly more affluent city of Amarillo, Texas. Despite his parents' worries that Woody would have trouble adjusting to the new town, he adored Amarillo, so much so that in later interviews he occasionally claimed to have been born there.[7]

His family's move did have one curious effect on the young Wood. Forced to make friends in a new town, he courted them with his lariat. On the day the Wood family moved into a new rental, Woody met a neighborhood boy named Eugene Lemmon, whom he would later call by the nickname Doc. Hoping the neighborhood kids would like him, Woody dressed in his Tom Mix cowboy duds—a leather vest and sheepskin chaps, as well as boots. Toy guns were holstered on his belt. As Doc Lemmon recalls: "To my complete surprise and envy, he began to twirl the rope and jumped through it as he spun it from side to side."[8] Lemmon was so impressed that even as a boy he knew that there was something special about C. V. Wood. Woody, he understood, was going places.

◆ ◆ ◆

In school, Woody was an average student, though close friends remember him as one of the brightest individuals in their class and particularly quick with numbers. Friends recall that he could perform three-digit multiplication in his head. By the tracks, he regularly bet adults ten cents that he could remember all of the numbers on the boxcars as a train pulled through town—a trick that brought him a good deal of pocket change.[9] But as his friend Jim House explains, Woody was bored with academics because he was thinking of other things: "He basically went through his public school . . . on cruise control."[10] In place of academic studies, Woody ran about town with his classmates, trying to find new ways to earn money because, even in elementary school, he no longer wanted to appear poor. Aside from the boxcar wagers, one of his early ventures was to set up a neighborhood store, whereby he bought candy and packaged cookies from a downtown grocer and sold them to neighborhood children at a profit. Being only nine years old when he started this business, he obtained the candy by "charging" his purchases to his parents' account. At the end of each month, he was careful to repay all of his debts before his mom received the grocery bill.

Later that same year, he entered an amateur talent contest held at the movie house, where he twirled his lariat for the judges, jumping through the hoop and roping members of the audience as though they were cattle. During the finale, he performed the wedding ring, a favorite trick, the rope rotating around his body like a giant belt. At the end of his performance, he stood center stage, his rope coiled in one hand as the audience cheered loudly for him.

He waited in the theater as other children sang and played musical instruments, but at the end of the evening, he was called back on stage where he was awarded first prize, beating out children who had received professional training in ballet, piano, and voice. He stood in a hoop of light as one judge handed him a blue ribbon and the applause of the audience again swelled through the auditorium.

Noticing the achievement of their son, Woody's parents contacted his grandmother in Los Angeles, who later made arrangements for Woody to appear in a local vaudeville variety show. During his eleventh or twelfth summer—as well as the one that followed—Woody traveled to Los Angeles, using a free train pass from his father. He spent most of his days in a pool hall, owned by one of his grandmother's boyfriends, where he learned the basics of pool-hall life, which included running games and trading jokes with older men. As one friend recalls, "He was at the height of his glory, hanging around the pool hall."[11] But at night, his grandmother took him to the theater, where he performed his rope tricks for city folk, which no doubt included some people from the film community. Again, he was greeted with enthusiastic applause—not just for his rope tricks, but for his curious accent and Texas sayings. Such appearances told Woody in very clear terms that the public liked him, especially when he used his Lone Star charm.

At the age of twelve or thirteen, he developed close relationships—ones that would define his later life—with a group of restless boys he met mostly through the Boy Scouts, which included his longtime friend Doc Lemmon. Originally the group called themselves "the Four Bombers," which was a reference to a World War I movie in which four bomber pilots were as close as brothers. But the concept of the Four Bombers quickly swelled to include nine boys, at which time they became simply the Bombers.[12]

For the most part, the Bombers came from poor or middle-class households, with many of their families struggling through the Great Depression, though at least two of the Bombers came from reasonably prosperous backgrounds. Earl Shelton's father owned the town's creamery, and Charlie

Thompson's family owned a downtown hotel called the Herring. For his part, Woody did not come from a well-off family. As one of the Bombers, Paul Skillman, explains, his family was mostly supported by Hunky's railroad salary: "And a guy with the railroad wasn't making all that much money. But at least he had a job."[13]

Without exception, the boys dreamed of becoming rich and having a good time. "The nature of Wood was tremendous loyalty," his business partner, Buzz Price later wrote in his memoir. "He was a rascal, but capable of total loyalty."[14] For Woody, the Bombers were quickly becoming his true family—their antics replacing the workaday tediousness of his home life.

The social arrangement of these boys also cast Woody as a leader of sorts. Though officially they considered themselves all "vice presidents" of the Bombers, without doubt, Woody was the main Bomber. He arranged pranks; he figured out ways to get booze; he pushed his friends to enjoy life, even if that meant acting rowdy or boisterous.

"Wood had a rather unique way of preparing for a Boy Scout hike," one of the Bombers later revealed. "Where everybody else took along canteens, tents, stakes, and things like that, Wood usually started out with a half gallon of wine." Another Bomber explained Woody's role more simply: "He had something the rest of us didn't have"—by which he meant the ability to ignore those in authority and live by his own rules.

For fun, Woody would fill his water gun with ink, throw water balloons at passing cars, drive through the poor sections of town and call everyone a bastard before quickly driving away. Along with other Bombers, he staged butter fights inside the Shelton family creamery; he organized mud-ball attacks against boys who ridiculed the Bombers; more than once he asked his friends to distract a teacher while he quietly left a tack on the man's chair.

Most memorably, when the rival football team from Lubbock came to Amarillo for a north Texas grudge match, Woody went downtown and bought three cases of rotten eggs, which he then carried to the railroad crossing at Thirty-sixth Street, where he met up with the Bombers. "When the Lubbock special came by after the game with all of those windows up," one of the boys recalls, "we thoroughly raked those spectators over with rotten eggs, except for one little item. Earl Shelton threw one egg, and he hit some girl right in the mouth."

The boys, all of them, simply died laughing.[15]

On warm spring nights, Woody, in his one good suit jacket, attended church revival meetings, where he pretended to accept the preacher's call for salvation. He was a master of rolling on the floor, screaming in tongues, and completely disrupting the service to the amusement of his friends. "[Preachers] used to hit you over the head and say, *you're saved, you're saved*. So [Woody] went and did one better," one of the Bombers recalls. "I remember him picking up a mandolin and hitting somebody over the head, claiming that he was saving them."[16]

To get into the movie theater without paying the five-cent admission, the nine Bombers would line up single file, leaving the chubby Charlie Thompson at the back. When each boy approached the box-office window, he'd say, "You see that fat boy back there. He's got my money." At which time, Thompson would hold up a dollar bill. The first eight boys would pass into the theater without further questions, but when the woman in the box office asked for the money, Thompson would indignantly exclaim, "Why, I've never seen those boys before in my life. I was holding up the dollar for my mother, who's already come to take it."

Once inside, the antics didn't stop. When the house lights would come on at intermission, one Bomber, named Curt Bellis, would call out, "It's all gone. It's *all* gone." Earl Shelton, who had earlier moved to the front row, away from the group, would reply, "*What's* all gone?" To which Bellis would point to a bald man sitting a few rows away. "Why, the hair on this guy's head!"[17]

Though this routine was initiated by Bellis, such practical jokes almost always were dreamed up by Woody. "These ideas never cropped up among the rest of us," John Bryson later explained. "Wood was the one who brainstormed all these things."[18]

But along with his natural leadership ability, his friends also noticed one other dominant quality in Woody: his ability to mask feelings of insecurity and shame. As was their habit, the members of the Boy Scouts, which included the Bombers, gave each other nicknames. John Bryson became Redwood; Eugene Lemmon became Doc; Paul Skillman became Beetle; and chubby Charlie Thompson became Bloto. Initially, the name the boys gave Woody was Foghorn because of his booming voice. "He had this big, deep loud voice. Teachers would call roll the first day in class, and when they got to C. V. Wood, you'd hear this guy in the back yell, 'HEEEERE!'"[19] But over time, the boys changed his name to Foggy because, even then, they understood that there was a fog around Wood, a warm expansive personality that could conceal his true thoughts. "Wood had this false front," explains Paul Skillman, "this typical bravado."[20]

As a teenager, he chased local girls and regularly reported the details of his sexual escapades to the Bombers. Down by the army base, he attempted to visit prostitutes and became such good friends with the local madam that she occasionally asked about him when she saw the Bombers in town. For spending money, he convinced his friend Earl Shelton to steal bottles of milk from his father's dairy only to dump out the milk and return the bottles for the ten-cent deposit, which they spent on snacks and gas. During these same months, however, Woody diligently completed the last required merit badges to become an Eagle Scout because he believed such distinction would help him get into college or find a high-paying job later in life. He also worked on his lariat tricks, occasionally performing with the school's marching band, where he was admired by both schoolgirls and members of town. He was the embodiment of opposites, a paradox even for those who knew him: "I remember him with some awe as a baby-faced gangster," one classmate recalls. "He smoked, drank gin, did unspeakable things with girls, and stole his folks' car for joyrides. But then strangely at the other end of the pendulum he was an Eagle Scout."[21] He was a boy who wanted to live without regard for traditional rules, yet a boy deathly afraid that he would be poor like most people he knew in Amarillo. On his best days, he felt pushed toward some important destiny, some glimmering future he could not yet see, but in his darkest moments, he suspected he was headed toward sure failure.

Before graduating high school, the Bombers made an adolescent pledge: the first person to make a million dollars would give $10,000 to each of the other members. The gift was seed money, an opportunity for each boy to overcome childhood poverty and finally earn his millions. On the night of the pledge, the boys shook hands, each of them solemnly understanding that in the world of the 1930s Depression, they would need to look out for each other because their parents might not be able to.

Years later, Doc Lemmon would sum up the Bombers' close bonds with each other in simple language: "We were like brothers."[22]

In certain superficial ways, C. V. Wood's childhood was similar to that of Walt Disney. Both boys came from working-class families in rural towns. Wood's father was a conductor and brakeman on the Amarillo-Waynoka leg of the Santa Fe Railroad;

Walt's father managed a failing farm and later supervised a newspaper delivery business.[23] Both boys loved to entertain. In college, Wood became the star of the Hardin-Simmons University Cowboy Marching Band, where he performed the last of his lariat tricks.[24] Walt performed skits at school, most famously reciting Lincoln's Gettysburg Address while costumed in a dark jacket and a stovepipe hat. They carried the imprint of their childhood identities for life—Walt, the reserved Midwesterner who loved to tell stories, and Woody, the boy from Texas who yearned to make his life *into* a story.

Though they dreamed of rising above their initial circumstances, they were yoked to their childhoods as well. During his film career, Walt continually dipped into the rich well of youthful experience, setting early cartoons on farms that reminded him of rural Missouri. Woody, however, desired a more portable connection to his childhood. Throughout his life, he hired his childhood friends, the Bombers, asking them to move with him from one job to the next.

From an academic standpoint, his time at Hardin-Simmons College was not remarkable, though it's hard to imagine a more unlikely candidate to attend a religious university than C. V. Wood. While there, he maintained his adolescent role as the leader of the Bombers, twirling his rope and arranging elaborate pranks, many of which were now aimed at those who attempted to control him.

Early in his college career, he sensed that the dean did not like him—particularly his late-night drinking, his constant smoking, and the reports of women going to his room. In the college chapel, Woody noticed a portrait of this same dean hanging on the wall, a portrait that presented the man behind a mahogany desk, holding a leather-bound book (most likely a Bible), so the night before a traveling revival service arrived at the college, Woody pasted a photograph of a whisky bottle clipped from a magazine onto the portrait so that it appeared as though the dean were not holding a book but instead toting a bottle of booze. He also attached a stick of white paper to the dean's lower lip, cut to look like a hand-rolled cigarette. In effect, he turned the dean into an older version of C. V. Wood.

During the revival service, while the dignitaries were seated near the altar, a few students started tittering, their heads angled up toward the portrait. The laughter quickly grew. "It was a human wave," one classmate recalls. "It spread and spread until the whole chapel was laughing."[25] In many ways, this was C. V. Wood's adolescent dream: to live in a world where people were just like him—to live in the world of the Bombers.

He lasted barely two years at Hardin-Simmons, though from his academic record it is unclear if he was even continually enrolled during that period. He took mainly general education courses—and curiously one course in journalism—earning many low and failing grades.[26] "He was a troublemaker from the day he hit school," his friend Roy Lofton later explained. "He was smart enough. There wasn't any real doubt about that. . . . The only way he ever made it through college was because he could throw that goddamn lariat [with the marching band] . . . His conduct was bizarre. He'd do everything from paint the dean's house to blow up the barn. He was constantly up to pranks. He just had that look about him: that sweet, kind face, and the mind of a goddamn criminal."[27]

Repeatedly he was suspended for his high jinks, though he was never actually expelled. Sensing trouble on the horizon, Woody applied to and was accepted by the University of Oklahoma, which was a big step forward in his college career. He entered the school immediately after leaving Hardin-Simmons, in the summer of 1939, and set about to earn a degree in—of all things—petroleum engineering. As neither he nor his family was able to fully afford tuition and fees, a good part of Woody's education was paid for by one of his aunts, an arrangement that must have told Woody in clear terms that he did not have much of a financial cushion on which to fall back if he did not succeed at this new school.

He began on the right foot in Oklahoma because, as one of his friends observed, "he knew that he needed to turn around a little bit."[28] He didn't want to end up like a lot of other people back in his hometown, living in a small house bordered only by an apron of dirt. He wanted something more for himself: good meals, nice clothes, and long vacations. To this end, he attended classes, even joined Phi Kappa Sigma, where many of his fraternity brothers were successfully moving through difficult programs of study. In his classes, he again found that he was good with numbers. He could do most calculations for the entry-level engineering courses in his head.

But over long weekends he felt that old restlessness. With friends, he hitchhiked to nearby cities, such as Galveston, Dallas, and Houston, attempting to learn what he could about the world. Often he would spend the night in a hotel but leave early in the morning without paying the bill, creating the only vacation he could afford, one without cost. But even these wayward trips were more of a vacation than some of the Bombers had known as children.

Officially, he separated from the University of Oklahoma in December of 1940, though some of his friends remember him hanging around campus for the rest of the school year. With very few options left to him, he began to apply for jobs—pretty much any job he thought would pay well. In the spring of 1941, he applied to be an hourly wage riveter at Consolidated Vultee, which was a company that manufactured aircraft in Texas, though the company is perhaps better known by its later name, Convair.

Nearly broke, Woody showed up to the interview in his best clothes, looking more like a college student than a blue-collar worker. He considered the position a temporary solution—assuming he was hired for it—until he could find a better job.

Yet the events of that Consolidated interview formed a story he would tell for years, the strange tale of how he entered professional life.

One version appeared in a 1969 issue of *Esquire* magazine:

In this version, Woody described himself as a "newly graduated engineer" who "tried to pass himself off as a riveter" at Consolidated Vultee. But the personnel committee was so charmed by him that when he finally "confessed to his diploma," they decided to hire him anyway. Perhaps they were taken with his confident manner, perhaps with his desperation. But they didn't hire him as an hourly wage riveter, rather as an entry-level engineer in the inspections department—a job that wasn't even advertised. In short, they hired him for a position that most University of Oklahoma engineering graduates could only dream of being offered.[29]

There was only one problem.

Though it is true that Woody applied for a job as an hourly wage riveter and it is also true that he was hired to work in the inspections department as an engineer, it is not true that Woody possessed a degree in engineering—or any other such college degree for that matter. He had left Hardin-Simmons without a degree, and later, left the University of Oklahoma without a degree as well. Moreover, his combined college credits would, at best, give him junior standing at most universities. At some point during his job interview, he must have sensed that it would be advantageous to claim he possessed such a degree. He presented the claim; the personnel committee believed it; no calls were made to the university to confirm his status as a graduate; and within days, he was working as an engineer for one of America's leading aircraft companies.[30]

In 1941, a new graduate of the University of Oklahoma's engineering program would earn about $20 per week. But by the time Woody finished talking with the personnel committee, he had convinced them that he would be such a valuable asset to Consolidated that he was offered $40 per week to start. Plus overtime.

From that day forward, Woody would tell all of his coworkers, friends, and even the Bombers that he was in fact a graduate of the University of Oklahoma's prestigious engineering program. Though one or two of the Bombers privately doubted the validity of this claim, none of them ever challenged him. The information concerning his college degree would exist inside the shimmering mist of C. V. "Foggy" Wood for the rest of his life.

There was, however, one catch: this new job at Consolidated would not be located in their Texas facilities. It would be at their plant in San Diego, California.

As a young man, away from the Bombers for the first time, Woody threw himself into his work, most likely hoping that his enormous efforts would successfully disguise his lack of proper training. "One time at Consolidated," one Bomber explains, "he was supposed to make a report that his boss thought would take a week or more. He worked that day and that night and the next day and the next night, then he had it complete. He didn't work on it six hours or eight hours a day. He worked on it twenty-four hours a day," completing a seven-day project in about two days.[31]

His first boss, Fred Schumacher, was impressed by Wood's efforts. Moreover, he took an immediate liking to Wood. He liked Wood's attitude and his racy jokes. He liked his exaggerated Texas accent, such as how he pronounced *po*lice with the emphasis on the "po" and how he called soda "so*dee* pop."[32] He liked how Wood fit in well with the other guys and the unusual sense of determination that emanated from him.

Within a few months, Wood felt comfortable in his job, sure that no one would ever check up on his bogus degree. He abandoned his temporary lodgings and found better accommodations at the La Jolla Beach and Tennis Club, whose back doors opened to the sugar cane sand of the Pacific. Yet he experienced moments of loneliness so strong that, by the end of summer, he was actively soliciting jobs for other Bombers— particularly those who, with *actual* degrees, had not yet been able to find meaningful work after college.

He brought good friend Earl Shelton out to San Diego, then Robert Lemmon, who shared his apartment at the Tennis Club. One evening, Woody called Quentin Lewis, a young man who had actually graduated from the University of Oklahoma in Engineering. "Come on out to California," Woody told him. "I'll get you a job working at Consolidated tomorrow, making a dollar an hour. And all the overtime you want."[33]

For Quentin, the decision was easy. Despite his degree, he was managing a service station, making $75 a month. Along with the satisfaction of finally becoming an engineer, he was taken with the impressive salary: the offer represented a pay raise of roughly 125 percent.

Not long after Quentin Lewis and his wife left for San Diego, Doc Lemmon and his wife, Mary Jo, made plans to move there as well, as Woody had also found Doc a job at Consolidated.

By the end of the year, half of the original Bombers lived in San Diego, all thanks to the efforts of Woody. At least one more Bomber, Charlie Thompson, would soon come to California as well. In effect, Woody had recreated his childhood gang inside the offices and manufacturing plant of Consolidated Vultee. But the Bombers noticed some changes in Woody. Though he still loved to have a good time, C. V. Wood was more work-oriented than he'd ever been back in Texas. "He wasn't quite as wild," Quentin Lewis observed. "He had calmed down a little."[34]

As fall gave way to winter, Woody noticed that many of his friends were married, including many of his new business associates in California. "He always thought that Shirley and I had just such a good deal being married," Quentin Lewis recalls, "that he decided that he wanted to be married." With his vacation time, Woody planned to return to Amarillo, where a few of the Bombers still lived, but before leaving he told his friends in California his specific plans: "I'll go home and get married and have a wife before I come back."[35]

In Amarillo, he visited the remaining Bombers, telling them about the good life he was enjoying in California. He also returned to his old haunts, which included the Herring Hotel owned by Charlie Thompson's parents. While at a hotel Christmas party, he fell for a local girl named Margo Dickinson, who was four years younger than him. The initial meeting was most likely made while Woody was talking with Curtis Bellis, one of the Bombers still in Texas, as Curtis was presently dating Margo. But Woody's attraction was so strong that he began to flirt with Margo even while Curtis was in the room. Margo felt a similar attraction for Woody, a boy about whom she had heard many stories.

The courtship began slowly, with Curtis Bellis conceding Margo's affection to the more prominent Wood, even though Bellis's emotions for her ran deep. Wood saw her repeatedly while he was in Amarillo. He made at least one more visit (and likely a few more beyond that) to Amarillo until in 1942 he proposed marriage.

The wedding was planned as a formal affair, though everyone soon learned that the celebration itself would involve the Bombers almost as much as it would Margo.

On the night before the wedding, the Bombers took Woody out for an endless round of drinks. After he passed out, they stripped him and painted his body with household paint, including his private areas (they attempted to paint his left testicle red and his right one green), the colors so deep that the following day, beneath his tuxedo his body still bore the rich insignia of the previous night's festivities.[36] At the ceremony,

Woody naturally chose Bombers as his best men. And for the photographer, he chose a "Junior Bomber" named John Bryson; that is, he chose one of the younger boys who used to hang around with the Bombers.

As the couple exchanged vows Woody understood what he most wanted from this marriage, a union to solidify the intimate community of his youth no matter where he moved in the future.

After the honeymoon, Woody returned with his bride to San Diego. His friends all believed that Woody and Margo were happy for a time, Woody being a romantic and Margo enamored with her new life in California. But Woody also loved work. He loved the sense of accomplishment it gave him and the camaraderie with other men.

But success at work came with a price. "Margo was lonely because Wood was a workaholic," explains Shirley Lewis, who was the wife of the Bomber, Quentin Lewis. "About every other day she would call me and want to know what I was doing."[37] The loneliness was probably nothing more than the sense of isolation many young housewives felt in the 1940s, but still it was there, that separation, creating small tensions for the newlyweds.

At work, Woody was receiving promotions and was now a supervisor. Ironically, he oversaw individuals who were far better trained and educated than himself. With the Bombers and with new friends, he went out to bars, where he drank, flirted with women, then slunk home late at night. Even then, he must have felt that old wildness slowly seeping back into his life.

Around Consolidated, he would pull pranks—such as leaving a thumbtack on the chair of a colleague or stapling shut the sleeves on a coworker's suit jacket—but people loved his antics. These practical jokes were part of his charming Texas personality. Every few months, he and his friends would escape to Mexico, where they would behave like bachelors, eating spicy food, drinking all night, chasing beautiful, dark-skinned women, and chatting up hookers.

Still, his one significant problem remained the divide between work and marriage. "He put the job ahead of Margo," Quentin Lewis explains, "which he's going to do. You can bet on that. And she was never very happy with it." He also put his friends ahead of his marriage, as the Bombers were still his true family.[38]

This point was made clear when John Bryson, who was still known by his Junior Bomber nickname of Redwood, announced that he was coming to California. He had been working as a photographer for *Life* magazine in Chicago and was being promoted to their Los Angeles office. As he was driving cross-country he read in the Tucson paper that a minor earthquake had just hit San Diego. Believing that he might match the self-congratulatory antics of Woody, he sent a telegram to his old friend: "Even the earth trembles when the great Bryson approaches." After explaining the situation to a Western Union clerk in Arizona, he said: "Now let him top that!"

The next day, as Bryson drove toward San Diego, he thought he saw a small hand-painted sign at the side of the highway announcing "Welcome Redwood," but by the time he turned to get a better look, it was behind him. Then he saw another sign, slightly larger this time, nailed to a tree, reading, "Welcome Redwood." Then mile after mile, hour after hour, there were signs all over the highway. "Sure enough," he later recalled, "I came around the corner in some little hamlet not far from San Diego and there, stretched across the highway, was a huge banner saying, 'Welcome Redwood.' Beneath it was an open convertible containing Wood in a top hat playing a trombone, [Doc] Lemmon playing a guitar, and the rest of the Bombers playing I don't know what. They had worked for days on this. They had painted; they had planned; they had driven out into the desert and put the signs up."

For Bryson, the point of the story was obvious: Woody's extraordinary resolve and determination, his love of spectacle, and his loyalty to his childhood friends. When asked about the incident, Bryson exclaimed, "You can't top the son of a bitch. He's always planning ahead."[39] But there was another point missed by Bryson: Woody's gestures of love were far grander when they were directed at his friends than they were when directed at his family. He was good at work, good as a friend, but he was not particularly good as a family man.

At the age of twenty-seven, Woody received a significant promotion at Consolidated and became the chief industrial engineer to supervise construction of the B-24 Liberator Bomber. Again, this promotion placed him in charge of individuals who were far better trained than he was. But already Woody understood that his natural abilities lay not with the minutiae of projects, but with people. Despite his boisterous manner and love of dirty jokes, people liked him. They liked the way he drew out his words with a theatrical Texas accent. They liked the way he looked at them with his steady, good-natured gaze. They liked the way he greeted them, a hand on their shoulders or upper arms. Most of all, they liked the way he laughed with a series of loud guffaws. They found it contagious.

As part of his new position Woody made regular trips to Washington, D.C., acting not only as project manager but as a type of salesman and junior executive, smoothing out problems between the Pentagon and Consolidated. The men at the Pentagon liked Woody a great deal, more so than most men Consolidated sent their way. Woody found that he liked the officers at the Pentagon as well. The military, he discovered, was just another men's club.

Early one morning, after boarding the midnight flight from San Diego to Washington, D.C., he felt once again that his life was directed toward some grandness. He was sleepy, a little tipsy, but he felt strong. He was ready for whatever life would throw his way. As he looked out the curved cabin window, he saw a cluster of city lights far below him. From the airplane, those lights appeared like a faraway galaxy. He was somewhere over the middle of the country. For all he knew, above north Texas, thousands of feet above the small house his parents once rented. Down there was his old life. In this plane, his new one. Strapped into his airline seat, he felt a strange sensation expand in his chest, a carbonated emotion he'd first experienced as a teenager in the Boy Scouts: he felt the finger of providence pushing him toward a destination he could not yet see.

The stewardess interrupted his thoughts to ask if she could take his empty martini glass.

Only if you plan on refilling it, he said.

She laughed, possibly flirting. He waggled the glass playfully then handed it to her. He watched her walk away, her navy blue skirt shifting back and forth over hips as she moved up the aisle. He loved the way women looked on airplanes.

He stared out the window again, hoping to see those same lights, but they were gone. The ground was black. The only thing he saw was the moon, like a perfectly carved hole in the sky.

Three
FROM ANIMATION TO AMUSEMENTS

In the years after Walt Disney's death, company publicists would present an image of their founder as a man driven by a lifelong obsession with animation. The real Walt Disney was not propelled by any such single-minded desire. For Walt, the golden years of animation were the late 1920s and the 1930s, when his studio continuously pushed the boundaries of animation—producing the first synchronized sound cartoon (*Steamboat Willie*), the first full-color cartoon using the three-strip Technicolor process (*Flowers and Trees*), and the first hand-drawn animated feature (*Snow White*). For these films, Walt meticulously supervised each step of production, reviewing scripts, storyboards, rough animation, pencil tests, soundtrack scores, and final scenes.

The developing Disney style could be defined as the advancement of cartoon realism, using the techniques of high art in a commercial animation studio to create a new type of theatrical experience. In part, these advancements were made possible due to the Great Depression, when men with formal art-school training were unable to find other work in their fields. One Disney animator would later claim that "the Depression was the greatest thing that could ever have happened to Walt. There was no employment for these young [artists], including myself."[1] Capitalizing on this opportunity, Disney heavily recruited from art schools to build a stable of classically trained artists now employed as commercial animators. Under the guidance of these skilled men, the early Mickey Mouse (whose limbs resembled rubber hoses) evolved into a mouse whose flesh was draped over an anatomically correct human skeleton and whose face could communicate subtle emotion. Bambi and his mother appeared as lifelike deer inhabiting a realistic forest. Most impressively, human figures (such as Snow White, the Prince, Geppetto, Stromboli, and the real-boy Pinocchio) moved with an identifiable human acuity and grace that allowed audiences to relate to them as they would actors, rather than as funny drawings.

But as the 1930s came to an end, Walt suffered a number of setbacks at work.

With the profits from *Snow White*, he built a new studio complex, one that resembled a college campus. Though it provided technically superior facilities for animation, the work environment was so large that the studio lost the camaraderie of its early years, the close-knit community of artists unraveling into various factions. Walt Disney Productions was now a company with hundreds of employees and, after the sale of stock in 1940, a company with a board of directors. In 1941, Disney employees organized a strike in order to form a union and bargain for better wages. By the time the strike was over, the studio had lost over 300 artists, storymen, and camera operators. A few months later, the studio lost many more to the military when the United States entered World War II.

After the war came to an end, Walt's interest in animation began to wane. In part, he understood that his most important work was now behind him—landmark films that pushed the technical boundaries of animation, such as *Snow White*, *Pinocchio*, and *Fantasia*. Because of restricted finances and a limited ability to distribute overseas, his studio currently only produced cartoons and short subjects. Those feature-length films it did release during the mid-to-late 1940s were mostly cobbled together collections of cartoons and shorts referred to as "package films," such as *Saludos Amigos*, *Melody Time*, and *The Adventures of Ichabod and Mr. Toad*.

Even if the studio were able to return to true feature-length animation, Walt could, at best, hope to create films similar to earlier works, such as *Snow White*, as the studio lacked the resources and manpower to significantly expand the artistic achievements of animation.

Though he remained active at the studio, particularly in regard to story meetings, Walt's attention drifted away from animation now that there were no large projects to claim his ambition. While once he had spent most every weekend at the studio, he now began to spend his weekends away from work. He dedicated months to minor home improvement projects. He took his family on vacations. He considered buying a second house. He threw himself into old hobbies, the most prominent of which was his boyhood love of trains.

His collection started innocently enough with the purchase of a Lionel model train as a Christmas gift to himself in 1947. In a letter to his sister, Ruth, who had grown up with him in near poverty, he described the model train as "something I've wanted all my life."[2] At first, he set up the track in one of the rooms outside his office so he could tinker with it when he wasn't otherwise occupied at the studio. With the help of a studio machinist and special-effects expert named Roger Broggie, he soon expanded the layout so that it included multiple trains, tunnels, hills, elevated bridges, artificial landscaping, and miniature buildings—most of which Walt built himself.

His interest in tabletop model trains quickly developed into an interest in scale-model railroads—ones large enough to carry people seated on boxcars, cattle cars, and gondolas around the perimeter of his backyard. He initially directed one of his studio employees, Dick Jones, to look for a used eight-gauge or sixteen-gauge train, but after visiting a nearby railroad fair, he decided to build the train at his studio. Again with the help of staff in his studio machine shop, most notably Roger Broggie and Eddie Sargeant, Walt learned to work with sheet metal and also to use the metal lathe, the miniature drill press, and the milling machine. In the evenings and on weekends, these men spent hours slowly crafting parts for a backyard train, with Walt contributing decorative items (such as the headlights, a smokestack, and the cab's woodwork) while the machinists fabricated the valves and a patternmaker designed and cast the wheels. The engine, itself, would be named after Walt's wife, Lillian: it would be called the Lilly Belle.

At the site of his new home, Walt, Broggie, Sargeant, and other men from the studio laid out 2,165 feet of track that curved around the five-acre plot, looping through the lower gardens and slowly climbing a raised earthen berm to the main house. The track passed over a forty-six-foot wooden trestle and through a ninety-foot underground tunnel. As for the surrounding landscape, Walt added rolling hills spotted with miniature trees and a manmade canyon bordered by rows of alabaster rocks, making his scale railroad far more elaborate than any railroad featured at a local amusement park or carnival.

During the summer of 1950, Walt and the men from his studio spent a great deal of time with the train, particularly on weekends when the Disney family opened its house to guests. Animators from the studio, along with their children, came to ride the train, as did executives from other studios and even Hollywood celebrities, such as Mary Pickford, Candice Bergen, Red Skelton, and Salvador Dali. These guests arrived in the morning to find dozens of cars already parked outside the Disney house. Just beyond the back patio, they could see the train, usually with Walt at the controls, a striped engineer's hat shading his eyes, his feet resting on special pegs, as he captained the engine around a curve. They watched the chuf-chuf of the train as it moved through the yard, listened to the sound of hissing steam and a blast of the four-tone whistle as the engine pulled into the station. Only then, with the train so close, could they smell the coal smoke and lubricating oils.[3]

More than once, guests wondered why the president of a successful animation studio would spend so much time and money on a backyard railroad. "He seemed totally disinterested in movies," one visitor later wrote, "and wholly, almost weirdly, concerned with the building of a miniature railroad engine and a string of cars in the workshops of the studio."[4] But to those who knew him better the answer was obvious: Walt had grown restless and needed a new project on which to lavish his creative attention. He needed to expand beyond cartoons and into a field that he had not yet conquered.

In the early 1950s, Walt set his sights on his own amusement park.

He had been considering the idea in fits and starts for years, an amusement park that might be named after his best-known character: Mickey Mouse Park, a relatively quiet facility, designed for families, without thrill rides or roller coasters. Attractions would include miniature cars, a carousel, and, of course, a narrow gauge steam train similar to the one in his backyard. But when Walt outlined his plan, his brother, Roy, wasn't enthusiastic. Roy was convinced that Walt's interest was transitory and perhaps dilettantish. "Walt does a lot of talking about an amusement park," Roy wrote in a letter, "but really, I don't know how deep his interest really is. I think he's more interested in ideas that would be good in an amusement park than in actually running one himself."[5] But instead of directly objecting to Walt's proposal, Roy suggested that he put the idea aside for a few years, citing the company's troubled finances. In 1951, the company was in debt to Bank of America and still recovering from wartime losses.

Walt walked away from the meeting frustrated and perturbed.

He immediately put Roy's advice aside. In private, he began to develop practical strategies to build a park within the company's limited budget. In one early plan, Walt considered building his amusement park on the studio's backlot—specifically, on two-and-a-half acres of land used to store old sets. Walt visited the location repeatedly, trying to envision it there. Once satisfied with his idea, he told Bill Anderson, his studio production manager, to leave the land empty, free of storage sheds, parking lots, and any other development. "I'm going to build my park there." But as he mapped out the space needed for trains, cars, and various attractions, he realized the area was too small, adequate for a playground but not an amusement park. Within two months he abandoned the backlot proposal. In its place, he focused on sixteen acres the company owned on Riverside Drive, a weedy parcel of land directly across the street from the studio.[6]

The showpiece of this park would be a new scale-model railroad—one far more elaborate than the backyard setup he presently owned. In December of 1951, he approached the city manager of Burbank about the possibility of building "an eight-mile railroad in Griffith Park with a terminal point right at [the Disney property]."[7] But as a studio animator recalls, the railroad would not merely provide a simple excursion into the wooded beauty of the park, but would connect the studio to the Griffith Park carousel, including track set alongside a golf course where Walt planned to erect "a chain link fence to make sure people in the train don't get hit by golf balls."[8] Two weeks later, Walt's plan was presented to the city's Parks and Recreation Board, who looked on it favorably.

During all of 1952, Walt developed the concept for his park, adding in a paddleboat, a petting zoo, and a carousel. At one point, he also considered adding a soundstage, perhaps for a future television show. Repeatedly he met with city officials in Burbank to discuss his plans. Over the summer, he petitioned the help of the superintendent of parks to prepare a persuasive outline to win the approval of the full Burbank City Council. These initial meetings between Walt and the park board were so congenial that one of the members noted the "Disneys seem very willing to cooperate and that the Board should cooperate and do all possible to see that the project becomes part of Burbank."[9]

But financing remained a problem. "I couldn't get anybody to go with me because we were going through this financial depression," Walt later confessed. "Whenever I'd go down and talk to my brother about it, why he'd always suddenly get busy with some figures. I didn't dare bring it up."[10]

The lack of interest from Roy—as well as from Disney stockholders—depressed Walt. As was often the case, no one seemed to understand both the attraction and the practicality of his creative vision. Likewise, no one wanted to pay to develop it. From this point forward, Walt understood that his largest obstacle would be money. For the most part, his brother, Roy, oversaw the studio's finances. But for this new amusement-park project, Walt would need to handle the financial development as well. Essentially, he would need to do the whole thing on his own.

At first, Walt believed that a Disney-designed TV show would create a revenue stream large enough to finance his amusement park. It was an idea with obvious merit, even if he hadn't fully considered the long-term consequences of producing entertainment for the small screen. In October of 1952, he entered negotiations with the literary agent Mitchell Gertz to obtain the television rights to the Zorro stories. But a TV series about Zorro couldn't officially be produced by Walt Disney Productions, as Walt needed the profits to fund his personal amusement-park project. So on December 16, 1952, he established his own private company to produce this TV series, a company that would technically exist as a separate entity from Walt Disney Productions.

In many ways, this was an absurd proposition: Walt was developing a second Disney-based production company because he had lost absolute control of the first. But it was a necessary step. In addition to the *Zorro* series, Walt would use this company to develop his amusement park, as Walt Disney Productions wanted nothing to do with that as well.

The company's original name was Walt Disney Enterprises. But, within a few weeks, Walt learned that the name was far too close to Walt Disney Productions for the comfort of some stockholders. Irritated, he changed the name to Walt Disney Incorporated, likely in defiance of stockholder concerns. Eventually, though, Roy persuaded him to use a name without the word Disney. Walt begrudgingly settled on the name WED Enterprises, a name that did not appear to trade on the notoriety of the Disney brand. But Walt was merely complying with the letter of the request, not its spirit. WED was the initials of Walt's full name [Walter Elias Disney]—with "Disney" (or at least the suggestion of the Disney brand) cleverly tucked into this made-up word.

Though Roy believed that even this name might aggravate some board members, he let it pass. It was a problem he could deal with later.

At the start of the New Year, Walt's private company was entirely housed in a broken-down wooden bungalow toward the edge of the backlot. Though the studio had moved during the late 1930s, Walt had transported a few buildings from the old lot to the new location, including this dilapidated two-room shack. Without heating or air conditioning, it would serve as the first planning office for Walt's experimental amusement park. "It was a god awful place to work in," recalls one of the original designers. "Just a plasterboard building. In the winter it was colder than a brass monkey. In the summer it was too hot."[11] But Walt loved being there because it reminded him of the studio's early years—back when he produced animated films that deeply mattered to him.

Unlike Walt Disney Productions, a company that had been publicly traded for over a decade, Walt now exercised complete control over the fledgling WED Enterprises, just as he once had over his animation studio.

Slowly, he began to move a few company men over to the WED payroll. One afternoon he approached Harper Goff, a storyboard man and illustrator who was presently designing Captain Nemo's Nautilus submarine for the film, *20,000 Leagues Under the Sea*. Not quite sure how to begin, Walt awkwardly asked if Goff had ever visited a local amusement park called Knott's Berry Farm. Knott's was an Old West town with a stagecoach ride, pack mules, and a steam train. "Have you ever been to Knott's Berry Farm? It's fun, isn't it?"

Confused as to Walt's sudden interest in this Old West park, Goff was silent. He wasn't sure how to respond.

"I've been thinking that I'd like to have something like that," Walt continued. Then, placing his hand on Goff's shoulder, he guided the illustrator back to his office to discuss the matter in private.[12]

On February 19, Walt finalized the contract that gave him the screen and merchandise rights to fifty-two of the Zorro stories, a deal that he now believed would create a revenue stream large enough to develop his park. To manage the Zorro project, Walt transferred his brother-in-law, the quiet and reserved Bill Cottrell, over to the WED payroll specifically to oversee a small staff of writers. Under Cottrell's supervision, these writers were supposed to develop scripts for the first fourteen episodes.

With a future source of funding tentatively in place, Walt began to move beyond the "dream" stage and into actual development. To create a master plan for Mickey Mouse Park, he hired the architectural firm of Charlie Luckman and Bill Pereira. Luckman and Pereira were chosen primarily because their firm was also designing the grounds for Marineland, an oceanographic park slated to soon open on the other side of Los Angeles. From Twentieth Century Fox, Walt recruited an art director, Dick Irvine (who had previously worked on Disney's *The Three Caballeros* and *Victory through Air Power*), to serve as a liaison between WED and the architectural team. Often described as intense and serious, Irvine was a determined individual who was perfect for the job, as Walt wanted a man with show experience to oversee the architects.

During their first formal meeting, Walt described in great detail to Luckman and Pereira his plans for an amusement park where children would be able to meet his animated characters. In response, Luckman asked where Walt was planning to build it.

Leading his guest to an office window, Walt pointed toward a small patch of weeds across the street from the studio. "I've got the site right next door," he said.

When Luckman suggested that this site might be too small, Walt simply responded, "You and Bill can do it," as though a careful master plan would somehow solve the problem of inadequate space.

For the next month, Luckman and Pereira developed preliminary concepts for the Disney park packed into seven acres—allowing the rest of the Disney-owned land to be used for parking—but after reviewing the plan, Walt admitted that seven acres was not enough. Luckman and Pereira then produced plans for a ten-acre park and finally for a park that would use the entire area, allowing that parking happened elsewhere, each time suggesting that the land was still not large enough.[13] The plans showed both the placement of individual buildings as well as water, sewer, and electrical lines. But Walt found their designs unimaginative, though in retrospect the problem may have been more elementary: Walt was not used to people telling him that his ideas would not work, which was what Luckman repeatedly expressed.

After only a few meetings, Walt concluded that WED might be better off without an outside architectural firm. That is, without *any* outside architectural firm. Instead, he would rely on studio men more familiar with his ideas and creative process, believing that his own people would better know how to design a Disney-style park and also solve the problem of space. In doing so, Walt flirted with an idea that would prove either extraordinarily brave or ridiculously foolish: that men without formal training in engineering, architecture, and site planning would be able to design an experimental amusement park.[14]

But from Luckman and Pereira, Walt did embrace at least one important idea: "Bill Pereira said that anything, a pier, a circus, or anything, should have [only] one entrance, so that you have a way to get in and a way to get out," thereby controlling how guests experienced the park, much in the same way a movie controls how an audience experiences the story. "If you had more than one entrance," Pereira told Walt, "you would never be a success."[15]

On Saturdays and Sundays, Walt and his new WED employees began their great experiment: the quest to see if men with absolutely no experience in the amusement industry could teach themselves how to build an amusement park that would rival the most famous parks in the world. They visited parks in Southern California, including the Los Angeles Fair in Pomona and Knott's Berry Farm in Buena Park, both for inspiration and to better understand the site layout of such facilities. "Funny thing," Marvin Davis later revealed, "we visited Knott's Berry Farm, and at this time they had no idea of what was going to happen. They were so congenial and pleasant to Walt and all of our group, you know, and showing us *everything*."[16] Walt was particularly interested in traffic flow, the way people moved through open space and narrow streets, what grabbed their attention, how landscape and architecture affected their mood. Early on, he wanted his park to put its guests at ease, urging them to feel both curious and comfortable.

In addition to the larger parks—such as Knott's Berry Farm—Walt regularly visited at least two corner amusement parks in the Los Angeles area. Bud Hurlbut, the owner of one of these amusement parks remembers those days that Walt used to come by, often with his two daughters: "I saw him just sitting there, looking at the rides." After the third or forth visit, Hurlbut went over to talk with Walt, taking a seat beside him on the bench. "Looks like you're interested in rides," he began.

"Just kind of looking," Walt said.

But over time, Walt confided in Hurlbut his dream of building an amusement park on a little strip of land across the street from his studio. Once Walt learned that Hurlbut, a machinist trained in the aircraft industry, now built many of his own rides, he took a deeper interest in the man and his work. Walt invited Hurlbut over to his office and then, subsequently, to his house. "I spent several Saturdays over there," Hurlbut later revealed, "and it was just like being with an old neighbor. Walt would sit on the floor and just relax. And we would talk about trains and other amusement rides that he was interested in."[17]

The other corner amusement park Walt regularly visited was located in Beverly Hills, operated by Dave Bradley. With Bradley, however, Walt's interest was more focused on layout and site planning: "Walt Disney would come over on Sundays with his kids and ask all sorts of questions about guest flow and capacity."[18] Bradley's answers were so insightful that Walt eventually hired him as a consultant. He also sent Bradley overseas with a camera to photograph rides in Europe.[19]

During weekends, Walt spent hours on the Riverside Drive property, walking off its dimensions, imagining its future buildings, picturing the transition from one themed area to the next. Often he would crouch down so he could see how the fantasy environment would appear from a child's perspective. Inside his mind, he would shift the buildings, widen and then narrow the walkways, add and then subtract various plants. "I lived on Riverside Drive back then," explains Disney designer John Hench, "and I remember several Sundays seeing Walt across the street . . . stepping things off in the weed-filled lot, standing, visualizing, all by himself."[20]

In its initial months, WED's function was twofold: to plan a family-friendly amusement park, and to find a means to pay for its construction. To this end, Harper Goff created a meticulous aerial map of Mickey Mouse Park, detailing the location of rides, green space, and even a lake, all of which was to be built on the sixteen acres across the street from the studio—with the possible exception of a miniature railroad that might still travel into Griffith Park. "I was young," Goff explains, "and awed by Walt. He had given me more responsibility than I had ever had and . . . I was afraid of not living up to his expectations."[21]

Dick Irvine contacted machine shops and identified ride manufacturers with the ability to build amusement cars, boats, and a carousel.

Walt himself focused on funding by securing personal loans and pushing Bill Cottrell and his small staff of writers to finish scripts for the first fourteen episodes of the proposed *Zorro* TV series. Cottrell oversaw the development of the scripts. He also visited shooting locations, including Mexico, and considered actors who might play lead roles.[22]

In the early 1950s, network television was managed to a significant extent by men who either owned or used to own theater chains. As these men visited the studio, Walt would routinely escort them to his little plot of land across the street. One of these visitors, David Wallerstein, who was making the transition from theater management to network TV, remembers the day that Walt first told him about his amusement park. Wallerstein was talking to Walt about the opportunity presented by television, hoping to persuade him to show his cartoons and animated features on the ABC-Paramount network, when Walt interrupted him to say: "Come with me."

Together, the two men crossed Riverside Drive. "This is going to be [my amusement park]," he told Wallerstein, then proceeded to describe where he would put the carousel, the train station, and the lake for his scale-model riverboat. Walt attempted to focus the conversation on his *Zorro* series, a series that was fully owned by WED, but like the other network executives, Wallerstein was far more interested in acquiring the Disney studio animation library. When asked how he would build this park, Walt explained, "I'll need financing. So that'll be one of the conditions when I sell any of my stuff."

Somewhat confused but still hoping to acquire the rights to televise Disney animation, Wallerstein asked, "Well, what'll I do now?"

"Just rely on me," Walt said, rather cryptically. "I'll call you."[23]

The network executives left the studio mystified by Walt's obsession with an amusement park, though they appeared interested in this possible arrangement so long as Walt Disney opened his film library to TV. The only person to actually offer Walt financial support was a local investor named Charles H. Strub, who had learned through friends about Walt's curious plan to build an amusement park.

Strub had originally made his money by opening a chain of "painless" dentist offices, then by owning a minor-league baseball team. But in Los Angeles he was best known for partnering up with movie mogul Hal Roach to develop the wildly profitable Santa Anita racetrack. With the support of his company, Strub approached Walt with an offer.

He had become so intrigued with the concept for this park, Strub explained, that he would partially finance its construction, with the condition that Walt build it down by the ocean, next to one of the popular beaches. That, Strub continued, was the way to make money off of amusements. After due consideration, Walt turned Strub down, explaining that the beach "was the one place where I would not build it" because he didn't want his amusement park to become the type of low-class tourist trap that littered coastal cities throughout the country.

Beyond this, Walt also might've had doubts about joining with a company that made its money primarily from gambling.[24]

At the studio, Walt worked to persuade Roy to support his amusement park. One of the better-known stories from this period involved the studio nurse, Hazel George, who was also one of Walt's close personal friends. As the story was often told, one afternoon Walt explained how hard it was to raise money for his park. The following day, Hazel George solicited financial commitments from fellow employees—nothing more than $10 or $20 from most—to support Walt's vision. But according to a recently discovered interview with Disney executive Card Walker, the employee investment strategy was really a ploy devised by Walt to cleverly shame Roy into the amusement park business.

"[Walt] did a lot of funny things to needle Roy," Walker began, "to make sure that Roy understood how serious he was about going forward with [the park]. Like one time when he told Hazel George, our nurse, 'I'm not getting any place with the financial people. . . . Now, you go around and get the different people at the Studio to make commitments. 'Like, 'I'll commit $10 or $100,' something that ridiculous. Walt was smart enough to know that wasn't the answer either. But it was the needle." And the needle was used on Roy in a public forum, to make him believe that he was letting his brother down.[25]

While George worked her way through the studio, asking for small commitments and explaining Walt's financial difficulties, Walt continued to refine his concept of Mickey Mouse Park into a cinematic environment to better amuse adults as well as children, theming its various areas to resemble sets from a movie. Its plans now included a Mississippi steamboat, a frontier town, multiple railroads, a stagecoach, a country fair, a farm exhibit with livestock, in addition to miniature cars and a carousel. With this larger plan fully outlined, he admitted that he no longer had enough land for both his park and for a parking lot.

"There were some narrow strips of land around there that weren't being used," Harper Goff recalls, about ten acres to the north of Walt's property and ten to the south, all of it owned by the city. Walt believed that the city might offer him use of the land at little or no charge, with a ten- or twenty-year lease, simply to keep Walt's amusement park—and its tax revenues—in Burbank.[26] But this plan proved more complicated than Walt anticipated; it would need to be approved by the Burbank City Council.

To prepare for this meeting, members of the Burbank Park Board helped Walt solidify his formal plans. One board member worked with the city of Los Angeles to finalize lease terms for a miniature railroad between the Disney property and the park, as the park itself was owned by the city of Los Angeles, not Burbank. Pressured by Burbank officials, Los Angeles representatives eventually agreed to lease the land to Walt at a rate of $1,000 per month—though the city also appeared willing to reduce the lease rate if WED beautified portions of the lands with new trees and groundcover. The chairman of the Burbank Park Board himself worked with Walt to develop a final proposal, which would be both acceptable to the board and hopefully acceptable to the full Burbank City Council as well.[27]

Fifteen months earlier, when Walt first presented his "miniature railroad" park to the city, both the park board and the Burbank City Council had viewed the plans favorably. Over the intervening months, however, the plans for Walt's small park had grown from a "miniature railroad" park with three or four rides to a full-scale amusement park with many attractions. The Burbank Park Board was universally supportive of the larger park, believing that it would bring added revenue to Burbank, but the city council remained skeptical, unsure if it wanted to sanction a large outdoor amusement facility.

To convince city officials that his amusement park would not be anything like those dirty parks one finds down at the beach, Walt requested a meeting with the full city council.

While Goff displayed preliminary illustrations drawn by himself and Don DaGradi on a presentation easel, Walt enthusiastically explained to the Burbank councilmen how his park would transform the amusement industry by creating a clean, well-landscaped environment that would not only entertain children but also educate them about their national heritage. To illustrate this point, he gestured to the Old West town on Goff's map, then to a turn-of-the-century main street, describing the authenticity of its details right down to the wooden sidewalks and the gold lettering on each shop window. Furthermore, he attempted to quell their initial concerns by explaining that his park would be a small, wholesome enterprise, content with making a small profit or operating on a public-relations basis, "rather than on a full-bore moneymaking scale."[28]

But despite his promises, Walt sensed continued reluctance in the council members that frustrated him because he was unaccustomed to having his ideas questioned, particularly by strangers. After his presentation, he returned to his chair, trying to hide the telltale signs of anger: more than once he raised an eyebrow; he repeatedly tapped his fingers against the leather arm of his chair; lines of frustration were scribbled across his forehead. He waited quietly as the councilmen discussed the matter amongst themselves. Finally, one rose to vocalize their decision. "We don't want the carnie atmosphere in Burbank," he pronounced. "We don't want people falling in the river, or merry-go-rounds squawking all day long." The councilman stood there, dressed in a dark suit and tie, leaning authoritatively across his desk, a clear invitation for Walt to respond.

Walt unbuttoned his jacket. He looked from one councilman to the next. He folded his arms then unfolded them. But instead of arguing his case, he told Goff to pack up the damn artwork. Together, they left the room, the wooden doors swinging shut behind them.[29]

Goff later related his impression of the evening: "Some of the city council sneered at us," he said, as a way of describing the overt animosity that Walt now sensed between himself and the council.[30]

Walt drove home alone that evening. His route would've taken him past the vacant lot on Riverside Drive—a lot full of weeds and a few stakes to mark locations. While planning the park, Walt had traversed the land so often as to create paths among the weeds. Even from his car Walt could see those paths—one path defining the park's grand entrance, another to the edge of a manmade lake. But without the twenty acres from the city, this property was not large enough for both amusement rides and for parking. Despite his penchant for big ideas, Walt was a practical man. He could feel it now, the boundaries being placed around his current dream. As it was now evening, he most likely did not stop at the studio but continued driving, the vacant lot—once so filled with promise— growing small in his rearview mirror.

At about this same time, Roy became curious as to how Walt was paying for all the design work. Roy was, of course, aware of the WED team and the architectural firm his brother had hired. "But I didn't ask," Roy later explained. "It was his baby."[31] As Walt's efforts with the amusement park grew, Roy finally decided to call the family banker, who explained that Walt had hocked his quarter-of-a-million-dollar life insurance policy and also arranged a number of personal loans. In all, Roy learned that his brother had raised—and likely spent—at least $100,000 so far.

The failed presentation at the Burbank City Council, along with the news that his brother had borrowed against his life insurance, forced Roy to take another look at this strange amusement park.

On more than one occasion, Walt publicly commented that, from his vantage point, Roy restrained him. Once, when asked about his ambition to develop an amusement park, Walt replied: "I believe that the worst thing you can do is sit still. Roy used to try to hold me back. But I think I finally convinced him that it takes money to make money."[32]

"Roy finally became a convert," Bill Cottrell, an early WED employee, recalls. "He realized that nothing could stop Walt from pursuing his desire for the park. But he objected to Walt's plan to locate the park somewhere in Burbank."[33]

In the spring of 1953, the two brothers talked again about the amusement park. Roy understood that the stockholders would most likely still not support its development; moreover, he believed that some stockholders might even file a suit against Walt Disney Productions, charging that WED created a conflict of interest for its president. Yet, as Walt discussed the problems with the Riverside Drive parcel, Roy stopped him. "Oh, we can't do that," Roy said, referring to the proposed site across from the studio. He put his arm on his younger brother's shoulder. As young boys, they had shared a farmhouse bed. He leaned closer, his voice soft, finally supportive. "We should do it in a bigger way."[34]

But plans for a bigger park created the need for even more money—not to mention a new site. Roy believed that banks would refuse to loan Walt money to build the amusement park without sufficient collateral and prejudicial terms. At present,

the studio owed $3.1 million to banks, and with both the extrav-
agantly envisioned 20,000 *Leagues Under the Sea* and *Lady and
the Tramp* being produced in CinemaScope, the studio would
need to borrow another $2 million over the next six months
simply to complete these films.[35]

Walt suggested a partnership with a television network to
develop multiple shows to help finance this venture. Studio
documents from that time reveal that Walt was now considering four shows beyond the *Zorro* series: a one-hour series that
would use footage from the Disney film library, a half-hour
show devoted to True-Life nature programming, a half-hour
show that would explore the future of mankind (such as space
travel and cities under the sea), and a fifteen-minute program for children called *The Mickey Mouse Club*. Television, he
explained to Roy, would get them the money they needed to
build the park.[36]

But despite their hopes, both brothers understood the inher-
ent risk of allowing the studio—or anything related to Walt
Disney—to partner with a television network. Threatened
by the new medium, prominent theater chains—specifically,
those chains not associated with the major networks—had
recently promised to boycott any studio that produced shows
for TV.

Members of WED searched for a suitable new location for the
amusement park near the studio, including thirty-two acres
of farmland in Chatsworth and an open valley in Calabasas,
California. Both of these sites were less than twenty-five miles
from Burbank.

With the possibility of more land, Walt revised his concept
for the amusement park, asking an art director named Marvin
Davis to draft tentative site plans for a larger facility. He also
reconsidered the park's name. The initial name, Mickey Mouse
Park, suggested an amusement park developed primarily for

children. But Walt now planned something larger, a park consciously designed for both adults and children. He tried out new names, including the name Disneyland.

Making good on his promise to help, Roy Disney went so far as to purchase forty acres in Calabasas to protect a possible later purchase of land in that area. But almost immediately, Walt and Roy began to doubt the wisdom of building in Calabasas. More to the point, they began to doubt their ability to select a good site for an outdoor amusement facility, as neither man knew much about traditional amusement parks, nor did they know much about real estate developments north of Los Angeles.

Before purchasing additional land, they made the decision to seek outside help for both site selection and design parameters of the park, which led Walt to casually pursue these topics with his friends at architectural firms. While at a cocktail party, he struck up a conversation with Charlie Luckman, one of the architects who had created early (but abandoned) plans for Mickey Mouse Park. After discussing his current problems—specifically, where to build the park and how much land the project would require—Luckman told him about a firm called the Stanford Research Institute (more commonly known as SRI), which he had recently used while developing a football stadium in Hawaii. Before leaving, Walt wrote SRI's phone number on a piece of paper and then slipped it into his wallet.

The following day, Walt told Nat Winecoff, a man who functioned as his executive assistant on the amusement-park project, to call the people at SRI and find out exactly what they did. More to the point, to find out if they knew anything about amusement parks. That afternoon, Winecoff called the local office of SRI and talked to an economist named Buzz Price. In doing so—quite by accident—he pushed the first domino that, years later, would lead to a great proliferation of American theme parks.

As a promoter by nature, Winecoff was often out-of-step with the Disney organization. Regularly dressed in a black jacket and red vest, he appeared ostentatious, with his slicked-back hair and pencil-thin mustache. He was direct and, occasionally, confrontational. Presented with the task of calling a little-known research firm, Winecoff got right down to business: "What the hell do you guys do for a living anyway?"

Hearing Winecoff's firm tone, Price responded softly: Let us come down tomorrow and we'll show you.

That night, Price drafted two proposals, the first for a site location report and the second for a study on the park's economic feasibility.

The following day, most likely June 3, 1953,[37] a Wednesday, Price had a noontime appointment to meet with Walt. The meeting itself wasn't held in the studio proper. It was held in the small WED bungalow, a building that Price would later describe as "a trailer."[38]

The Los Angeles branch of SRI was a serious scientific, technical, and economic research firm, whose recent work included studies on the causes of smog and on the future demand for newly developed color television tubes. For the past three years, their economic division had also compiled information on the markets, population, and industry in California, which was primarily used for large companies wishing to expand or establish new west coast branches. The call from Nat Winecoff about Walt Disney's amusement park most likely garnered some chuckles from other researchers at SRI accustomed to more serious assignments.[39]

Representing SRI economics division at the meeting were two men in their early thirties, both dressed in gray suits, white shirts, and dark ties. The first man, Buzz Price, well-educated and cautious by nature, was the serious numbers man who would do most of the actual research. The second man was "the presenter," a man who did not appear to be a researcher at all but did most of the talking. Though thirty-three years old, this "presenter" possessed a soft face and coal-black hair that made him look more like a man in his mid-twenties. His most memorable feature was his curious accent—a strong Texas inflection that, by turns, suggested control, joviality, and determination. It also gave one the impression—wrongly so—that he had enjoyed a privileged childhood and a broad cultural education.

The man firmly shook Walt's hand, then Roy's hand,[40] finally the hand of Nat Winecoff, before formally introducing himself. His name was C. V. Wood, which he pronounced with a noticeable twang. But most people, he added, just called him Woody.

During the first meeting, the Disney brothers found Woody enthusiastic, even exuberant. More importantly, they felt that Woody understood Walt's vision for the experimental amusement park while at the same time realizing the fiscal difficulties of building such an enterprise. The park, as Walt explained, would include customized rides adapted to various themed areas. Unlike other amusement parks, which spent little or no money on landscaping, his park would develop storytelling environments that might even include a western fort, a Victorian station for a steam train, a monorail concourse, and a medieval castle. Walt told his guests that they had recently purchased a small piece of property north of the San Fernando Valley, with an option to buy more, but now questioned that location.

As the meeting progressed, Buzz Price explained that SRI would be able to complete not only a land-use study to help determine where best to build the park but also a feasibility study. "We could study market behavior in other amusement parks and public attractions and use it as a basis for judgment in developing an economic feasibility model," Price explained.[41] Before the initial consultation ended, they all agreed that these studies should be quietly completed so as not to call attention to the company's objectives and inadvertently inflate real estate prices. They also agreed on a consulting fee for SRI's initial twelve weeks of service—$10,000 for the site study and $15,000 for the feasibility report, which was a substantial sum in 1953. Conflicting reports set the final bill, including expenses, at either $28,000 or $31,000.

But there was something that the Disney brothers did not yet understand about Woody. Though Woody had been raised in a working-class family, he longed for the notoriety and security that came with wealth. While working at SRI, he had developed the unique ability to make eccentric, wealthy men feel as though he understood their plans, no matter how unusual these plans appeared on paper.

Before leaving, Price asked, "Do you have any bias, any opinion on where [the park] should go in Southern California. The study area you are talking about is big."

"Absolutely not," Walt insisted. "It's wide open. You tell me."

"No bias? No predetermined interest?"

Walt shook his head.

"What about the [land] that you own north of the Valley?"

"Don't bother with that," Walt said. "I want your opinion about where this park will work the best."[42]

Though the initial meeting went smoothly, the first disagreement between Walt and Woody occurred only a few days later, mainly because Woody didn't understand the financial limitations of WED. SRI's preliminary findings advised Walt that he would need more land than he expected. Woody simply asked, where would customers park their cars if all of the available land was used for attractions? Walt responded with anger, then silence, because funding was still an obstacle for his proposed park. Later that day, Walt exclaimed to one of his WED employees, "They think I'm making a lot of money, and they're trying to get me to spend a lot. I can't go into a big thing like that."[43]

Eventually, Walt was convinced that he needed about 150 or 160 acres, as opposed to the 80 or 100 originally proposed. He was also convinced to keep the new "larger" park a secret, even from general studio employees, until a site was purchased. From that point forward, the only people with access to Walt's revised plans were Walt, Roy, the small WED team, the SRI economic consultants, and, of course, C. V. Wood. The issues concerning the proper size for the amusement park were settled quietly and with civility—though already Walt had the sense that Woody was more opinionated than he had appeared at their first meeting.

At times, Walt believed that Woody's independence and direction would help his amusement-park project. Other times, he was less sure.

In both the SRI office and in their official logbooks, the Disney contract quickly came to be known as "Project Mickey"—a name hinting at the less-than-serious nature of the assignment.[44] For the remainder of June and much of July, C. V. Wood and Buzz Price evaluated seventy-one possible sites for Disneyland in five southern California counties—Los Angeles, Orange, Ventura, Riverside, and San Bernardino—though they quickly narrowed their selection area to five miles on either side of the proposed expansion route of the Interstate 5 freeway.[45] The most bizarre location they considered was undeveloped land owned by a cemetery; the most lavish, a private club near Santa Ana. Price did most of the hard research, evaluating each site against a number of factors, such as SRI's data on climate, population growth, land values, and proposed expansions in the freeway system.

During excursions to examine specific sites, Woody was the talker, the raconteur, the person who chatted up property owners and realtors to get inside information. But aside from participating in the research trips, Woody's "contribution on the studies was light," Price recalls. His primary job was to bring new contracts to the firm, particularly government and military contracts.[46]

To determine the best location for Walt's park, Price estimated the center of population ten years into the future, which he believed to be south of Los Angeles—in the direction of the Whittier-Norwalk area and Orange County. After a July 14 meeting, at which Wood and Price presented their information to Walt and Roy, Price was given the green light to further study possible locations in the Whittier-Norwalk and Orange County regions, looking at specific cities that offered favorable tax codes, zoning ordinances, and utility rates.

Using county records, Price looked for large parcels of land owned by a single owner. A grouping of family orchards with multiple owners was avoided due to the problems with motivating multiple owners to sell their land to a single buyer at the same time. But a local real estate man, Fred Wallich, suggested that Price might find more favorable land by working with a grouping of owners—particularly a grouping of small parcels in Anaheim alongside the proposed path of the Golden State Freeway. "This site," Wallich explained, "was not on your search through Orange County records because there are 17 parcels involving many owners. I know that many of the owners are considering selling to a housing subdivision."[47]

Over the following week, Price evaluated the combined parcel using the criteria he'd developed for the other possible sites. The land was flat and ideally suited for development, and the climate was slightly milder than that of other possible locations. But the surprising factor was its overall cost. Though the parcel abutted up against the proposed freeway expansion, Price calculated that the land in this unincorporated section of Orange County, just outside Anaheim, should cost roughly $4,800 per acre, compared to $5,000 per acre in nearby Santa Ana or $5,500 to $6,000 in La Mirada. Price also learned that the parcel near Anaheim had a lower overall tax rate of 5.26 percent, compared to rates of 6.8 percent and 6.95 percent in neighboring areas. In short, it was a bargain.[48]

To present their findings, C. V. Wood and Price invited the Disney brothers out to Los Angeles, to their office in the Pacific Finance Building. The meeting took place in the conference room, with maps and diagrams displayed on the walls. Price explained all of their data: temperature, projected population growth, tax rates, etc. With the maps, he discussed the projected freeway expansions—explaining when each leg of the new system was expected to be finished.[49] "Twenty-four sites were considered worthy of further investigation," Price later wrote. "A tour was made of these sites, with Disneyland representatives, and the choice was further narrowed down to four sites" in the Anaheim, La Mirada and Santa Ana regions of Orange County.[50]

"We gave Walt and Roy four choices," Price recalls. "They said let's go for number one."[51]

Presumably it was at this same meeting that Walt received copies of the SRI report for himself and the WED team—copies that WED employees reviewed carefully. Existing copies of the SRI report hold few notes, with only a handful of phrases underlined for further discussion. One of the underlined phrases, highlighted with a quick swipe of Conte crayon, would turnout to be prophetic, a phrase in which Buzz Price described one of the key variables—"A determination of owners' willingness to sell"—as if he was able to sense the coming trouble.[52]

At the end of the week, Walt, Woody, and Nat Winecoff drove out to the Anaheim region to view the 139 acres on Ball Road: seventeen individual properties, most of them family farms, though one was used for vehicle storage. They drove slowly down Winston Road, looking from one side of the thinly paved street to the other. Outside the car, they saw rows of citrus trees as well as elegant two-story homes. Some had chicken coops, others ornamental palm trees, still others windmills.

At one residence, farm children looked out the front window to see the unusual car crawl up the road. "[The dark car] would just stop in front of our house," one local resident remembers. "But we would never see who was in the car."[53]

After Walt had thoroughly viewed the combined parcel of farmland, the driver parked the car on the dirt collar of the road, where the men discussed their strategy.

Even if they could convince all seventeen owners to sell, there were still many obstacles—namely, the city would have to agree to provide a water main, a sewer line, and enough electricity to power the park. At present, the land received its water from local wells and dispersed sewage into the ground without the aid of a modern sewer system.

But the WED team did have one small bit of luck—or, at least, what they believed was "luck." A few months earlier, the city of Anaheim had requested help from the Disney studio to expand its annual Halloween parade, making it the centerpiece for a multi-day festival designed to put Anaheim on the map.[54] Disney had agreed to contribute floats to the parade, beautifully decorated platforms that would include scenes from *Snow White*, *Pinocchio*, and *Peter Pan*. Disney's offer quickly expanded to include an entire parade unit, with six floats total. Animator Roy Williams would draw up plans for the unit, dubbed Walt Disney's Fairyland. One float would even feature Cinderella's storybook castle—a structure strikingly similar to the one that Walt wanted to place in the center of his amusement park. In short, the parade unit would not only be a goodwill gesture, but also a stealthy preview of the type of dimensional entertainment Walt wanted to permanently bring to the region.[55]

As a reward, the city of Anaheim asked that Walt select one of his employees to be an honorary judge for the parade. Walt chose Nat Winecoff, an extremely practical decision considering his options. In his ridiculous red vest and black suit, Winecoff looked like a creature from Hollywood, someone entirely consumed with the business of motion pictures. Each morning, Winecoff manicured his mustache to a neat pencil-line. He wore flamboyant ties and spoke with a slight affectation. No one would ever suspect that he was in Anaheim to secretly gather information about a possible land deal. Specifically, Winecoff's mission was to inquire about variances to the zoning code and the expansion of city utilities without revealing Walt's intention to build an amusement park in Orange County.

Pending positive reports from Winecoff, the WED team intended to use a third-party agent—namely, John Gilcrist at the Los Angeles office of Coldwell Banker—to option the land, so as not to inadvertently inflate real estate prices. Since the loss of even one of the seventeen parcels could destroy the deal, they decided to tell no one in Anaheim their intentions until the land was secure—not the city, not the county, not even the chamber of commerce.

On that first trip, Walt and his men remained in the car for nearly an hour, discussing their plans. Before driving back, Walt looked again at the land. He could imagine it here, this place he was beginning to call Disneyland. His image of the park changed from day to day, though presently he pictured it as a turn-of-the-century street leading to a frontier town and a riverboat landing. The sound of the car engine broke his reverie, so that he focused again on the actual orange grove before him. The sun was low in the sky, half-hidden behind the trees. Long shadows reached across the dirt and, with something that approximated prophecy, almost touched their car.

As the driver pulled away, Walt watched the land grow small, the trees on those seventeen parcels becoming distant, blending with the rows of orange trees on other parcels, until it seemed this entire area, this great swatch of land that lay just outside

Anaheim, was one large farm. He let the quiet excitement set-tle inside him—a turbulent peacefulness that reminded him of the early days at the studio. The other men felt it, too—this blend of anticipation, excitement, and satisfaction.

For a few golden moments, they all believed that the land deal was as good as done, that the site selection was now over.

Four
THE MONEY AND THE LAND

Even without Walt's amusement park, Anaheim was a city on the verge of transformation—from a rural to a suburban economy. The state's main arterial freeway was scheduled to expand south, connecting Los Angeles to San Diego, cutting directly through the center of town. Based on this information, land developers and speculators were purchasing large parcels near the proposed freeway expansion, mostly with an eye toward building suburban housing tracks, shopping centers, and motels for travelers. The town's modest population (then roughly 30,000) was poised to explode.

In August or September of 1953, a pair of realtors from Coldwell Banker (hired by the Disney brothers) approached the seventeen landowners at the Ball Road site to acquire purchase options on their property. Based on later records, it seems clear that the realtors were attempting to purchase the farmland slightly under market value, at roughly $4,000 per acre with additional money offered for structures and improvements. In short, they were trying to get the land on the cheap, as the land was worth between $4,700 and $5,000 per acre. There was, however, one exception to this strategy of lowball offers. The Viking Trailer Manufacturing Company occupied the largest parcel, a particularly desirable property as it was situated directly next to the proposed freeway expansion. For this parcel, Disney authorized Coldwell Banker to offer $5,300 per acre plus an additional $100,000 for the assets of the trailer company itself.

In line with this strategy, Coldwell Banker realtors approached the owners of both the Viking land and the Viking Trailer Manufacturing Company (as the company was owned separately from the property) and successfully purchased an option on the land as well as drafted an agreement to acquire the assets of the company. The option cost WED a total of $10,000 and guaranteed them the right to purchase the entire parcel at $5,300 per acre, assuming they could convince the other sixteen land owners to sell their property, thereby placing the entire 160 acres in Disney's hands.

But shortly after the option was signed, without the knowledge of Coldwell Banker, a land speculator purchased the property next to the Viking site. In all likelihood, this speculator had heard that the Viking land had been optioned—perhaps from one of the Viking employees—and believed that the land was destined to become a large subdivision of ranch-style homes. One can assume that this speculator hoped to make a substantial profit by withholding the property until the developer agreed to a much higher price per acre.

Feeling both naïve and hustled, Walt was furious when he learned through Coldwell Banker of the developments. He quickly decided to walk away from the Ball Road site—even though that would require the forfeiture of the $10,000 already paid for the option on the Viking property. "Some S.O.B. . . . picked up some property at the same location," Nat Winecoff later explained. "It messed up the whole deal. They figured we would pay any price for the land. We found out the person bought 20 acres. He thought he was going to make some money out of it. . . . We dropped [our interest in that site] and lost the deposit." In short, Walt "got annoyed."[1]

Immediately following the loss of the Ball Road site, Woody, Buzz Price, and Nat Winecoff began to explore nearby sites in the cities of La Mirada and Santa Ana, all of them next to the proposed route of the new freeway. This time, however, they were careful that no one—not even the landowners—understood how many acres they were attempting to buy.

There was only one problem, as they soon discovered: the price of land in La Mirada and Santa Ana was more expensive than land in and around Anaheim. Moreover, the long-term tax and utility rates in La Mirada and Santa Ana were higher—meaning that not only would the land cost more upfront but an amusement park in those cities would cost more to operate as well.

For the cash-strapped WED Enterprises, this was a significant problem—one left to Woody, Buzz Price, and Nat Winecoff to solve.

In September, Roy Disney arranged to meet with executives from at least two—if not three—of the four national television networks in New York to solve the growing financial problems associated with Disneyland. Both Disney brothers believed that a network sponsorship would be their best and perhaps only opportunity to secure adequate funding to build the park.

Along with Walt, five men from the studio assembled a pitch book that included a typed description for both the proposed Disney TV show, originally called *Walt Disney Presents*, and for Disneyland itself. One man at the meeting, Harry Tytle, recalled that Walt was unusually emotional that day, firing off one idea after another: He "was very 'hot' with his suggestions," Tytle later wrote, indicating that Walt clearly understood the importance of the meeting.[2]

In the pitch book, Walt explained the concept of Disneyland: the frontier town, the World of Tomorrow, and the kingdom for cartoon characters. In recent months, he'd been playing with the idea of a permanent circus area, complete with sideshows and animal acts, which he now included in the description of his park. In short, direct paragraphs, he highlighted the potential profitability of Disneyland by using figures from the original SRI report. But he still didn't have an estimate for construction costs. As potential investors would need this information, Walt approached Bruce McNeil, a contractor who was building a new soundstage at the studio. Walt explained the concept for his amusement park, reviewed the type of buildings needed, and then shared preliminary layouts for the acreage.

Like everyone else at the studio, McNeil had no previous experience with outdoor amusements. In all likelihood, he assembled a loose estimate using construction costs for similar projects, such as a mall, a county park, and possibly a group of studio buildings. A few days later, he returned with his answer: six million for land preparation and construction costs.[3]

This enormous sum, surprisingly, seemed reasonable to Walt.

A few days before Roy's departure, on Saturday, September 23, Walt decided that his typed description of Disneyland in the pitch book was inadequate to convey the grandness of the project to network executives in management and finance. These executives, Walt believed, possessed little imagination. Without adequate illustrations, they might assume that Disneyland would be just another carnival or Coney Island.

Walt also worried that the lack of a physical site might suggest the Disney brothers were not yet fully committed to the park.

As Roy was leaving in two days, Walt met with his WED design team (Bill Cottrell, Marvin Davis, and Dick Irvine) on a Saturday morning to discuss the pitch book. In the WED building, they explored the issue for a couple hours before settling on a plan. They determined that a large rendering of Disneyland as an aerial map with particular attention to individual attractions would not only depict the uniqueness of the proposed park, but also craft the illusion that the park had a definite location, even if that location existed only on paper. To create a map that would incorporate individual ride concepts into a unified image, they needed an experienced illustrator who could convey the emotional texture of Walt's park through a line drawing. But most of the men present were only trained in architecture and set design. They didn't have the right skills to create this map—especially as it would need to be completed in less than thirty-six hours.

A single, flawless draft—there was time for nothing else.

While reviewing the names of local artists, Irvine suggested an old friend at Twentieth Century Fox, Herb Ryman, an illustrator whose quick fluid pen glided effortlessly over the page. He would be fantastic, Irvine explained. There was only one problem: Ryman, once one of Walt's favorite artists, had walked away from the Disney studio years ago and now worked for its rivals. After some discussion, Walt agreed that they should at least call Ryman to see if something might be worked out, as Walt, too, knew that Ryman was perfect for this job.

With a wave of his hand, Walt asked Dick Irvine to initiate the call.

In the late 1920s, as a teenager, Ryman had been trained at the Chicago Art Institute, where he'd developed exceptional skills as an illustrator and atmospheric artist, but during the Great Depression, he had found few options for employment outside of the film industry. He began his career as a story illustrator at MGM in 1933, styling such films as *David Copperfield* and *Mutiny on the Bounty*, but even during this period he continued to work on his own paintings. For two years in the late 1930s, he lived in the Orient, an experience that greatly influenced his painting style. When he returned to America, his oil paintings and watercolors were accepted for gallery shows in New York and Los Angeles. In 1938, he again found himself employed by a studio—Disney's this time—where he worked in story development and as an art director on *Pinocchio* and *Dumbo*.

In 1941, Walt organized a good will trip for roughly one-dozen artists to South America, a trip that would become the inspiration for many Disney cartoons and features, most notably *Saludos Amigos* and *The Three Caballeros*. Among these artists personally selected by Walt was Herb Ryman. Together, Walt and the artists spent three months in South America, visiting Brazil, Argentina, and Chile, representing both the studio and the good will of the United States government, a trip that solidified many strong bonds between the artists and Walt himself. At the trip's conclusion, Ryman returned to his job at the studio, where he worked as an art supervisor on *Saludos Amigos* and a layout artist on *The Three Caballeros*. But in the late 1940s, as Disney struggled financially, Ryman quietly left the studio to work at Twentieth Century Fox as a technical advisor and an art illustrator on *Anna and the King of Siam*. With the money he earned on this film, he left Hollywood for two years to pursue his own work, this time following the Ringling Brothers Circus in an attempt to document the grotesque beauty of carnival clowns and of circus life through a series of paintings. When he returned, he did not seek employment at the Disney studio; instead, he accepted higher-paying work at Twentieth Century Fox and MGM.[4]

On the Saturday morning Dick Irvine called him from the WED bungalow, Ryman was at home, ten miles away, leisurely working on one of his circus paintings. Irvine's voice was nervous, tentative. "We're over here at Disney studios," Irvine began, "and Walt would like to talk to you."

Ryman waited, listening as Irvine passed the phone to Walt. For years he had believed Walt was likely mad at him for leaving the Disney studio.

But instead of anger, Walt's voice was casual, even friendly. "Herbie, whatcha doing?"

"I'm working on my circus pictures."

Walt exhaled as though he were carefully considering his next line. "Can you come over to see me?"

"But it's Saturday."

"Sure, it's my studio. I can work on Saturday."

"What do you want to talk about?"

"I'll tell you when you get here."

Ryman looked down at himself, realizing that he was still wearing his nightclothes. "But I'm not smartly dressed."

"Come as you are," Walt replied, his voice still cheerful and expectant. "I'll be out front waiting for you."

Without changing his clothes, Ryman drove up Riverside Drive to reach the studio, only to find Walt standing alone at the main gate, his arms crossed, his eyes anxiously fixed on the distant foothills. It was late morning, the sun slanting down from the east. Even from inside his car, Ryman could see that Walt's face was dusted with faint stubble. It was unlike his old boss not to shave. Beyond this, he was tapping his fingers nervously against his arm. Ryman knew that Walt was a man of many moods, but he didn't know how to read his present disposition.

He parked in the nearest spot. "What's on your mind, Walt?"

"I want to talk to you about an amusement park."

"You mean you're going to go ahead with your idea across the street?" Ryman nodded toward the vacant property opposite Riverside Drive.

"No, it's not going to be like that," Walt said, then lowered his voice, his tone becoming conspiratorial. "It's bigger than that."

Curious, Ryman moved close.

For the next five minutes, Walt explained his plans for Disneyland, offering examples of the different themed areas as well as the rides. He explained that his brother, Roy, was going to New York on Monday morning, hopefully to secure money from a TV network to help build the park. "My brother has to take a large rendering of Disneyland with him to show the investors," he explained. "You know, most financial types don't have much imagination. Roy has to show them what we're going to do before we can have any chance of getting the money."

Not quite sure how to respond, Ryman asked, "Well, where are these drawings? I'd like to see them?"

Walt lowered his eyes so that his gaze met Ryman's directly. "You're going to make them."

Many years later, Ryman would explain his motivation for what happened next: he could not see how he could possibly translate Walt's idea into a rendering in only two days. It was as though Walt didn't understand the enormity of such a request. But on that Saturday morning, he simply said, "No."

Ryman witnessed a change come over his old boss, some of the rosy confidence leaking from his face. "Will you do it if I stay?"

Ryman was quiet. After a moment's consideration, he recognized that Walt was not angry. Rather, in his own limited way, Walt was pleading, which was a disposition that Ryman had never seen in him. "Yes," he finally agreed, "if you stay Saturday and Sunday night."

From there, Walt led Ryman into the WED bungalow, where Bill Cottrell, Marvin Davis, and Dick Irvine showed Ryman individual pieces of conceptual art, area site maps, and architectural renderings that they, along with Harper Goff, had produced for the park. They explained each of the proposed themed sections, paying particular attention to an early version of Adventureland called True-Life Adventureland (named after a series of Disney nature films), the turn-of-the-century promenade called Main Street, and a rather large area called Lilliputian Land.

The name, Lilliput, was, of course, borrowed from the classic novel *Gulliver's Travels*; it was the land of the little people. But for Walt, this name also held a second meaning because it contained the word "Lilly," as in the Lilly Belle, the name of the locomotive he once helped build. Lilliputian Land, therefore, would be a land of miniature storybook cities that also contained track for a 1/8th scale railroad, much like the one in Walt's backyard.[5]

Along with these imaginative realms, the WED designers explained the more practical areas of the park, such as an area called Holidayland, which featured a dining and reception area for guests to celebrate children's birthdays and other holidays. The park might also contain a world shopping bizarre called International Street. Together, the WED designers explained the park's concept: a single street as the main entryway, the circular hub, the castle serving as the park's focal point, around which were organized the major themed lands. After they finished their presentation, Walt asked the WED designers to leave so he and Ryman could work alone.

The studio was unusually quiet, Ryman noticed, the only sounds being outside traffic and the buzz of electricity passing through nearby lines. Sitting at a drafting table, he closed his eyes and brought his folded hands to his mouth as he attempted to visualize this strange park. Again, he looked at the individual drawings left by Davis and Irvine, but to him, they appeared an odd assortment of cars, boats, turn-of-the-century stores, and a medieval castle. He also looked at partial plans, though now abandoned, that had been created by a local architectural firm, as well as preliminary site designs completed by Davis. Walt had ordered dozens of preliminary site designs. These plans included not only the buildings, but markings for sewer and water lines. The enormity of the project unnerved Ryman. "I can't do anything between now and Monday morning," he finally announced. "I need time to think about it."

Walt, who had been sitting close by, rose up, his face creased with frustration. "Herbie, this is my dream. I've wanted this for years, and I need your help. You're the only one who can do it."

Walt stood quietly, his eyes a little damp, his arms loose at his sides. He waited a minute, maybe two, before Ryman finally lifted his pencil.

For most of Saturday, Ryman experimented with quick sketches, guided by Walt's corrections. "When we worked on the castle," Ryman later recalled, "Walt wanted it to be hundreds of feet high. He said, 'When people get near us, I want them to say, Look, there's the castle; that's Disneyland; let's go over there.'" On one sheet, Ryman drew a castle that, in real life, would be well over 500 feet tall. Behind Main Street, he added a few buildings for the international area, and next to the World of Tomorrow, he added Lilliputian Land. He drew the Jungle River ride, where boats floated past live zoo animals arranged on islands. With each subsequent sketch, he gained a slightly better understanding of how the park might be pictured in the form of an aerial schematic map.

Walt ordered a mid-afternoon lunch of tuna salad sandwiches and malted milk to be delivered to the WED bungalow. Hours later, he ordered dinner. Late on Saturday, Ryman copied Marvin Davis's most recent site plan for the park into the corner of a large sheet of tissue paper, and then began the first full visual interpretation of Walt's park. He worked with carbon pencil and darkened in a few areas for depth. An enormous project, measuring almost four feet by six feet, this aerial view of Disneyland clearly showed the train station, the steamboat, the Moonliner rocket, the Jungle River, and over a dozen other attractions—all intricately set into a unified drawing.

The two men left the studio late Sunday night, both of them exhausted.[6]

Reports differ as to how the map and final pitch book arrived in New York; some people remember Roy taking both the map and the pitch book on the plane, while others recall that the items were sent by courier. Either way, within twenty-four hours of the map's completion, Roy had the large-scale illustration and presentation materials in New York. The pitch book described Disneyland as "a new experience in entertainment," an educational amusement park where guests would find "happiness and knowledge."[7]

In New York, both Roy Disney and Dick Irvine knew that their goal would be very difficult to accomplish: to convince a TV network to co-invest in Walt's theme park using a Disney-produced television show as collateral. The financial numbers behind the arrangement were staggering. In 1953, Walt Disney Productions was on tract to make a net profit of roughly a half-million dollars, meaning that the cost to build Walt's park (now estimated conservatively at $6 million to $10 million) could consume up to twenty years of profits from the studio.[8]

Though Roy was not expecting the meetings to go smoothly, he hoped to receive some interest from both CBS and NBC because during the previous year, Walt had talked to executives at these networks about his park. But the trip went worse than planned. Roy was refused almost immediately by CBS. At NBC, Roy talked with David Sarnoff (an iron-willed executive better known to his employees as General Sarnoff) who initially showed interest, but quickly passed the project along to two junior executives, Joe McConnell and Pat Weaver, most likely hoping that these junior executives would somehow be able to capture the Disney TV deal without entangling the network in an amusement park.

Over the following week or two, McConnell and Weaver found themselves taken with Disney's approach to TV as well as the amusement park. But talks soon stalled after Weaver took a slightly revised Disney proposal back upstairs to General Sarnoff.

According to Weaver, he explained to the general that Roy Disney was proposing that his company break ranks with other Hollywood studios and offer the network access to their film library as part of a weekly series, but there was one significant stipulation: in addition to payment for the series, NBC would need to purchase a 25 percent interest in a new Disney amusement park.

"I can't do that," Sarnoff said. "It would put me in show business."

"General," Weaver countered, "what business are we in now?"

"Communications," he replied, bringing the conversation to a decisive close and allowing Weaver to return to Roy.[9]

Roy was fond of relating a slightly different version of these events. After the project stalled with the general's underlings, he finally had a showdown meeting with Sarnoff himself (probably during a subsequent New York trip later that fall), at which they both agreed to call off the entire arrangement because plans for both the TV show and for the amusement park were not moving forward fast enough.

Turned down by NBC—either by Sarnoff directly or by Weaver—Roy ended his workday earlier than he had planned and returned to his room at the Waldorf Astoria. Later that day, he called Leonard Goldenson at the underdog network, ABC—a network that both Walt and Roy initially had perceived as being less able to help with Disneyland than either CBS or NBC.

Beyond ABC, Disney had no real possibilities. There was a fourth national network, the DuMont Network, but by 1953, it was already in the early stages of its death throes and therefore not a viable option.

"Well," Roy said to Goldenson over the phone, "you once said you wanted to make an arrangement with us, are you interested?"

"Where are you?"

Roy told him that he was in New York. At the Waldorf, to be exact.

"I'll come right over," Goldenson replied.[10]

For the past two years, Goldenson had been looking for a way to better compete with NBC and CBS, both of which enjoyed a substantially larger list of affiliate stations and therefore more viewers and higher advertising revenue than ABC. In 1953, NBC had sixty-three primary stations (a combined total of affiliate stations plus those it owned-and-operated), CBS thirty, ABC fourteen, and DuMont a paltry six, only three of which were true affiliates. Because of this, Goldenson was interested in— or at least curious about—a possible commitment with the Disney brothers for both the park and the TV show, not only to compete with the more successful networks but also to save his company from a DuMont-like failure. From conversations with an ABC executive named David Wallerstein, Goldenson already knew a few things about Walt's amusement park before his meeting with Roy and had cautiously expressed interest in a possible Disney-ABC deal.

"How much is Disneyland going to cost?" he asked Roy, who sat opposite him in a dimly lit room, as waiters cleared their lunch plates.

"Walt figures from two to five million to get started," he said. He took a drink from his water glass then set it back on the table before looking directly at Goldenson. "But I figure maybe ten million."[11]

Even with those astronomical numbers, Goldenson was not deterred, sensing that this might be his one chance to bring cinema-quality entertainment to his struggling network. He believed his best chance to catch-up with the other networks was to incorporate familiar movie personalities, such as animated characters from the Disney studio library, into ABC's programming. He nodded and signaled the barkeep with a pair of fingers to bring another round. He knew that the Disney offer had been turned down by the other two networks, and from friends in finance, understood that banks would not underwrite an amusement park without ample security. "ABC," he later wrote, "was really Disney's last hope."[12]

Though Goldenson never publically acknowledged this, Disney was also ABC's last, best hope as well.

Over the next two days, Roy developed a handshake deal with Goldenson. Though the terms were not yet solidified, the two men agreed that ABC would make a direct investment in Walt's park and also guarantee financing to finish its construction. In the initial agreement, ABC would find a way to guarantee $2.5 million in construction loans for the completion of Disneyland, though that amount was quickly raised to almost $5 million. Exactly how ABC would guarantee $5 million of financing outside of the usual circle of investment bankers remained a significant problem. In return, ABC would become a part owner of Disneyland and receive a weekly program for their network, produced twenty-six times each year.[13]

There was one catch, however: the deal needed to be approved both by the board of directors for ABC and the board of directors for Walt Disney Productions. Roy returned to California with the news. Though it would be months before the deal could be finalized, both Walt and Roy saw the development as a bit of good luck—perhaps the only good luck the Disneyland project would experience for months.

In October of 1953, the city manager of Anaheim was Keith Murdoch, who at the age of thirty-four was relatively young to hold a position of such importance. For the past three years, he had been watching contractors pave over farmland to build new houses for America's quickly expanding middle class. He was generally aware that speculators and developers were purchasing land inside the city and in nearby unincorporated areas of the county, though he had no idea that anyone was eyeing his sleepy little city for one of the largest amusement parks in the world.

Having failed to purchase the original Ball Road parcel, C. V. Wood, Buzz Price, Nat Winecoff, and Dick Irvine decided to change strategies. After assessing the risks and benefits of confiding in key city officials, they agreed to discuss their project with at least one person in Anaheim. The first meeting would take place shortly after Winecoff finished his work as an honorary judge for the Anaheim Halloween Parade.

On Saturday, October 31, Nat Winecoff drove to Anaheim, most likely with one or two other members of the Disney public relations team. He walked through the outdoor festival, passing carnival-style food booths and games of chance. The day's events included a children's parade, a "Wiskerino" contest to identify the man with the bushiest beard, and a beauty pageant to announce the festival queen. In the afternoon, Winecoff joined the other seventeen judges to award prizes to the best floats—that is, floats that would later appear in the festival's fabulous evening parade. Included in the group were those created by Disney: on one, Cinderella stood before a fairy-tale castle; in another, Mickey Mouse and Donald Duck rode an amusement-park coaster called "Tunnel of Spooks." It was as though, through these artistic contributions, Disney was hinting at its larger aims.

The judges fell, by and large, into two groups: members of the Hollywood entertainment community, such as Winecoff, and members of companies looking to expand their manufacturing business in California, such as two executives from the Ford Motor Company. All of the judges were selected for the same reason: to introduce business executives to the town of Anaheim.[14]

After finishing his duties as a judge, Winecoff quietly explained to Earne Moeller, a member of Anaheim's chamber of commerce, Walt's plan to build an amusement park in Orange County. Understanding the importance of this conversation, Moeller asked if it would be all right to include City Manager Keith Murdoch in their discussion. Winecoff agreed.

But even here, it is unclear exactly who was playing whom. For months, Winecoff had made trips to Anaheim, helping to organize Disney's participation in the Halloween festival, while slyly asking Earne Moeller and others about zoning ordinances. But years later, one city official would confess that Moeller was also playing Disney in that he had known about the amusement project for months, most likely from a local realtor: "When Earne Moeller, who was the executive secretary of the chamber of commerce, heard about Disney's interest in establishing a park, he invited Walt's personal representative for this expansion—a fellow by the name of Nat Winecoff—to come to the Halloween Parade to be a judge." So it's possible that the chamber of commerce (without Keith Murdoch's knowledge) had been quietly feeding Winecoff information about Anaheim with the hopes of bringing the now-secret amusement-park project to their city.[15]

Late in the afternoon, as the autumn sun sent long shadows across town, the three men sat in a parked car, hidden away in an alley behind the Chamber office building. Once settled, Winecoff relaxed, his demeanor becoming more casual, his body turned in the driver's seat to face Moeller and Murdoch. He explained Walt's problems in detail, specifically that sections of the parcel recommended by SRI had been bought out from under them, requiring them to search for a new site. The new site, Winecoff explained, needed to be located close to the freeway expansion. It needed to be relatively flat as Walt intended to build a lake on it large enough for a steamboat. It also needed to be free of electrical lines and other tall structures, allowing Walt a clear shot to send television signals from the park to the signal antennae atop Mt. Baldy. Though it's unclear exactly how much information Moeller had previously possessed about the Disney park, both men were surprised by the enormity of the plan. Moeller and Murdoch agreed to search for other possible sites within or near the city limits and report back to Winecoff in a couple of days.

"We outlined two likely sites," Murdoch later wrote, "which met Disney's criteria of about 160 acres near to and accessible from a freeway. One was along the west side of Euclid, north from Ball Road. The other was bound by La Palma, Magnolia, Crescent and Gilbert. Both sites were mainly orange groves with few buildings."

The following Saturday, Walt, along with Dick Irvine and Nat Winecoff, drove to Anaheim in a family-style station wagon to view the sites with Moeller and Murdoch. Murdoch took them down Euclid to the first site, though along the way, they passed a cemetery owned by the Los Angeles Diocese that had fallen into disrepair. Weeds grew waist-high and nearly covered some grave markers. Walt viewed the cemetery with disappointment, lowering his eyebrows and shaking his head. Noticing this, Moeller explained that the diocese had already promised to clean up the site, but this did little to mollify Walt.

"I wouldn't bring my guests past this for love nor money," Walt said. Without even stopping to consider the area, he asked, "Do you have another site?"

"Yes, we do," replied Murdoch.

The next site, located on La Palma Avenue, pleased Walt— it was a large tract of land filled with orange trees and other produce. The land appeared flat and held few structures. They parked on a strip of bare dirt beside an orange grove. Once outside, they walked down dirt avenues between rows of trees. Moeller indicated that the owners would most likely be cooperative and willing to sell at a reasonable price. Excited again, Walt took his men out to a celebratory lunch, though the only restaurant he knew in the entire area was the famous fried-chicken diner at Knott's Berry Farm—the same restaurant where he had eaten a few meals the previous year while researching the amusement-park business. Over lunch, Walt spoke in a soft, enthusiastic tone, describing how his park might appear on that piece of property.

At a nearby table, however, sat a local realtor, who understood enough of Walt's conversation to discern roughly where this new amusement park would be situated. The following day—while Walt was developing a strategy to secure this new site—this realtor quietly approached landowners, explained that a large company was interested in their land, and obtained listings on some key parcels.

"When Disney found out about that action," Murdoch recalls, "he was infuriated. . . . He was already a little touchy because of [the loss of the original Ball Road site], and so when the second one [was lost] in much the same manner, he would have no part of it. . . . He decided not to proceed."[16]

In years to come, Walt would rarely talk about this second site for his amusement park, presumably embarrassed by his mistake and continued naïveté, but once, when directly questioned, he explained to a local reporter: "We found one tract [in Anaheim] but when people found out what it was for, the price went up."[17]

With the initial Ball Road and the La Palma sites now lost, Disney and SRI decided to investigate other locations near Anaheim. Though a site in Santa Ana had ranked high on an earlier list of possible locations, Nat Winecoff specifically recalls: "We then shifted to Garden Grove," where the team began to consider sites with slightly higher land values.[18]

Back in Anaheim, Keith Murdoch and other city officials continued to search for an alternate location so as not to lose Disney's amusement park to another city. "The effect of the leakage of the well-kept secret at Knott's," Earne Moeller later wrote, "and the threat of competition for the location of [the amusement park] elsewhere acted as a catapult, for my office became more resolved than ever to hold onto the most promising prospect of putting Anaheim on the map and establishing a sound economic base for the ascending and inevitable growth and transformation from a small quiet agricultural-oriented settlement into a robust dynamic city."[19]

For residents of Anaheim, the break came a couple weeks later, when after church one Sunday, Murdoch was sitting alone in his office, staring at an area map tacked to his wall which identified all of the land parcels in northern Orange County, as well as their exact acreage and the names of their owners. "I kept looking at that doggone map," Murdoch remembers, "thinking where can we locate it?" By chance, he happened again to study the original Ball Road site, located just outside the city limits, and as he did, he realized something important about the property: the land speculator had only purchased twenty acres, leaving a great deal of the original site available to Disney. His eyes followed the property lines south, noting again that the original site ended at Cerritos Avenue. But on the other side of Cerritos Avenue, he found more family farms, most of which he thought could be purchased for a fair price. Then it occurred to him: the county would only need to close Cerritos Avenue to interest Disney in this area again. Because the land was just outside the city limits and located in the unincorporated territory, city officials didn't have jurisdiction to close the road by themselves, but Murdoch was fairly sure that county officials would agree to close that section of the road, so long as Disney owned all of the surrounding land.

Consulting a book on municipal law, he read the procedures required to close a section of a county street, only to discover that he had been correct. If Disney owned the surrounding land, the county should agree to abandon a section of a street for a purpose beneficial to the region. Believing his plan had the potential to locate Disney's park on land that would most likely become part of Anaheim through annexation, he called

Earne Moeller, who excitedly agreed to call Nat Winecoff and Dick Irvine the following morning.

That week, Moeller and Murdoch met with Walt, Irvine and Winecoff at the Burbank studio. Using a map, Murdoch outlined his plan to create a new site for Walt's amusement park by using part of the original site combined with additional property south of Cerritos Avenue. The new site would effectively be located one block south of the original Ball Road location.

Guarded but interested, Walt asked, "Can you do that?"

Murdoch explained the procedure to close a portion of a street located in an unincorporated section of Orange County.

Walt studied the map, tilting his head, before turning his attention back to Moeller and Murdoch. "If you can close that street, we've got a deal."

Walt extended his hand, and with that, the assembled men began to smile. On the basis of Murdoch's presentation, Walt was drawn back to Anaheim—specifically to fourteen family citrus, walnut, and sweet potato farms along the proposed route of the new interstate freeway. A good mood moved through the conference room, though the enthusiasm was muted. By now, everyone understood that, even with a new site identified, they were still a long way from securing the land for Walt's park.[20]

During these same months, while some Disney men worked to lock up a site, Walt expanded the WED team to better design his park. Though in its early months, WED had been comprised almost entirely of architects, live-action art directors, and set designers, Walt now brought in studio animators and artists more familiar with his animated films to design individual attractions. In a projection room, these animators and artists reviewed many classic Disney features—such as *Snow White*, *Pinocchio*, and *Dumbo*—looking for ways to adapt story elements into two- or three-minute amusement rides. The men were given, what was later called, a "blue-sky" period in which they were encouraged to express any idea, no matter how outlandish, as a concept for an amusement ride. Using the creative process familiar to animators, these men illustrated their ideas for each sequence of a ride on rectangular sheets of paper, then tacked them up to corkboard, just as they would when arranging the scenes for an animated cartoon. Each afternoon, Walt would examine their illustrations, juggling some around and removing others to refine each ride's basic concept. Walt later explained this period of the park's development to a newspaper reporter: "We just started dreaming a lot of storyboards with notes on them, the way they do in typical Disney fashion."[21]

But such straightforward descriptions remove the intimacy of these storyboard sessions. Many animators recall how Walt would pantomime the gestures of characters in each ride, acting out each part with an actor's precision. "Walt would get enthused about any one of these [possible rides] we happened to be discussing," Marvin Davis later recalled. "And he would throw himself into the story and he would visualize himself going through this ride."[22]

Of these animators and artists transferred to WED, no one was better skilled at imagining cinematic rides for children than Bruce Bushman, a man who had once worked on *Fantasia*. He was a large man who was occasionally teased about his weight—however, in the business culture of the 1950s, it was not considered inappropriate to call a heavy man "fatso" so long as the insult was offered with affection. More importantly, unlike the other artists and animators, Bushman seemed to intuitively understand how children would respond to these themed fantasy environments.

For over a decade, Bushman had dressed up as a convincing Santa Claus for local charity events. Seated on his red velvet throne, behind a snowy beard, he saw how children lost themselves inside a make-believe Santa's village. He observed children as they wandered through the fairy forest, the way they liked to be both tickled by the friendly elves and scared by the elves who were mean. Through this experience, he was able to create ride concepts for Fantasyland that seemed more generously imagined than those developed by other artists.

During this "blue-sky" period, he developed the spinning teacups concept into a swirl of pastels, oversized cups on a yellow-and-purple platter. Though never built, in the Bushman version, a twelve-foot-high Mad Hatter and a menacing Marsh Hare were seated in the center of the Mad Tea Party, forever hoisting cups to children, as the ride platter circled around them. His initial pencil drawings for the Dumbo Flying Elephant attraction used a series of frightening pink elephants—taken from the highly stylized nightmare segment of the film—as the ride vehicles, instead of the child-friendly gray elephants that were later built.

He drew concept art for a Donald Duck bumper boat ride and a windmill Ferris wheel, neither of which were built. He believed that the pirate-ship restaurant at the edge of Fantasyland should be mounted on an enormous turntable, allowing diners slowly to take in a view of the entire park—an idea that Walt liked, but proved too expensive. In his initial version, the Fantasyland canals didn't feature canal boats, rather bathtubs (a la "rub-a-dub-dub, three men in a tub"), but after a European vacation, Walt believed that canal barges would prove more elegant.

Bushman's most elaborate idea for an attraction was a Pinocchio thrill ride, called "Monstro the Whale," in which guests, loaded into boats, floated by scenes inspired by the movie that featured Jiminy Cricket and Geppetto. At the ride's conclusion, the boat splashed down a twenty-foot flume formed by the angry mouth and extended tongue of Monstro, the demonic whale from the movie's frightening climax, as though the boat were being expelled from his sour mouth.[23]

But Bushman's contributions extended beyond his ability to imagine unique rides based on Walt's films. Within weeks of joining the WED team, he began to refine ride concepts, such as the Peter Pan and Mr. Toad attractions, attempting to stage each as though it were a movie, every room a new scene, creating drama in addition to beautiful scenery. For the Casey Jr. Circus Train, he colored-up each car to resemble the palette used in *Dumbo* but also to complement the palette of other Fantasyland attractions. In general, he worked to unify Fantasyland as a place where the rides together offered a cohesive statement—as opposed to a carnival where rides offered visual confusion.

At the suggestion of Anaheim officials (specifically, Earne Moeller and Keith Murdoch), Walt agreed to abandon his relationship with the realtors at Coldwell Banker, in favor of using two local realtors, Frank Miller and Ed Wagoner, who already had the trust of many Anaheim residents and understood the needs of farmers, to pursue purchasing options on the new Ball Road site. Moeller and Murdoch felt that Walt stood a better chance of not only acquiring the fourteen properties on Ball Road by using local realtors but also keeping the exact nature of the amusement project under wraps until the land had been fully optioned. Of these realtors, at least one—Miller—had been previously successful in acquiring multiple parcels for industrial developments and therefore understood how to operate in an environment of secrecy.

But these measures did not go far enough for C. V. Wood. Having repeatedly learned his lesson about opportunistic speculators and realtors in Southern California, Woody moved into high gear: he protected the new site by leaking a story to the press claiming that Disney's true intentions were to build an amusement park in the San Fernando Valley, roughly fifty miles east of Anaheim. It was through actions such as these that Walt began to understand why his brother so liked C. V. Wood: Woody could manipulate the press and perhaps other individuals to save an important business deal.

Even before purchase negotiations could begin, Walt asked his friend and radio personality, Art Linkletter, to join him on a trip to the new Ball Road site. Along with Woody and Buzz Price, Walt drove Linkletter out to Anaheim. Once there, they parked at the edge of the road, walked through the orange trees, following paths and irrigation lines used by farmers, to get a feel for the location. Before leaving, Walt climbed a small mound of dirt to better see the surrounding area. He stood there for many minutes, surveying the land, imagining how he might transform it. "We were all sworn to secrecy about this place, Anaheim," Linkletter recalls, "and I remember thinking to myself, 'These people are crazy . . . we're 30 or 40 miles from the city in a sleepy backwoods. Who's going to come way out here?'"[24]

Though C. V. Wood made many trips to the new site in Anaheim—including some to talk with landowners—his primary responsibility for the final months of 1953 was to oversee a study to investigate the feasibility of operating a year-round amusement park in Southern California. In general practice, a feasibility study determines if a commercial project will be "feasible" and "profitable," though in this situation, it was virtually a foregone conclusion that, if Walt had his way, the park would be built. So, instead, the study adopted a unique slant: to forecast the number of seasonal visitors and estimate their total expenditures. The finished report would be used not only to refine the plans for Walt Disney's amusement park, but also to entice new corporate sponsors to invest in the project. Though no one said as much, everyone knew that the report might also prove useful in closing the deal with ABC, as the ABC board of directors had not yet approved the development agreement with Disney.

Beyond these initial problems, Woody faced a more serious challenge: no one at SRI—or more bluntly, no one at *any* economic forecasting firm—had ever completed a feasibility report for the type of large-scale outdoor amusement facility envisioned by Walt. To determine Disneyland's economic possibilities, Woody and his lead economist, Buzz Price, visited more than ten major amusement parks, museums, and zoos in the U.S., as well as Tivoli Gardens in Copenhagen, Denmark, paying particular attention to crowd densities, traffic flow, and sales of individual ride tickets. "We studied attendance peaks, seasonal variations, per capita visitor expenditures, on-site crowd densities, required ride capacity as a function of attendance and investment levels," Price explains. "At the time we did not have names for these things. They had to be invented."[25]

One of the most interesting things Woody and Price discovered while visiting these parks concerned the importance of a line. It was Woody's observation that it didn't matter how good a ride was, if it didn't have a line, people wouldn't buy tickets for it. And so, as plans for Disneyland developed, Woody looked for ways to ensure that every ride would most always have a line, even if that line was comprised of just a few people. One of his suggestions was to open rides gradually, managing the number of customers they could accommodate each hour. For that Jungle River ride, maybe the park could run just two or three boats in the morning, when the park was empty, allowing the line to build. As more customers entered the line, more boats could be added, keeping the line at about 150 people. Woody believed that "the line" was magic: people attracted more people.[26]

Woody and Price also discovered ways to manage ride capacity. If you built a park for 20,000 guests per day, you would need to have enough rides so that, during peak times, each guest could ride between one and two rides every hour—that is, an overall ride capacity to accommodate 30,000 riders per hour. With this, they were fairly sure that the park would need to have more attractions than initially planned. As Disneyland would earn most of its money through ticket sales, Woody and Price understood that if the park didn't have enough rides it would not optimize its income potential.[27]

Along with the exploration of rides and attractions, the WED team explored ways to create what, essentially, would be an outdoor mall (Main Street) and food-service counters. In the fall of 1953, Disney approached John Gostovich, general manager of the Los Angeles Farmers Market—an outdoor market so large it was, in essence, one of the city's most significant tourist attractions. Gostovich recommended a "high entrance fee to the park to keep out the loafers and undesirable characters." Among the problems with the LA Farmers Market, in his opinion, were some regulars "who have nothing to do all day but sit around on benches . . . watching people walk by." He believed that shops should be small and situated on a single level: "people will go in a small store with a few people in it," he explained, "because it looks crowded." He felt that the concept of the Main Street area to be very good, so long as the stores sold high-quality merchandise and the food vendors offered an "assortment of different kinds of food" in various price ranges. The WED team typed up Gostovich's observations into a multi-page memo for Walt.[28]

But none of this information yet answered the big question: how to design the park to ensure a yearly profit?

Relying heavily on attendance patterns for the San Diego Zoo, Price estimated that January would be the slowest month (accounting for only 4 percent of the annual attendance), while July would be one of the busiest months (accounting for 12 percent). He estimated each guest would spend between $2.50 and $3.00 on admission and rides while visiting the park and that in its first year of operation the park would receive between 2.5 million and 3 million guests. But these estimates came with a caveat: the Disney park would need to have the right number of rides so that people could spend between $2.50 and $3.00 per person. If the rides appeared empty, people wouldn't be attracted to them and therefore spend less. If the lines were too long, people would spend too much time waiting in line—as opposed to buying and using additional ride tickets.

The information came back to WED in driblets, observations slowly arranged into a report. But because these estimates were based largely on other amusement facilities, no one at WED knew how much weight to give these numbers in terms of developing an operational plan. Would the Disney park really follow the attendance patterns of traditional amusement parks? Or even a zoo? By and large, the WED team began to incorporate Price's estimates wholesale, mostly because they had no alternative.[29]

In an attempt to confirm some of his underlying economic assumptions, Price made an appointment to meet with Walter Knott, the owner of Knott's Berry Farm, who by now knew a few things about Disney's interest in the amusements industry. Price arrived early, carrying with him material that would illustrate Disney's proposed amusement park—a park the WED team hoped to build a mere seven miles from Knott's Berry Farm. At the time, Knott's was the largest outdoor amusement operation in the region, receiving about one-and-a-half million guests each year. Knowing this, Price assured Knott that the combination of Disneyland and Knott's Berry Farm would be synergistic, creating a larger total market. "Like two department stores together," he repeatedly told the older man. But as Price continued, the weary Knott sat stiffly behind his desk, becoming increasingly concerned and suspicious about this new amusement complex now tentatively slated to be built in his own backyard.

"I left with none of the data I was looking for," Price later revealed, giving the WED team no choice but to blindly trust his economic forecast and its underlying assumptions.[30]

To further investigate the potential profitability of the park and also to better understand ride-design, in late November, C. V. Wood and Buzz Price accompanied three WED employees (Dick Irvine, Nat Winecoff, and Bill Cottrell) to an amusement-industry convention, called the National Association of Parks, Pools, and Beaches, held at Chicago's Sherman House Hotel. The three men from WED attended primarily to meet representatives from companies that manufactured rides for amusement parks, hoping to develop a workable plan to create custom rides for Walt's park, whereas the two men from SRI attended to gather more information for their feasibility report. On the first day, Irvine talked to a number of sales representatives, most of whom had booths, and examined their brochures. Some companies displayed sample vehicles, mostly kiddy cars and roto-planes, designed for the type of corner amusement parks that were popping up by the hundreds in postwar suburban neighborhoods. A few companies had previously contacted Walt Disney Productions by letter or phone, hoping to win contracts to supply rides, as it was generally known that Walt was now interested in the business of outdoor amusements. At one booth, Irvine saw two photos of a steamboat built by Arrow Development, which was one of the companies who had previously contacted the studio. The photos, presented with a soft focus, showed a Mississippi steamboat propelled by a paddle-wheel. It was hard to gauge its exact dimensions, but in terms of design, the boat was very close to the type Walt wanted for his frontier river.

Irvine talked to one of the four joint owners of Arrow Development, a man named Bill Hardiman, who told him that the boat had only been recently finished and therefore they did not yet include it in their brochure. Better quality photographs would be ready soon. Before leaving, Irvine got the contact names and the address for Arrow Development. Luckily, the company was located in California, a quick flight from Los Angeles.

In many ways, the WED men felt out of place at the conference, which was more or less a fraternity of amusement-industry professionals who had known each other for years. The conference culture was more business-oriented and less creative than the studio culture they were accustomed to in Hollywood. But toward the end of the week they were able to persuade seven men central to the industry to attend an evening presentation in their hotel suite to review the overall concept of Disneyland.[31] Though the WED team believed that they were luring the industry men with the promise of Chivas Regal, fine cigars, and caviar, the men mostly came because they were curious about this thing now being called Disneyland.

During the presentation, the WED team, assisted by Woody and Buzz Price, outlined their plans, as they existed in late 1953, for an amusement park by showing artists' renderings and sketches for individual rides and Herb Ryman's bird's-eye map of the park. The attendees, most of them millionaires who owned carnival-style amusement parks with bare-bones mechanical rides, included Harry Batt (owner of New Orleans' Pontchartrain Park), William Schmitt (owner of Chicago's Riverview Park), Ed Schott (owner of Cincinnati's Coney Island Park), and George Whitney Sr. (owner of Whitney's Playland at the Beach in San Francisco). Their reaction, which was tape-recorded by the men from WED for accuracy, was unanimous. They agreed that the Disney plan would be a financial disaster: the experimental rides would cost too much to build and maintain; the lavish landscape design would not increase attendance; the attractions would not accommodate enough guests to make them profitable; many aspects of the park, such as the proposed pirate ship and castle, would produce no revenue whatsoever; the sit-down restaurants would remain empty as people tended to eat hot dogs and drink beer; and guests on the Jungle River ride would see no wildlife as most zoo animals tended to sleep all day.

After their guests left, the WED team and the two men from SRI sat quietly, stunned by the harsh criticism. "It was a chilling evaluation of a new venture that was essentially already underway," Price recalls.

No one looked forward to delivering the bad news to Walt.[32]

But the following week, upon receiving it, Walt was frustrated but not deterred. He simply shook his head in anger and grumbled, "To hell with them," before putting the report aside.[33]

In the days that followed, after his temper cooled, Walt returned to the report, taking what he could from it, particularly the advice about ride capacity and the use of live animals on the jungle attraction. For the past few months, he had been toying with the idea of using the giant squid built for the movie 20,000 *Leagues Under the Sea* for a park attraction. Made from rubber and other synthetics, the squid could be operated through a system of wires and engines, though in daylight, its mechanics would be visible. But now he believed he might adapt the concept of using synthetic, mechanical animals to the Jungle River attraction. "Walt wanted to use the squid from 20,000 *Leagues Under the Sea*," Bill Evans discussed in a 1990 interview, "but it was in bad condition and the wires that pulled the tentacles would have been hard to hide . . . [and so] we began to think of hippos and other animals which could be operated without wires and still have animated elements."[34]

Beyond the actual report, Walt also looked over the brochures that Irvine had acquired at the convention from manufacturing companies. None of the iron rides—with their bare swing systems and exposed tracks—appealed to him.

He wanted rides that were entirely new and beautifully ornamented—nothing like those that existed at other amusement parks.

Even Walt understood the enormity of this request.[35]

After the convention, word was out within the industry that Walt Disney's interest in outdoor amusements was on the rise, his sights now set on a unique park significantly larger than the one he'd originally planned for Burbank. Companies from as far away as Europe sent brochures describing their rides. Salesmen regularly dropped by the studio, wishing to talk to Disney in person. A handful of representatives from a German manufacturing company went so far as to arrive with a prototype miniature car created especially for Disneyland. Though the vehicle appeared more or less like many carnival kiddy cars, the German company had inscribed its green-and-cream hood with the word Disneyland as well as placing Donald Duck's surly image on the trunk. But as WED employees tested the car in the backlot, the vehicle provided a noisy, jittery ride—like so many other stock carnival contraptions.[36]

In general, Walt was disheartened by these salesmen and their tacky brochures. Typical iron rides with their exposed machinery (such as the Octopus, the Scrambler, or a set of swings hanging from a spinning platform) appeared cheap. These rides provided thrills but did not engage the mind or the imagination. But Walt also understood that his crew of animators, art directors, machinists, and special-effects men could not fabricate amusement rides by themselves. In light of this, he contracted with manufacturing firms to provide technical information—including the Cleveland Tram Company, which provided an aerial track system for the Peter Pan ride.[37] He also negotiated with what he felt was the best of these ride manufacturers, the Eyerly Aircraft Company of Oregon, to build a ride based on the movie *Dumbo* in which park guests would ride inside flying elephants.

Lee Eyerly, of Eyerly Aircraft, proposed to adapt the steel mechanism of the rotating Octopus ride, popular at traveling carnivals, for the Disney park. Only instead of the familiar egg-shaped cars, Eyerly would use cars shaped like elephants, each with an interior bench large enough for two people. His men produced at least two miniature models of the proposed Dumbo ride, closely following concept art produced by Bruce Bushman. But after viewing them, Walt believed that the Eyerly models appeared too much like a stock carnival ride, with lots of steel and exposed machinery. The models did not incorporate the sense of whimsy and playfulness evident in Bushman's draw-ings. As with other aspects of Disneyland's design, Walt now believed that he would need to closely supervise the construc-tion of unique attractions, perhaps fabricating them in the same studio machine shop that had once produced his backyard train.

But at the urging of Dick Irvine, Walt agreed to visit one last amusement-ride company with the purpose of inspecting a paddle-wheel steamboat that, at least in photos, appeared similar to the one Walt wanted at his park.

From previous correspondence, Irvine knew that Arrow's cus-tom-built steamboat, powered by a gas motor, was capable of offering guests a scenic tour of a lake. He also understood that the craft was significantly smaller than the one Walt desired, but he was hoping that the design of the boat could be adapted or resized to suit Disneyland. In preparation for a possible visit by Walt, some of the men from WED, including Dick Irvine and animator Bruce Bushman, flew up to San Francisco to inspect the rides at the Arrow plant. They viewed cars, small-scale trains, and carousels built for other parks, though the paddle-wheel boat remained at a city lake forty miles away in Oakland.

Following a positive report, Walt flew with Bushman and Irvine to San Francisco, where they rented a car to visit the Arrow plant. As Walt drove his men to Mountain View, they had a chance to discuss problems with the Disneyland project, primarily how long it was taking to secure options on all 150 acres in Anaheim despite using local realtors. As the men approached the town, the conversation turned just as quickly back to the job at hand. Irvine felt confident that the Arrow steamboat, once adapted and enlarged, would satisfy Walt's desire to have a Mississippi paddle-wheeler at Disneyland, but as the rental car pulled up to the Arrow buildings, he saw that the boat, newly repainted and displayed on wooden stands, was much smaller than he'd expected—little more than twenty-five feet in length. It was clear now that the boat was designed exclusively for children, not families. Unlike the photos in which the boat appeared stately, in person the boat appeared flashy, lacking attention to historic detail. "Lil' Belle" was spelled in thick black letters across the bow. Rising from its roof were two crown smokestacks disproportionate in scale to the rest of the boat. Just below the miniature wheelhouse was a highly polished brass bell. It was this detail—the oversized bell—that made the boat look cheap.

Walt did not spend much time examining the Lil' Belle. "He didn't even take notice of it," recalls one of the men at the site.

Instead, Walt briefly talked with the four joint owners of Arrow, including a balding man named Karl Bacon and a younger man named Ed Morgan, before his attention was drawn to a set of kiddy cars fashioned after old Model Ts. Bushman noticed Walt's interest gravitate toward the cars. Walt stopped ten feet from them, specifically to regard one from a distance, before examining it up close. Unlike the stern-wheeler, the cars were better detailed, but still not what he wanted for his amusement park.

"I had no idea of the scope of Disneyland," Ed Morgan, co-founder of Arrow, admitted decades later. "Of course, there is a great bit of difference between our boat and the boat they would build for Disneyland. No one had heard of a theme park at that time."

Walt, who had mostly soured on amusement-ride companies, was ready to leave the Arrow plant when Bruce Bushman approached him alone. Like others at WED, Bushman believed that studio artists simply couldn't build an amusement park by themselves. They would need the help of an experienced ride design team. Bushman told Walt that these Model Ts were not terribly different from the cars that Bushman had himself designed for the Mr. Toad ride—a ride in which cars would careen through English country streets. Despite his reservations, Walt agreed that these cars might somehow be transformed into vehicles for the Mr. Toad ride.

With Walt's reluctant approval, Bushman walked across the empty workroom, to the far corner, where Karl Bacon and Ed Morgan stood, their hands in their pockets, both of them slightly nervous. Bushman showed the two men a preliminary sketch of the vehicle for the Mr. Toad ride—a colorful drawing that lacked the specific detail and perspective of a proper rendering—and then asked if Morgan could turn this drawing into a workable car.

Morgan considered this. He would later call this vehicle a fired-up hot rod. But these drawings were nothing more than concept art. Cartoon images, really. He would not only have to build the car, he would have to do a great deal of design work as well. From his perspective, the men from Disney seemed utterly unaware of the effort it would take to turn these loose drawings into an amusement vehicle. "Yes," Morgan finally said, "I think we can."

Bushman nodded his head, then returned to the place where Walt stood, only to find that his boss's arms were now crossed, one eyebrow slightly arched, betraying agitation. For all present, Bushman's role was now clear: he was the mediator, carefully nudging Walt to hire an experienced ride manufacturing company despite obvious reservations. "He had a fairly brief conversation with Walt," Morgan remembers, "then came back to me."

"Well," Bushman said to Bacon and Morgan, "I think what we'd like to do is have you make one of the cars from the sketches I've brought with me. Don't assume these are final. But they pretty much show what we're looking for."

While walking to the rented car, Bushman handed Morgan a folder that contained all of the drawings for the Mr. Toad car. They said their goodbyes and left. Only later would Morgan realize that the men from Disney had departed without offering a formal contract, discussing price, or even the possibility of work beyond this initial car, a mere prototype. Morgan knew exactly what this meant: the Mr. Toad car needed to be perfect if Arrow wanted to do more business with Walt Disney.[38]

Back in Anaheim, the problems of acquiring the new Ball Road site were quickly becoming larger than anyone had imagined.

C. V. Wood and Bill Cottrell worked with the two Anaheim real estate agents to secure the initial 150 acres of land, attempting to arrange individual deals with over a dozen separate owners, some of whom lived as far away as Ohio. Many of the landowners saw strange cars repeatedly passing by their property. From rumors, they gathered that someone was trying to buy individual farms in a group purchase, though no one at that time suspected it was anything more than a housing developer.

Again, the realtors were directed to make offers slightly below a fair market value for the land—offering an option of $100 per acre against a purchase price of $4,000 per acre.

The realtors explained how the contract worked to each owner: the owner would receive $100 per acre up front if they agreed to give an unnamed buyer the option of buying the land at $4,000 per acre later in the year. The $100 per acre was theirs to keep, even if the unnamed buyer decided not to purchase the property.

Each deal presented its own problems, but Woody and Cottrell, along with the two local realtors, worked to bring the combined parcel intact to Disney. The realtors told everyone that they would get the same price per acre, $4,000, but within that, for hesitant sellers, they decided to offer generous sums for structures and other land improvements, effectively paying more for some acreage while creating the illusion of equality between all landowners. "We felt that by then working with them individually on their houses," C. V. Wood later explained, "that this would give us a way of compensating some of them who obviously didn't want to move or were a potential hold-out."[39] Some owners were given upwards of $15,000 for worthless old farmhouses, destined to be torn down. Beyond this, as negotiations continued, Disney authorized the realtors to offer a few holdouts a price noticeably higher than the original $4,000 per acre. At least one owner received $5,000 per acre, simply by threatening not to sell.

Aside from financial incentives, Woody and the realtors enticed many sellers into signing through special provisions, each handwritten into the contract. In retrospect, these individual meetings between Woody and the sellers were essential to closing more than one deal, and without them, the entire site might've been lost. In reviewing the contracts, it seems clear that Woody would have OK'd almost any request, no matter how crazy, so long as the amendment produced a signature on the option contract. One coworker later explained Woody's loose and borderline shady dealings to assemble this parcel: "He was young and charismatic, and he could charm farmers out of their orange groves with his Texas talk. I don't know . . . and I don't even want to know . . . about some of the ways borders were changed and people were persuaded to sell their land to Disney."[40]

One seller reserved the right to remove all of the wall-to-wall carpeting from the house, as well as to remove select shrubbery and equipment used to raise chickens. One owner wanted to relocate his entire house. Another seller requested the right to remove wind machinery—with a removal date as late as August 1, 1954. The Dominguez family agreed to sell only if the "unnamed owner" promised to preserve a large palm tree given to the family in the late 1890s as a wedding gift. (The tree could be somehow incorporated into the jungle attraction, Woody reasoned.) But the most elaborate request was made by a family who owned twenty acres central to the site. They agreed to sell their farmland only if their daughters could continue to live in the house at its current location once the new project was built—meaning that they would live on land presently earmarked for the edge of Disneyland's parking lot. Even this ridiculous request was OK'd by Wood in order to preserve the deal.[41]

Though Buzz Price estimated that the original Ball Road site would cost an average of $6,200 per acre, mainly due to the high cost of purchasing the Viking land, Wood worked to acquire the new site well beneath this estimate, at an average cost of just under $4,600 per acre. As he acquired a prime site for Disneyland—a site only a stone's throw from the original location—Woody began to suggest to both Roy and Walt that he might be interested in leaving SRI to build this experimental park. He was growing tired of SRI, with its rules, strict organization, and lack of further opportunity for advancement. He wanted to have more freedom in his work life. Plus, as general manager of Disneyland, he would be able to hire some of the Bombers to work with him again, once more recreating the rambunctious social life he had so loved in high school.

Though Woody was young and somewhat inexperienced, Roy Disney understood that he now possessed a working knowledge of amusement parks from his research trips for Walt. Additionally, from his days at Consolidated, Woody had gained experience as a project manager and a company planner. In his best moments, Woody appeared to revel in Walt's vision for the park. But unlike Walt, he possessed real-world experience in construction and manufacturing. Most importantly, he had a natural sense about business: he knew how to create and save deals, even if some of his methods were unusual, unconventional, and perhaps even somewhat unethical.

The only other inside person who might have been considered for the lead role at Disneyland would've been Nat Winecoff. Presently, he was exploring the possibility of leasing space inside Disneyland with both local and national companies. Included in these early talks were Ford, General Electric, General Motors, and Coca-Cola. When corporate executives were in Los Angeles for a convention, Winecoff quietly invited them to the studio to discuss Disneyland in private, often promising them a tour of the animation facilities as a bonus. By and large, these discussions went poorly.

On March 18, three members of the Coca-Cola Company visited the studio, where Winecoff pitched a Coca-Cola "bottling plant" and exhibit in the Main Street section of Disneyland. The executives, however, appeared confused as to the nature—and cost—of participation. They wanted to know how big the park would be and if Winecoff had any mimeographed maps. The Disneyland concept was so foreign that Nat Harrison, a leading adman at Coca-Cola asked, "People will be able to go into these stores?" as he thought the Main Street section might be exterior facades—much like a movie set.

There would be plenty of indoor space, Winecoff explained.

He then outlined the cost structure for lessees, which caused
one of the execs to murmur: "Sizeable amount of bucks." This
same exec also suggested that sponsors, such as Coca-Cola,
might be more valuable to Disney than Winecoff realized and
might be invited—at a greatly reduced cost—to participate.
"Don't you imagine," he offered, "your exhibitors would send
out a lot of advertising pieces, saying, 'Come and see us in
Disneyland?'"

At times, the Coca-Cola execs expressed enthusiasm, calling
the park a place for "a wonderful afternoon." They also voiced
concern: "I can't see how you can build it and get it in operation
in a year, though." As with all of Winecoff's sales attempts, the
talks broke down with no firm agreement in place, not even
a subsequent meeting scheduled, just Winecoff's promise to
send more materials. The Coca-Cola meeting ended when Harrison, having seen enough, asked: "Could we go through and
see how a Disney picture is made?"[42]

By mid-March, 1954, only two barriers stopped Walt from
beginning work on his park in Anaheim: the first was the pending partial closure of Cerritos Avenue to create a unified site,
the other was the unsigned contract with ABC.

Though, in theory, the quarter-mile closure of Cerritos Avenue seemed to be a foregone conclusion once Disney acquired
option contracts on all of the surrounding land, in practice
the closure did not go as smoothly as Anaheim city officials
had promised. By late March, even Anaheim city officials were
concerned because the County Board of Supervisors had yet to
begin the legal proceedings necessary to abandon this section
of Cerritos Avenue as requested. From the perspective of Anaheim officials, "the project hinged upon a decision of this body
of lawmakers, and it had to occur without further delay."[43]

The problem, city officials soon learned, was that the County
Board of Supervisors had not obtained sufficient proof that

the road closure was justified. To rectify this situation, Earne Moeller and Keith Murdoch, along with Anaheim mayor Charlie Pearson, arranged a meeting between two county supervisors and Walt Disney so that the project could move forward as soon as possible.

On one afternoon late in March, Moeller drove the two county supervisors in his car from Orange County to the Disney studio in Burbank, while Murdoch and Mayor Pearson followed in a separate vehicle. Once at the studio, they were met by Walt and Roy as well as high-level managers, including publicity department director Joe Reddy. The supervisors were given a general briefing on the state of the proposed amusement park, as well as a full tour of the studio, which included enormous sets for 20,000 *Leagues Under The Sea*. Finally, the supervisors were guided into the studio projection room where, in anticipation of a general announcement, Walt had already begun to display colorful drawings of the rides planned for the park, as well as Herb Ryman's aerial site map. With enthusiasm, Walt explained the ride or attraction in each drawing, and as he did, the board members betrayed signs of enthusiasm. Walt promised to run a clean park, one far different in conception than those noisy parks down by the beach.

The visitors had a number of questions, even going so far as to ask if the park would serve peanuts-in-the-shell, as one local amusement park was constantly littered with peanut shells.

Walt assured his guests that there would be no peanut shells in his park. He would even include this requirement in the contract of each lessee who rented retail or restaurant space at Disneyland.

Just before they left the studio, Joe Reddy, the publicist, quietly expressed Walt's deep frustration concerning the closure of Cerritos Avenue to Earne Moeller. Once in his car, Moeller explained to the county supervisors that plans to develop the park were presently stalled because of the issue surrounding Cerritos Avenue. Walt would not even issue a press release about his park until the county board reached a decision. Though Moeller never pointed out that Walt might leave Anaheim for another location, the board members now understood that this was a strong possibility.

On the drive back to Orange County, the supervisors discussed the matter quietly, until one of them—Supervisor Willis Warner—turned to Moeller with an expression of new conviction. "Earne," he began, "you see that telephone booth at the Standard Oil Company's station?"

Moeller nodded and slowed his car into the parking lot.

Handing Moeller a coin, Warner continued: "Call Mr. Reddy and tell him Cerritos will be closed."

Moeller happily made the call.[44]

While Walt was working to complete the site purchase, Roy aggressively struggled to finalize a contract with ABC—a handshake deal that had dragged on for nearly six months without resolution. For weeks, ABC executive Leon Goldenson had tried to persuade the network board that the Disney package would be a sound investment for the company, but many board members objected, using the rationale that if CBS and NBC had passed, then ABC should as well. Goldenson also discovered that even with ABC guarantying the loan, banks in New York and California would not loan the proposed $4.5 million to Disneyland, which led him to examine other possibilities.

At the time, ABC was co-owned by the Paramount Theater chain. There was a man in Texas, Goldenson knew, named Karl Hoblitzelle, who owned a few Paramount theaters and who also was the chairman of the Republic Bank in Dallas. Beyond this, Hoblitzelle owed Goldenson one large favor—which was enough to establish a $4.5 million line of credit for the ABC network as extending to Disneyland, Inc.

In both Hollywood and New York, rumors circulated that the Disney studio would soon license its films to ABC as part of a weekly show, though officials from Disney repeatedly denied these reports as unfounded speculation. On March 24, board members from both Disney and ABC finally agreed on the terms, with financing for the loan arranged through the Republic Bank in Dallas. The contract was signed by representatives from ABC on March 29, 1954.

Almost immediately a representative from Disney—most likely C. V. Wood—floated another bogus story to newspapers in Southern California, suggesting yet again that Disney would not build in Anaheim. The news ran in the March 31 issue of the *Anaheim Bulletin* under the headline: "Hopes Dim for Big Disneyland Project in the City." In retrospect, it seems that the bogus story had one intended effect: to keep land prices from escalating around the site. With the funds now insured by the ABC contract, Disney wanted to purchase more land—even land that did not adjoin the main site. Representatives of Disney would be successful in purchasing three more farms before land values went through the roof.

Though the contract could have been finalized by the end of March, last-minute wrangling on the Disney board delayed its formal approval until April 2. According to the agreement, ABC would become an investor in Disneyland, Inc., a company separate from Walt Disney Productions and WED, by investing a half-million dollars in the park, the first payment of $150,000 due at the execution of the contract. Beyond the direct investment, they would also purchase a weekly TV program from Disney, which in turn would help ABC develop a larger audience. In the first year of the agreement, ABC would pay Walt Disney Productions $50,000 for each television episode produced, $60,000 in the second, and $70,000 in the third. (In subsequent years, payment would be negotiated between the two parties.) Disney would also receive additional money from programs aired more than once. Though most of the contract revenue would go to the studio to pay for the TV shows, fifteen percent of the payments would be transferred to WED to finance Disneyland.[45] In all, the initial three years of the ABC contract was worth almost $7 million, but for Disneyland, more important than the actual payments was ABC's direct investment of a half-million dollars in the park and the promise to immediately guaranty up to $4.5 million in loans to finance construction. In exchange for its investment in Disneyland, ABC would receive a 34.48 percent ownership in the park and also the fast-food concessions for the first ten years of operation—little carts and lunch counters that they would run much like the snack bars in the Paramount theaters they owned.[46]

The pact between ABC and Disney was announced to the press over the weekend of April 3 by Walt himself, who was careful to stress that "his confidence in the theatrical motion picture [was] not diminished," rather that he was "convinced of the compatibility of films and TV." To minimize the backlash from non-network theater chains which still threatened a boycott, he reminded the press that his studio was currently producing the three most expensive theatrical films in its history: *20,000 Leagues Under the Sea*, *Lady and the Tramp*, and *Sleeping Beauty*. He further explained that all of them would be produced in CinemaScope, meaning that they were intended for the wide screens of theaters, not the boxy screens of home TVs.[47]

Almost instantly, the deal between ABC and Disney exacerbated the troubled relationship between movie studios and theater owners, leading Thomas M. Pryor of the *New York Times* to point out the obvious—namely, that Walt Disney was "to become the first leading Hollywood producer to enter into a formal alliance with television."[48] Though Columbia and Republic Pictures had produced material for television, they had consistently done so by using subsidiary production companies to protect the distinctiveness of their trademark names.[49] In response to the ABC-Disney announcement, officials at most every Hollywood studio reaffirmed their loyalty to the American movie theater. No one was more vehement in his support than Spyros Skouras, president of Twentieth Century Fox. "We have been approached [by TV networks]," he told the press shortly after the ABC-Disney announcement, "and we have refused because we believe the future is in the theater. If we were to sell our pictures today to television, it would hurt the box office. It would be very disastrous at this time to destroy the theater business."[50]

Though the contentious ABC deal occupied much of Walt's attention that spring, Disney also made a second alliance during those same months. Walt turned to its publishing partner, Western Printing. For the past twenty-two years, Western Printing had published all Disney materials for the United States, including a series of extremely popular Disney comic books. At the age of seventy-six, the company founder, Edward H. Wadewitz, agreed to a company investment of $200,000 in exchange for a 13.79 percent ownership of Walt's park. Additionally, Western Printing would receive its own bookstore on Main Street.

Wadewitz would only live a few more months, but after his passing, Western's president noted that "it was one of the last official acts of E. H. Wadewitz, too, which made Western Printing & Lithography Company an active and invested partner in Disneyland. . . . We are grateful for the foresight of such men as E. H. Wadewitz and for the confidence and friendship of Walt and Roy Disney and their organization." The statement was far warmer and more personal than those issued by ABC.[51]

The remaining investors were all in-house: Walt Disney Productions ($500,000 for a 34.48 percent ownership) and Walt Disney himself ($250,000 for a 17.25 percent ownership).

◆   ◆   ◆

With secure funding in place, Disneyland's prospects were finally on firm ground—even if that success might damage the studio. Disneyland also had a definite location, an accomplishment that was made possible in no small measure by the efforts of C. V. Wood.

Over the same weekend—most likely Saturday, April 3—Roy met privately with C. V. Wood at a bar in Los Angeles. The purpose of this meeting was to discuss Woody's possible role in the further development of Disneyland, a discussion that Roy had initiated a week or two earlier. There are two possible rationales for excluding Walt from this meeting: (1) the general manager of Disneyland would be part of Roy's financial and management team, not necessarily part of Walt's creative team, and/ or (2) even here, in 1954, there were small but noticeable tensions between Walt and Wood. At the end of the meeting, now intrigued by the possibility of this new position, Woody's voice grew loud, its low tones filled with confidence. He concluded by listing those assets he felt he could bring to the park. "I can promote it," Woody said, raising one finger. "I can get the money for it," he said, raising another. "I can build it. I can manage it. And you and your brother can do all the dreams that you want." Woody sat there, a highball glass before him, four fingers raised in the air, as though claiming he could do the jobs of four men, not just one. Then his gaze settled back on Roy.[52]

In his best moments, Woody exuded self-assurance, an energy that those around him often found intoxicating. "He would look you straight in the eye and listen," one associate recalls. "It was like you were the only person who existed in the world."[53]

Needless to say, Woody could not support his promises with specific evidence, other than his work as a team manager at SRI and as a project manager at Consolidated. His promises were built mostly on confidence and personal conviction, but his grand self-assurance would be enough as no one on the Disney team had previously worked with any type of outdoor amusement enterprise.

But from Roy's perspective, there was this: Woody saw the project primarily as a for-profit venture, which might help balance Walt's overwhelming artistic and creative interest in the park. A man like Woody would look after the money, while Walt developed the vision. That the two men didn't always get along likely meant one important thing to Roy: Woody was capable of standing up to Walt.

On April 5, Roy Disney officially gave C. V. Wood the position he'd wanted: to oversee the development of Disneyland. He made Woody promise to stay with the park through construction and at least its first year of operation. In effect, Woody would be Disneyland's first actual employee, its general manager and executive vice president.[54]

Woody received the news early on a Monday morning, a day on which, for the first time, he knew that his future would now be inseparably intertwined with the development of Disneyland. The connection between Woody and the park seemed a natural extension of what he'd already done for the Disney brothers. At his office, he found his childhood friend, Doc Lemmon, who occasionally worked with him. "Doc," he called out, "I got the job of building Disneyland."[55]

The two men talked about the position for a few minutes before Woody went off to share his good news with others.

But Woody did not yet fully understand one of the essential political divisions at the studio—namely, that Roy hired key men associated with management and finance, while Walt hired creative men associated with film production. Because of this, Woody wrongly assumed that his appointment to vice president had been supported equally by both Disney brothers. That afternoon, after a celebratory lunch, Woody went to Walt's office to talk about his new position. They discussed his responsibilities and then reviewed the men Woody wanted to hire for his management team. Though publicly, Walt—or perhaps his publicists—would later claim that Walt welcomed Woody to the team by saying, "Since you [helped plan] this park, get it built," people close to Woody remember the meeting differently, without this warm, enthusiastic exclamation.[56] In their memories, Walt never welcomed Woody to the company with such aphoristic acclaim. Instead, the meeting was casual, yet tense at times, with Walt concluding the conversation on a note of sarcasm—with a line that begrudgingly welcomed Woody to the company yet let him know his place in no uncertain terms: "[Being vice president] doesn't leave much room for advancement," Walt said, as if to remind Woody that he already held the highest job he would ever hold at this new company and that all of his youthful ambitions should be focused on keeping this job rather than on rising from it. There was also a subtext: at this new company, creative individuals, such as Walt, would always be more important than the suits. Walt stood from his chair, said goodbye, then walked off to a production meeting, leaving Woody by himself to absorb his full meaning.[57]

Quietly, Wood walked out of Walt's office, saying a quick goodbye to the secretary. Alone now, he stood in the hallway, his hands in his pockets. Though he was generally good with people, he still could not read Walt Disney. His moods were too difficult. Woody thought about their conversation for a full minute before taking a pack of cigarettes from his pocket and setting one in his mouth. Artists were difficult, he decided. Slowly he walked back to a temporary office the company had offered him at the studio. Once there, he asked his new secretary to make some phone calls.

Now that he was general manager of Disneyland, he needed to build a management team. The problem was Woody had no close friends in the outdoor amusement business. He did, however, know one person who had worked at the New York World's Fair in 1939 and 1940, his old boss at Consolidated, Fred Schumacher. Though Schumacher's training was as an industrial engineer and though he was presently working in the auto industry, he was one of the first people—if not *the* first person—Woody called upon to join the Disneyland team.[58]

"He came over to my house on the same day he was hired, as best I can remember," recalls Schumacher. "He said, 'How would you like to go to work for Disneyland?' And hell, I didn't even know what that was." But ten days later, Schumacher was at the Disney studio, helping Woody to organize the team that would build the Disney park.[59]

Woody also brought with him three longtime friends from SRI—Bill Platt, Charlie Thompson, and Charley Wilkinson—who acted as executive associates, overseeing financial tasks and promotion while occasionally supervising some aspects of construction. He would soon hire other members of the Bombers, such as "Doc" Lemmon, who would become the fifth official employee of Disneyland and eventually oversee the lessees and storeowners inside the park. "If anybody wanted to go to work," Lemmon explains, "and he was a Bomber, he was in."[60]

But Wood did not bring his numbers man from SRI, Buzz Price. By his own choice, Price elected to remain at SRI, hoping to develop the economics office into a larger business. "Wood and I had an effective working association," Buzz later wrote. "I did the work and he operated. [But] I was not in his blood coterie," meaning that he was not part of Woody's inner circle of business associates and childhood friends.[61]

The two business partners remained sociable, but after some months, they drifted apart, each into his own area of specialization. Price returned to the world of financial reports, while Wood took his skills as a salesman and as a presenter to the world of constructed fantasy.

Five

AND STILL NOTHING IS BUILT

With the ABC deal approved, Walt finally revealed his secret project to studio employees not previously privy to the information. Up until this point, he had confided his true plans to very few employees, perhaps as few as twenty, and so in April, he finally told hundreds of other people who worked for him. For the occasion, he reserved the main projection room at the studio and filled its front seats with key members of his staff, executives from ABC, and officials from Bank of America, who now seemed willing to loan Walt money for his park. As studio employees filed in, they found renderings and concept art for the proposed park on easels displayed along the sides of the theater, including images of the castle, the Mississippi steamboat, a stagecoach, and the rocket ship. Most employees had heard rumors that Walt was working on a secret project, but for the most part they had assumed it was either a new series of live-action movies or a small kiddy park, much like the Mickey Mouse Park originally planned for Riverside Drive.

Walt waited as his employees moved around the room in groups to take in each drawing. Fifteen minutes after the hour, the house lights dimmed. Walt appeared at the front of the theater, wearing a dark suit and white shirt. Today, he appeared confident and relaxed, which was a change from his recent turns of manic energy and frustration. With the room now quiet, studio employees felt the electricity of the moment, as though they were all connected to the same live wire. "When

Walt spoke [at that meeting]," animator Bill Justice remembers, "everybody listened."[1]

Walt began by explaining his concept for a new type of amusement park—one without thrill rides and carnival barkers, one that was both entertaining and educational for children. A place the whole family could enjoy. It would be located in Anaheim, he said, which was an area that would soon have a freeway and many new suburban neighborhoods as well. Directing a pointer to Herb Ryman's aerial map, he discussed the park's unique layout: it would only have one entrance, leading to a turn-of-the-century main street that would in turn lead to a circular hub. From there, guests could go to the land of tomorrow, a fantasy kingdom, a jungle exhibit, a miniature train town, a western fort, or a street with international shops. As he discussed each themed land, he pointed to the corresponding section on Ryman's aerial map and then gestured to poster-sized drawings to illustrate key attractions.

Then came the section of the presentation that most concerned Walt. He explained that his studio would produce a weekly program for ABC for a total of twenty-six shows a year. Most of the men at the studio knew that some theater chains had threatened a boycott of studios that produced for TV, but he let this moment pass without commenting on it. Instead, he described the first weekly series the studio would produce. Though originally called *Walt Disney Presents*, it would now be called *Disneyland* to provide exposure for the park.[2] He outlined the other investors—Western Printing and the studio—then continued to talk about the arrangement with ABC. The weekly *Disneyland* program was only one of two projects that Walt hoped to develop for TV. A second was a daily variety program for kids that would feature talented youngsters as well as Disney animation—though the decision to develop a second show was not, at the moment, up to Walt. It was an option that ABC could exercise, assuming the first Disney show proved successful.

Walt made it clear that the studio was now moving away from its historical roots as an animation and film studio. The studio would keep working with animation and live action, but now it would also work with TV and build an experimental amusement park. To conclude his presentation, Walt promised that the studio expansion would provide great opportunities for many of its employees. Those assistant animators wishing to be lead animators may now have a chance to do so. The same for those lead animators wishing to direct. Similarly, some studio men would have an opportunity to work on Disneyland itself.

Applause grew slowly, but firmly. While in the theater, most studio men felt the excitement of the coming projects. It was only later—in some cases, days later—that they realized what these changes would mean for them at the studio. "After our initial shock wore off," Bill Justice recalls, "the full impact of what Walt said began to sink in. Our workload would increase dramatically. We'd have to turn out more film in a week than we had been doing in a year to support this TV schedule."[3] Another studio employee later explained, "We had to get ourselves in high gear, from a [studio development] program that included maybe three, four or five features a year to the prospect of twenty-six shows a year."[4]

But the workload was even larger than most employees initially imagined because the Disney brothers used many key men from the studio to develop Disneyland, shifting them from their company assignments to the WED or the Disneyland payroll, thereby depleting the studio of senior artists just as its production schedule was being stepped up.

A week or so after the meeting, when a sense of urgency again filled the studio, Walt approached the desk of John Hench, a longtime layout and background artist. Walt was no longer the casual, enthusiastic man his employees had seen at the formal presentation. He was directed, driven, once more worried about his amusement park. "I want you to work on

Disneyland," he ordered. "And you're going to like it." He kept right on walking out of Hench's department and into other wings of the studio, presumably to transfer more men to WED and Disneyland.

As Hench recalls: "I didn't even have a chance to answer."[5]

In those early weeks, Walt transferred (or partially transferred) dozens of studio artists to the Disneyland project, but even then, he understood that his own studio would not be able to build the park without additional help. To develop the various themed lands, he looked to art directors more experienced in live-action set design and real-world architecture than those he employed at his own studio. Over the phone, he delegated the responsibility of locating top-quality art directors to Dick Irvine. "I don't care what you have to pay for them," Walt said, "you go out and get the best."[6]

From MGM, Walt hired Wade Rubottom, once the art director for *The Philadelphia Story*, to design part of Main Street, and Gabe Scognamillo, a quirky art director who had a taste for sci-fi films, to design Tomorrowland. He also hired men who had worked with Irvine at Twentieth Century Fox, such as Sam McKim and Bill Martin, to develop the architectural facades of Frontierland and Fantasyland as well as their themed interiors.

When Bill Martin first reported to Dick Irvine's office, Walt told him, "This is not a lifetime job."

"I know," Martin said and then found a desk in the WED bungalow where he might store some of his things. Like most art directors, he was used to working on a project-by-project basis. Why would work on an amusement park be any different?[7]

At the studio, C. V. Wood quickly came to understand the sharp labor divisions inside the company. Though Woody liked to think of himself as a creative individual, he was not a member of the WED design team. In fact, he wasn't even particularly welcome in their social circles. "[Woody] brought his own crew in," observed Bill Martin. "They came from Texas and Oklahoma."[8]

In practice, the WED design team was the extension of Walt's creative authority; likewise, Woody's management team was an extension of Roy's fiscal authority. As Walt developed the creative talent to design the park and its rides, Woody developed a managerial team to build, promote, and run Disneyland, relying on many trusted friends, including coworkers from the Stanford Research Institute, engineers from the aerospace industry, and, of course, childhood friends from Texas. Some of these men would prove invaluable to Walt, but their loyalty for the most part would fall to Woody, not to the Disney brothers.

Woody hired longtime assistants, such as Earl Shelton, to work with him as Disneyland's site manager. He also used his position to payback business associates for old favors, even when those paybacks were not in the best interest of the park. One such apparent favor went to Brett Smithers and Bill Vanburgh in the form of a contract to provide Disneyland with souvenirs. Though Smithers and Vanburgh had absolutely no experience with either amusement parks or souvenirs, they hastily incorporated a new business, named American Souvenirs, Inc., and a few days later possessed a contract, signed by C. V. Wood, to be the exclusive provider of trinket souvenirs to both Disneyland itself and the various leased stores inside the park.

In exchange, Smithers and Vanburgh paid Disneyland (what one lawyer would later call) "some piddly amount" for a distribution deal that was estimated to be worth more than a million dollars.[9] Woody justified his decision by claiming one distributor was necessary for the "strictest control of the source, appearance, quality and design" of souvenirs, though, of course, that was merely his publicly stated rationale.[10]

As with most "friendship" deals arranged by Woody, the work was easy enough—even for a man such as Vanburgh, who had little or no managerial experience—because American

Souvenirs would not manufacture any souvenirs. Rather, as a middleman operation, American Souvenirs took orders from Disneyland and its leased stores, contracted for the manufacture of these souvenirs with third-party companies, then arranged delivery. In the amusement business, standard markup at the time for such a service was 20 percent to 25 percent above wholesale, thereby insuring that American Souvenirs would make a tidy profit for doing very little work.[11]

During these early months—when Woody was just beginning to oversee other deals that would benefit himself as well as Disneyland—he was also making an effort to endear himself to the Disney staff. He repeatedly invited members of WED to his house for dinner and drinks. He even invited Walt Disney's daughter, Diane, and her new husband, Ron Miller, to social events. "Diane and I went to Woody's house a couple times," Miller recalls. "Once for dinner, once for a larger gathering."[12]

But for top-level managerial positions, Wood did not simply hand off jobs to close friends. Though he did work almost exclusively within his network of business associates, he carefully identified men uniquely suited for these roles. A high-quality team of executive managers and supervisors, he understood, would be essential to his success as vice president of Disneyland. Though he never said as much, he must have understood that it would be essential because his own professional experience was limited to that of sales, planning, and team management. Like most of the men with Disney, he was learning about the amusement industry as the project moved along.

For the position of a special consultant to oversee construction of the Mark Twain steamboat, he wanted to hire a retired rear admiral named Joe Fowler, whom he had worked with a few years earlier. In the early 1950s, while employed by SRI, Woody's team of researchers had completed a study for the admiral to unify procedures for guided missiles between the air force, army and navy. From that experience, Woody understood that Fowler knew not only how to direct large projects and work with firm deadlines, but he also knew about the construction of large ships, as he'd managed the U.S. Navy repair shipyard at Mare Island during World War II.

But such an important hire would require personal approval from Walt Disney.

In 1954, Fowler was twenty years older than the average studio employee—he was fifty-nine to be exact—and already retired from a long military career. He was presently living in a large ranch house and overseeing the construction of housing developments just south of San Francisco. Like many construction bosses of the era, he tended to dress in dark jackets, gray slacks, and white shirts. He wore black-rimmed eyeglasses and dark felt hats. His face was comprised of soft, doughy features, which naturally conveyed sympathy, but on the construction site, he had a habit of watching workers from a distance, his hands placed in judgment on his hips, assuming the starchy posture of an admiral.

In early April, he received a call from his friend C. V. Wood to tell him about this new position he'd taken at a movie studio—to build, of all things, an amusement park. Their conversation was peppered with one-liners—as both men were in the habit of memorizing jokes—but Fowler also found himself intrigued by this movie-inspired amusement park. Woody was a good salesman, he knew, but this park interested him in a way he didn't quite understand. Its grandness, perhaps. It was just the type of thing old C. V. would throw himself into.

Before hanging up, Woody promised to send him some information about the park, particularly about this steamboat, in case he wanted to visit it someday.

For the rest of the week, as Fowler continued with his plans to build tract homes, he found his mind drawn back to Woody's crazy park. He reminded himself that it was also a Walt Disney project and, therefore, probably something that would actually make money. At the end of the week, he received another call from Woody. "Joe, I'd like to come up and see you," he said. He would be traveling with a friend or two to inspect a narrow-gauge railroad and other midway rides for that same amusement park. He was wondering if he and his friends might visit with Fowler—though he neglected to mention that one of his traveling companions would be Walt Disney.

"Gee, Woody, that's great," Fowler said. "I'd be glad to see you."

As was Walt's habit, he preferred not to mention the possibility of employment when hiring for top management, so the meeting in San Francisco was defined solely as a social outing, allowing Walt to make a judgment without the pressure associated with a job interview. On paper, Fowler appeared a promising prospect: during the war, he had built a fleet of cargo ships on a tight schedule, and after the war, he oversaw a committee to eliminate waste and unnecessary duplication in fifty-seven branches of the government, including the military. Since retiring from the navy, he'd found work in residential construction, overseeing the development of a new housing project in the Bay Area. On the morning of Saturday, April 17, Walt Disney, C. V. Wood, and Nat Winecoff, boarded a plane headed for San Francisco. They met Fowler at his house in Los Gatos, which was really a small ranch, where they talked briefly about Walt's amusement park before inspecting a locomotive at a nearby park.

When they returned, the Disney men shared a meal and some drinks with Fowler and his wife. Fowler talked about his years in the navy, and in turn, Walt talked about his studio—how it looked like a college campus—and then about his park, how he wanted it to be nothing like the noisy, dirty amusement parks seen in most large cities.

Initially, Walt talked about Disneyland in general terms. At one point, he even pointed to an impressive forty-foot olive tree just outside Fowler's house, commenting, "Boy, I wish we could move that down to Anaheim." But, gradually, he directed the conversation toward the Mark Twain steamboat—as he felt that Fowler, with his experience in shipyards, might be able to offer some specific advice for this project. Before stepping out the door, Walt shook Fowler's hand. "Joe," he said, "I'd like to have you come down next week and have a look at Disneyland. We'll send you a ticket."

The offer was repeated by Wood: "I'd like to have you get the feel of [the place]."

Fowler didn't know how to respond.

Later that night, he discussed the offer with his wife, understanding that Walt and Woody had vaguely suggested that he might work on the Disneyland project as a consultant, probably for this steamboat they wanted to build. For reasons he couldn't explain, he was curious about the place. "Well," he said, "I don't know anything about the motion picture business, but how do you turn down a personal invitation from Walt Disney?" As he fell asleep that night, he wondered what it would be like to be a consultant for a Hollywood movie studio—the idea seemed foreign and alluring to the old navy man. It was something he'd never dreamed of.[13]

In downtown San Francisco, the Disney men returned to their hotel, where C. V. Wood made a call to a man named George Whitney to confirm a meeting the following day. The primary owner of a San Francisco amusement park called Whitney's Playland at the Beach, Whitney was one of the seven men with whom Woody and Price had talked at the Chicago amusement convention the previous November. Out of the seven men, Whitney had offered some of the most practical suggestions to improve the early concepts of Disneyland.

The following day, instead of returning directly to Los Angeles, Walt, Woody, and Winecoff, drove to San Francisco to visit Whitney's amusement park. They could see Playland from almost a mile away: the canopy of its carousel, the scaffolding of its roller coaster, and a ten-foot clown that, like a child's recurring nightmare, crowned the entrance to the funhouse. As they sloped down a coastal access road, they heard the eerily cheerful calliope music and smelled the briny sea air that slowly entered their car. They parked two blocks from the amusements, as better spots were already taken, and walked to the first entrance, where they expected to meet George Whitney. But instead, Whitney sent his thirty-one-year-old son— George Whitney Jr., a tall, thin man with dark hair combed back from his forehead. Dressed in a suit and slender tie, he shook his guests' hands and then explained that his father was temporarily delayed. In his absence, he would guide them through the park.

Unlike the WED employees, George Whitney Jr., had grown up in the amusement industry. He'd spent his childhood in his father's shooting gallery, helping to collect pellets and repair damaged targets. After his father became the manager of the entire park, he worked in the various hot dog stands and pie shops. At first, Whitney did not want to follow his family into the amusement business. He went away to college, joined the army for two years, took a job at Bank of America in their foreign investments division, but eventually he realized that the amusement industry was in his blood. When he returned in the late 1940s to Playland, his father put him in charge of the midway, where he oversaw all of the rides and games.

As he guided Walt through Playland, he pointed out how the park's layout forced visitors to move from one attraction to the next, luring them with raised marquees, lights, sounds, and interesting buildings. The most popular games, he explained, were the ones where people could bet money, such as the spinning wheel of fortune. They couldn't bet more than two cents at a time, but they could bet multiples of two cents, which gave the spinning wheel an excellent hourly income. Most of the rides, he continued, were stock rides, purchased off the shelf from ride manufacturers—though the park had made unique improvements to its Laff in the Dark funhouse. The rides were mainly for the kids, he added; older people wanted to play bingo and skeet ball. The food sold well to people of all ages.

Though Walt was not interested in stock rides or midway games, he was interested in the park's layout. He asked again about traffic flow and how queue lines were best arranged for each ride. He inspected the merry-go-round and looked at Laughing Sal, a giggling, shrieking mannequin that beckoned people into the funhouse. He asked Whitney to explain other strategies the park used to move guests from one area to the next. In response, Whitney not only explained strategies for guest circulation, but discussed ways to increase a park's profitability by increasing the hourly capacity of each ride using a few simple steps that they had developed at Playland.

Walt was so impressed with the practical knowledge that George Whitney Jr. had of the business that, even while he was at the park, he considered hiring him as a consultant, though he wouldn't officially make an offer until the following month. As Walt reasoned, it would be good to have at least one man at WED with substantial experience in the outdoor amusement industry.

As it turned out, George Whitney Jr. would be the only one.[14]

On the following Monday, retired Rear Admiral Joe Fowler told his wife, "I don't know anything about the motion picture business. I'll be back tomorrow night."

At the kitchen table, he placed his hat on his head, picked up his briefcase, and stepped out the door. He flew to Los Angeles, with only a single change of clothes, and once there, he met

Walt Disney's son-in-law, Ron Miller, and one of Woody's men, Fred Schumacher, who drove him to the Burbank studio.

After a brief tour, Fowler spent thirty minutes with Walt in his office, discussing the Disneyland project as well as current films in production. Walt showed Fowler concept art for the park—in all likelihood, the artwork included multiple images of the Mark Twain steamboat—and in return, Fowler explained how such a boat might be built. Their conversation wasn't limited to the steamboat; it included other aspects of the park, but before their meeting concluded, Walt was called away to a screening room to watch the morning rushes. "I'll be gone for a few minutes," he said. "But help yourself to whatever you want." Pointing to the intercom, he added, "Push the button and get coffee." Their meeting was so pleasant that when Walt left the room, Fowler believed he'd soon return, perhaps with other executives, to continue the interview.

But when Walt didn't come back, Fowler walked over to Woody's office. The two men talked about the boat and other projects at Disneyland until Woody, too, was called away to an urgent meeting. Alone in the office, Fowler looked at some promotional artwork for Disneyland on Woody's desk. The painting appeared to be of a medieval castle, complete with flags and a drawbridge. He examined the intricacies of this building—the texture of the bricks, the shape of the windows, the way the scale of the structure had been altered to make the building appear taller than it actually was. He already sensed that this consulting job might include projects other than simply the steamboat.

After a few minutes, he returned to Walt's empty office, where he was met by one of the studio secretaries. "Is your name Joe Fowler?" she asked.

"Yes."

"I'm here to show you to your office," she said. "There are some contractors waiting to talk to you."

Fowler's face betrayed surprise. Only then did he realize that the interview was over—and that he'd been offered a position. Exactly what the position would entail, he didn't know. He took off his hat and ran his free hand over the smooth dome of his scalp. He stood there, considering his options. Briefly he looked out the window—studio buildings as far as he could see—before letting out a long, decisive sigh, believing he might at least talk to the men waiting for him.

"Come with me," she said, handing him a thick envelope. "Here're the keys to a car."

Without even discussing a consulting fee, he followed Walt's secretary down the hall to his new office where, he supposed, he would meet these contractors.

Though Fowler expected to stay in Los Angeles for just one day, he ended up staying for three weeks before returning home, talking to contractors and attempting to better understand Walt's vision for the entire park. Even in those early days, Fowler recognized Walt's great weakness: Walt surrounded himself with artists able to produce beautiful concepts of buildings and rides, but no one at the studio had a practical understanding of what it would take to build a sixty-acre cinematic amusement park—especially one designed to accommodate millions of visitors each year. During these initial weeks, he shared many meals with Walt and Woody, who gradually made the amusement park seem more interesting than the highly profitable housing project he was working on in the Bay Area.[15]

"Little by little, we got [Fowler] trapped into this thing," Walt later joked. "We got him so trapped that he said, 'To hell with the subdivision.'"[16]

When asked for a job description, Walt told him: "Now, Joe, I'll create in my mind all the things we're going to do, and your job is to make engineering realities out of them." Though, as Fowler would soon discover, those engineering realities never

once came with a full set of plans. Nor did they come with adequate funds. In practice, Fowler discovered that his job was not
only to convert Walt's dreams into reality but to secretly report
those dreams to Roy Disney, thereby allowing Roy the opportunity to keep the park within its budget.[17]

With a slightly better understanding of the proposed amusement park, four members of the WED team left the studio for
most of June 1954 to perform a second round of field research.
Though early trips to the Los Angeles County Fair and Knott's
Berry Farm had been structured as relaxing outings for inspiration, general research, and to informally evaluate the overall
concept of Disneyland, these later trips were filled with direction and purpose. "My wife and I traveled thousands of miles,"
Harper Goff recalls, "all over the United Sates, trying to find
information about, for example, what proportion should there
be of men's toilets to women's toilets. . . . How much thievery?
How much destruction? How many people come in a car? How
big a parking lot?"[18]

Mostly in pairs, the WED team traveled to dozens of fun
spots, including Williamsburg, Mount Vernon, Luna Park,
Coney Island, and Palisades Park. Much of their research
focused on the economics and land-use practices of successful
parks. "We would take pictures and come back and tell Walt all
about what [these parks] were doing," Goff recalls. "One of the
main things we tried to get was their 'gate' . . . how much they
charged, how many people came through, and how much they
made. Also what kinds of operating problems they had."[19]

The WED report on the Long Beach Pike reveals that George
Whitney Jr. and one other designer (probably Herb Ryman)
even timed the exact length of each dark ride. ("The Honeymoon Trail lasted 1 minute 38 seconds, Laff in the Dark 1 minute 34 seconds.") They counted the number of arcade machines
and measured the exterior of each building. They reported

ticket prices and hourly guest attendance for each ride—numbers that were acquired by standing near a ride's entrance and discretely counting the customers that passed through the turnstiles over the course of a few hours. More revealing than the statistics, however, was the tone. In a section titled "Midway Operations," these same designers suggested that Disneyland adapt Long Beach Pike attractions because, it is assumed, the time to design Disneyland was growing short: "Sling shots (with 6 marbles) shooting at bottles might be a Tom Sawyer type of concession in Fantasyland, or Frontierland."[20]

Similarly, Bruce Bushman believed that Disney might adapt the jet fighter ride (like the one at Riverview Park) to use the Little Pedro plane from *Saludos Amigos*. A minor Disney character named Susie the Little Blue Coupe could be featured in an auto ride. Lastly, an off-the-shelf mirror maze (like the one at Willow Grove Park in Pennsylvania) could be dressed up to more or less recreate the final sequence in *Alice in Wonderland*.[21]

But perhaps the most valuable lessons from these trips concerned how customers circulated through an amusement park. Early on, Walt and his men devised a layout for his park that would include only one gate that led to an entrance street and then a radial hub off of which roads, all of equal importance, opened to various themed areas. This radial design was an attempt to avoid the problems they'd witnessed at many amusement parks, in which guests clustered around the entrance plaza and avoided peripheral areas. "The things that we learned as you go to the 'Pike' . . . the main drag always gets the traffic," Dick Irvine later explained. "Anything off the main drag suffers."

Similarly, the WED team recognized that customers were attracted by elevated marquees, so they devised a system of elevated structures, which functioned as marquees, to draw guests to distant areas of the park. These elevated structures, easily seen from a distance, would include the train station on

Main Street, the castle, the Moonliner rocket, and the Mark Twain steamboat. Walt would refer to these elevated structures as "weenies."[22]

As a curious side note, in most of the Disney literature, the term "weenie" is compared to a "weenie" cart that would draw hungry people to the far end of a street, but Walt's use of the term "weenie" in the 1950s did not refer to a hot dog cart but to the hot dogs that Walt used to get his old brown poodle to follow him around the house, giving her small pieces of meat as a reward. The unique use of "weenie" as an architectural term does not refer to a sign that might make guests curious, such as a SALE banner, but rather a means of enticing guests to circulate through the park by offering them small rewards.[23]

During the first week of July, the WED team produced a bound report that systematically presented their findings— paying special attention to pricing structures for tickets, hourly guest capacity for each ride, the size of various show buildings and arcades, and the width and length of public thoroughfares. In places, the report also noted the reaction of amusement industry professionals to the concept of Disneyland when the WED team was able to sit down with an owner or a manager. "I went with Bill Cottrell, Bruce Bushman and George Whitney to places like Fairmont Park in Philadelphia," explains Bill Martin. "We took all these sketches being done for Disneyland with us and those people all said, 'This'll never go,' and 'It's never been done like this before.'"[24]

Unlike previous research trips, no one was worried about delivering this criticism to Walt. By now, Walt understood that no one believed in Disneyland, aside from himself and a few men at his studio.

As spring warmed into summer, Walt sent around another set of letters inviting companies to lease space at Disneyland. These letters were mainly sent to executives who'd previously

worked with Disney with hopes that their financial contributions would help ease the park's burgeoning construction
costs. Walt's tone was exuberant and expansive. Beyond this,
the letters showcased Walt's ability as a salesman. To Joyce
Hall of the Hallmark Company, he wrote: ". . . with all modesty,
I must say [Disneyland's] going to be one Hell of a show! I think
it would be a mistake, if you don't come over and get some
first-hand knowledge about Disneyland the next time you're
out this way. I definitely feel you will want a spot somewhere in
the setup. We have some big important concerns, who are very
excited about it, and we are 'booking' them in as they come."

Despite the letter's honest enthusiasm, there were still no
"big important concerns" lining up to lease space in Disneyland. Most likely Joyce Hall knew this, and so the Hallmark
Company—like most large American companies—turned down
Walt's initial invitation, believing that an amusement park could
do little to help an established firm with a good reputation.[25]

During these same months, as Walt came to grips with the
park's financial problems, he experienced long periods of frustration with how slowly his design team developed construction plans. Though the team had strong design plans for some
areas of Main Street and Fantasyland, designs for the rest of
the park were nowhere near finished. Frontierland was merely
a fort and a saloon. Tomorrowland was still a collection of
empty show buildings—with very loose plans for a Science &
Industry pavilion as well as a second structure for Technology
& Communications. But what would go in these pavilions was
anybody's guess?[26] Other sections—such as Holiday Land,
Lilliputian Land, and the land devoted to circus shows—had
been discarded or delayed to better focus on the most essential areas of the park. Despite such concerns—and despite
repeated suggestions by Joe Fowler to move more design and
manufacturing work to outside companies—Walt remained

determined to keep as much of Disneyland's development in-house as possible.

The extent of this control can be observed in his use of structural engineers. Though Walt hired an outside firm to complete the structural design work for the park, he insisted that this team of engineers work at his studio—as opposed to office space owned by the engineering company—so he could better review their work on a regular basis.

During the entire design and construction of Disneyland, there was only one large exception to Walt's control over the progress of his park—Arrow Development.

Since Walt's initial trip to Arrow earlier in the year, Ed Morgan had taught himself how to sculpt sheet metal, primarily with the use of aviation tin snips, through cuts and folds, into a workable vehicle that resembled Bruce Bushman's drawing of the Mr. Toad motorcar. Because Bushman's drawing was a piece of concept art, not a rendering, Morgan had been asked to both mechanically design and build a ride vehicle that was functional yet retained the whimsical feel of a cartoon. He had focused on the headlamps and grill to create a subtle face for the car. On the body, he mounted an oversized seat to an undersized frame, which in terms of scale created an amusing juxtaposition. The finished car looked nothing like the antique-style vehicles Arrow had manufactured for various kiddy parks. Once satisfied that the prototype incorporated the "spirit" of the drawing, along with many of Bushman's precise details, he called Dick Irvine expecting that Irvine might travel alone to Mountain View to inspect it.

But he did not travel alone: he was accompanied by Walt Disney and Bruce Bushman. Just outside Arrow's main building, Walt inspected the car, viewing it from many angles before testing its seat. The car was still unpainted metal. In practice, all the ride vehicles produced by Arrow would be later painted at either the studio or at the park's construction site. The men from WED conferred with Walt privately, and afterward Bushman approached Morgan alone. "Walt is very pleased," he said. "If you feel that your company can handle this, we'd like to have your company build the vehicles and support system for this ride." They discussed minor changes to the car so it better resembled the one in the movie, but before leaving, Bushman showed Morgan another drawing: a colorful sketch of the Casey Jr. Circus Train, a scale locomotive far more elaborate than anything the Arrow team had ever built. Bushman explained that they needed someone to build an engine car for this train, with all of its complex curves and unique metalwork.

Morgan signaled that his partner, Karl Bacon, should have a look. Bacon stared at the drawing for a while before nodding his head, promising that he would find some way to create a working version of this cartoon locomotive.[27]

As the Disney men drove away, Morgan had the vague understanding that Walt might offer him other contract work, though he had no idea how much. He also knew this: Walt would be a demanding customer. But the job would be unusual and challenging. It would also provide steady money for his struggling company.

Once inside the machine building, Morgan and the other men set about to making the changes Walt wanted. From there, Morgan created a plywood pattern, which he would use to create the remaining Mr. Toad vehicles. It would be some time before the men at Arrow could even begin preliminary work on the Casey Jr. Circus Train.[28]

By early summer, many individuals in the Los Angeles business community had heard that C. V. Wood, once a member of the prestigious SRI economics division, was working with Walt Disney on his strange amusement park. One of Woody's longtime friends, Van Arsdale France, was initially surprised at his decision to abandon SRI for a project as unconventional as Disneyland. France had met Woody at Consolidated Vultee, when France had managed the firm's training program and Woody had overseen its industrial engineering division. Since leaving Consolidated, France had moved to Los Angeles, where Woody had occasionally hired him as an SRI training consultant. "I first heard of this dream of Walt Disney's," France wrote in his memoir, "when C. V. Wood called to say he'd quit his job with Stanford Research Institute to become the first vice president of something called Disneyland." But France also thought Woody "was crazy to give up a secure job" for something like this.

On the phone, France was direct: "What the hell is *Disneyland*?" he asked.

To better explain what *the hell* it was, Woody offered France an invitation to the Disney studio the following week—probably August of 1954. At just after three in the afternoon, France drove from his office on Wilshire Boulevard and merged onto the Hollywood Freeway. A studio guard checked his name on a clipboard then directed him to the visitors' lot. After his car was parked, France walked down the center promenade, past streets with odd names, like Snow White Lane and Dopey Drive. The studio complex, he noted, was a collection of tall buildings arranged around manicured green space. On Mickey Mouse Avenue, France located the three-story animation building.

A receptionist led him into Woody's office, where he found his old friend leaning back in a swivel chair, his stocking feet characteristically kicked up on the desk—a managerial posture that also suggested self-indulgence. "Woody," France recalls, "had always been a bundle of energy wrapped in a deceptively laid-back personality." In other words, C. V. Wood liked to present himself as a man so important that he could casually disregard the stiff business customs of the era. The two men shook hands then took their seats, one on either side of the desk. Foregoing small talk, Woody told France about

Disneyland, claiming that it was far better than working for an aircraft plant.

"We have four million dollars to build this place," he explained. As was his habit, he overstated the project's good qualities, saying that Walt was "a wonderful guy" and neglecting to relate the underlying tensions between himself and his boss. "The studio is nothing like any place you or I have ever worked," Woody said. He even went so far as to say, "It's like a family" and "Walt treats me like a son," neither of which were true.[29]

Just as Wood and France were wrapping up, an older man dressed in a sport shirt and cotton pants walked into the room and reclined into an empty chair, his charcoal hair falling into his face. The man, France learned, was Walt Disney, who upon being introduced leaned over to shake his hand. "I expected the soft handclasp of an artist," France recalls. "Instead, it was the solid grip of a boy raised to work on a farm." As was his habit, Walt lit a cigarette and pulled an ashtray to the corner of the desk. But what impressed France most was the level of comfort and familiarity at the studio: even with the big boss in the room, C. V. Wood kept his feet up on the desk, a gesture that for the moment seemed to reinforce his earlier claim that Walt treated him as a son.[30]

For a while, the three men talked about the proposed park, but they were soon interrupted by Nat Winecoff, who wanted to review the purchase of horses for the park's stagecoach attraction. "As I listened to the report," France says, "and the ensuing conversation, I was struck by the sense of excitement Disney felt for this project. He even turned to me, an outsider, to present his thoughts. Perhaps he sensed my feelings of being uncomfortable in a strange situation. In the back of my mind, I remembered that Woody had been involved in some crazy ideas."[31]

As evening darkened to night, France left the studio, unaware that his visit had not been entirely a social affair. Woody was an excellent salesman; he was able to convey excitement for a project. He presented this amusement park as a unique and fulfilling work experience, even though that was, at best, only partially true for Wood himself. Woody's genius was that he was able to make someone desire an experience—such as to work on the Disneyland project or to become a corporate sponsor of the park—long before he came through with his full sales pitch.

That night, as France drove away, he wondered if Woody was on to something good. Woody could slant the truth, he knew that. It was hard to see past his enthusiasm. But, still, France sensed that there was something important in this project, something he couldn't quite name.

Six months later, after the idea of Disneyland had taken root in him, Van France received another call from C. V. Wood: "Look, we're building this place," he said. Woody then explained that he'd told Walt about France's experience at Consolidated Vultee, where he'd created a training program to transform thousands of cowboys, farmers, and homemakers into aircraft workers. Disneyland would need a similar training program to transform Anaheim locals into hosts, ride operators, and actors. "[Walt] agreed with me," Woody added, "that you sounded like the guy for the job."

The following day, France returned to the studio to talk further about the matter in person, only this time he found the office filled with frantic energy and urgency. His meeting had been sandwiched between other meetings, all of which were constantly interrupted by coworkers entering the office to ask questions and retrieve architectural drawings. When France was finally called into the office, Woody remained standing, which France took to mean that he shouldn't even consider sitting down.

"We have deadlines on top of deadlines," Woody began. "We have a firm opening date of July 17th. And we're concentrating on getting the place built and finding the money to build it. It's a tough enough job just keeping the construction on schedule. But we know damn well that people have to be trained to operate the place."

The two men made a quick handshake deal for France to begin immediately on a week-to-week basis. As he left Wood's office and entered the main studio, France felt the eager determination that filled the building: despite obvious problems, the Disneyland project was muscling ahead.

Only months later would France realize that he had been set up to take this position from the start, that Woody had carefully created then deepened the desire France now felt to work on this amusement-park project.

This ability to manipulate people, France suspected, somehow made Woody a genius.[32]

At the studio, Walt continued to encourage dozens of employees—men without training in architecture, ride design, or the management of an amusement park—to adapt their skills to design and build Disneyland, mostly as a means of keeping the Disneyland project in-house.

A team of studio artists focused their efforts to create concept art and later detailed elevations for Disneyland. But even with high-quality elevations, Walt was skeptical that architects and carpenters could translate these images into a set of themed buildings, so he asked Fred Joerger in the studio shop department to oversee the construction of detailed models for the entire park, land-by-land, street-by-street. Models, Walt believed, wouldn't lie.

Joerger developed models of Main Street, the boat ride in Adventureland, and the frontier fort. One model that was particularly important to Walt was the castle—a structure that was roughly modeled after the Neuschwanstein palace in Bavaria. Already Walt understood that the castle would serve both as a landmark and a logo for the entire park. Over the span of two or three weeks, he asked each WED employee to view the model and give his opinion.

Herb Ryman first saw the model with Dick Irvine and Marvin Davis. "I didn't like it," he later explained, "because it was such an obvious copy [of Neuschwanstein]. People would say, 'Walt's men have no imagination of their own—they can't even create their own castle.'" Ryman adjusted the model so he could better view it from a side angle, and as he did, he noticed that the top portion was a separate piece not yet glued to the bottom half of the structure. "I picked it up and moved the obvious Newschwanstien part that was facing Main Street, and turned it around to the Fantasyland side." This combination, the half-inverted castle, pleased Ryman.

As the men waited, Irvine became anxious, believing Walt would be unnerved by the altered model. "Dick said I'd better put it back. Walt would be back any minute. At that moment, Walt was standing behind me, hands on his hips." Walt stepped forward, betraying early signs of agitation, but as he examined the model, he found that he liked the half-inverted castle. Not only did the alteration partially conceal the Neuschwanstein influence, the model now appeared more inviting and somehow grander.[33]

As time wore on, Walt transferred more and more studio artists to the WED payroll in an attempt to better control the Disneyland project.

One steamy afternoon, he called Roger Broggie, head of the machine shop, to his office. Until then, Broggie had worked on special effects, repaired studio equipment, and assisted Walt in building his backyard railroad. After discussing the Disneyland concept in detail, Walt said, "You're off of this special effects work here. Now we're going to turn this machine shop into a manufacturing facility for Disneyland." In the coming year, Broggie would oversee the production of two steam engines, fourteen railroad combine, gondola and coach cars, the superstructure for the Mark Twain steamboat, and various other boats and vehicles—all of it completed without any specific training in train, boat, or automotive design.[34]

Ken Anderson, who held both an architectural degree from a European university and had once been an art director for *Snow White*, was added to the team that translated the animated films into dark rides—that is, rides that conveyed guests through the scenery and sets of famous Disney films. Claude Coats, whose painted backgrounds had established the emotional tone for many animated classics, reworked the design of each Fantasyland dark ride until it matched the emotional mood of the corresponding film. Studio effects man Bob Mattey mocked up a test track of the Peter Pan, Mr. Toad, and Snow White rides in the studio's special-effects building. When he was finished with that assignment, he set about to create lifelike animals for the Jungle River in Adventureland.

During these months many studio artists expressed deep skepticism about Disneyland's prospects: "Nobody believed in Disneyland to begin with," confesses Ken Anderson, "not even those of us who worked with Walt. We had only seen other amusement parks which had nothing special to offer."[35]

Similarly, lead animator Frank Thomas recalls Disneyland's development as a nuisance that interrupted work on the animated films: "We didn't have any sense of continuity with the [animation] projects going on around [the studio] in 1954 and 1955. We'd go over to Don Iwerks' building, for example, because of something to do with cameras or procedures, and we'd look into the carpenter's shop and see these giraffe's heads sticking up out of a bin."[36]

◆ ◆ ◆

At the construction site, efforts to clear the land progressed more quickly than did the studio's ability to finalize a plan for the park. Earthmovers and bulldozers arrived in either late July or early August, while some farm families were still in the process of moving to new accommodations. "The day we moved out in August of 1954, we were walking in ditches and holes," remembers Ron Dominguez, a teenager who had grown up on the Ball Road property. "Things were popping up around us because construction had to move ahead."[37]

Joe Fowler, who oversaw construction, later admitted: "I didn't know a damn thing about what we were getting into. At groundbreaking, I had a budget of four-and-a-half million dollars. That was before we had any plans at all."[38]

On Monday, August 30, a construction company supervised by Bruce McNeil—the same man who offered the original estimate for the construction of Disneyland—began to grade the site, paying special attention to the park's proposed lake and river system.[39] The dirt excavated from the Rivers of America was moved to the edge of the park, creating a continuous 12-to-20-foot raised earthen berm on which the railroad would ride. Throughout the park, channels were dug for sewer, water, and underground electrical lines.

One of the best-known stories about the land clearing concerns a colorblind bulldozer operator—though the official Disney version of that story is most likely embellished. In the official Disney version, the groundskeeping staff tied colored tags to all of the existing trees, one color indicating destroy, another relocate, and a third leave-in-place-for-later-landscaping-use; but a colorblind bulldozer operator was unable to properly distinguish between the various tags. Before the problem was recognized, he had removed a great many of the trees the staff wanted to save.

On the surface, the official version doesn't account well for the activities at the site. During this phase of construction, a work crew was not only clearing the land, but regrading it, raising some areas with fill dirt, lowering others through excavation. In short, the work crew could only leave trees in areas where the land was not altered.

A slightly different version came to me secondhand, originating from Van France. In the Van France version, there was a kernel of truth in this story—namely, that there was a colorblind tree cutter (probably a bulldozer operator)—but the trees that he mistakenly removed were limited to a small area in Adventureland, where Disney was hoping to reuse the existing greenery to help create a jungle. The problem was so small that even Bill Evans, the lead landscaper, didn't discover it immediately: "A few days later, we were walking through the area, and I thought this wasn't right. So I checked the blueprints, and a lot of the threes which were supposed to be there were gone."[40]

In 1954, this story was not reported in any paper, nor is there any mention of it in materials released by Disney. Likewise, it was not reported in 1955 or 1956. But in 1957, one of the Bombers, Earl Shelton, mentioned it in an employee newsletter: "One of the methods for saving trees was to place a red tag on those to remain un-cut. Only problem was that it was discovered too late that one of the tree cutters was color blind."[41]

Following the release of the 1957 newsletter, the Disneyland public-relations department got a hold of the story—and since the PR department had a mandate to release at least one news story about the park each week—they floated it to columnists, who printed it in local papers. From there, over years, the story took on a life of its own and was reprinted in papers across the country. In the popular version, the colorblind tree cutter was a bulldozer operator who removed many, many trees, expanding a minor mishap into Disneyland's first tall tale.

◆　◆　◆

As the land was being prepared and at Admiral Joe Fowler's insistence, WED redesigned key sections of the park, because Fowler believed that the initial plans were structurally inadequate for a large tourist facility. He convinced Walt to include a more substantial foundation at the base of Main Street. For the river, he argued that Walt should build a dry dock to assist with both the construction and maintenance of the Mark Twain steamboat. Fowler marshaled forth his usual reasons, explaining that there was a big difference between building a movie set of a steamboat and building an actual boat. "I had to have some place to dry dock it," Fowler later explained. "We couldn't lift that ship out and take it to the shop." Reluctantly Walt agreed, but because of the cost, each time he passed the excavation, he would turn to the members of his party with exasperation and say, "Aw well, here's Fowler's Ditch."[42]

As Walt visited the construction site, he attempted to hide his sense of discouragement, so his men would not know how close WED was to going bankrupt. The crew led by McNeil was supposed to complete both excavation and the installation of underground utilities by September 30, but in late October, they were nowhere near finished.[43] As it turned out, the sewer system alone would require 8,467 feet of clay pipe—with all of it needing to be installed before work on structures could begin in earnest.[44] To his design team, Walt repeatedly asked, "Will they ever get this [site] so it looks like something other than just a hole in the ground?"[45]

The early cost overruns were reported in the local newspapers, again suggesting that this amusement park would be Walt's undoing. A sassy columnist from *The Week* magazine went so far as to ask Walt point-blank if he would be able to build his park within the proposed budget. "I can stick to the budget all right," he said. "It's the fool people working for me who keep coming up with new ideas."[46]

One Saturday, after hearing that efforts to prepare the site were finally progressing with better speed, Walt arrived at the park only to find that it looked much as it had the previous week. "Not one goddamn thing has changed," he yelled as Earl Shelton drove him through the park in a company jeep.[47]

It soon became clear that it would be difficult—if not impossible—to complete Walt's original plan for Disneyland by July 17 of the following year. C. V. Wood argued that Walt should delay the opening of one land so as to better focus the design and construction resources on other areas of the park. The obvious choice was Tomorrowland, which lingered in a type of perpetual redevelopment, without firm plans for its rides and attractions.

After seeing how slowly construction efforts progressed at the site, Walt grudgingly agreed with Wood. Starting in September, Tomorrowland was removed from Walt's regular status memos, which now only offered updates on the other sections of the park. Though design and development continued on at least two Tomorrowland attractions (the theater-based Flight to the Moon attraction and the Autopia motorway), development on the rest of the area came to a halt. The new 1954 plans for Disneyland, explains Joe Fowler, "called for completing only the Main Street area, Adventureland, Frontierland, and Fantasyland" in time for opening. Tomorrowland, however, would be boarded up "with a fancy construction fence" and opened as an expansion area the following year.[48]

Throughout the fall, Walt experienced repeated episodes of doubt, understanding for the first time that his critics might be right. Disneyland could prove to be his folly. Since July, he had walked through the site with his team of designers and architects most every Saturday, but now he visited the site on many weekdays as well. By early December, he toured the site obsessively, noting that after many months of work, no buildings were complete, no asphalt or cement walkways poured.

Only on Main Street was there even the suggestion of structural work. At Fowler's insistence, a crew had poured the foundation and begun to frame in the Opera House. Though the Opera House would eventually become part of Main Street, Fowler wanted to use the building as a lumber mill and workshop to develop the rest of the park.

Beyond the foundation for the Opera House, Walt could only see dirt. By now, surveyors had been hired to stake building sites, but as land preparation had not been finished, caterpillar drivers continually backed over surveyors' stakes, making them worthless. "It got too expensive in time and money to have the surveyors keep coming out to replace them," Harper Goff recalls, "so Walt said, 'Harper, just eyeball it.'" With this, Goff used scale models from the studio to eyeball many sites—a practice that would later have unintended consequences. "I would . . . signal to the cat drivers to pile a little more dirt up there and level it here until it looked right to me."[49]

Slowly the land preparation was finished, but the site was still without structures. One Saturday, after most of his design team had gone home, Walt walked with Goff to the skeletal observation tower erected in the center of the park. Walt also used this same tower to house time-lapse cameras that would chronicle the park's development. These cameras served two purposes: the time-lapse film, which was date-stamped, verified the completion date of individual construction projects; later, used almost as an afterthought, this film, when set to music, would showcase construction efforts for home viewers on the *Disneyland* TV show. Together, the two men climbed the rigging to survey the site.

As Walt looked out at his property, he felt a stab of sorrow and regret, as he understood that even without Tomorrowland he had catastrophically underestimated the costs to build such a park. He would need millions to finish the project—money he didn't have. "What we were looking at that day," Goff recalls, "were the sewer systems, mounds of dirt from the river path of what would become Rivers of America, all the expensive innovative support systems we'd designed into Disneyland. Walt didn't see any *show*, and that bothered him."[50]

Walt was an intensely private man, rarely revealing his emotions to those outside his family. But according to Harper Goff, tears came to his eyes. The two men stood there for many minutes. "I have half of the money spent," Walt said, "and nothing to show for it." Out of habit, he touched the pack of cigarettes in his pocket, his fingers trembling. He repeated that final word. "Nothing," his voice trailing off into silence.[51]

The one true Disneyland success for those months had very little to do with the construction of the park: it was the *Disneyland* TV show.

By November of 1954, millions of Americans regularly tuned in each Wednesday. The show opened with a relatively new character named Tinkerbell making her glittering circuit around the Disneyland castle. (Months ago, the Disney brothers had decided not to use their better known characters, such as Mickey and Donald, in the shows credits, in case the park turned out to be a disaster.) On the show itself, Walt regularly displayed concept art for individual attractions and offered progress reports on the park's development—most of which led the American public to believe that construction of Disneyland was progressing at a faster pace than was actually the case. These segments also introduced the public to the highly themed environments in the park—environments where landscape design, architecture, and period props produced a cinematic reproduction of a frontier town and a turn-of-the-century main street.

For ABC, the *Disneyland* TV show proved to be an instant success, regularly drawing over half of the available audience for its timeslot, and would be ABC's only program that routinely placed in TV's top 25 for years to come. More importantly, the show helped ABC attract new affiliates to broadcast not only *Disneyland* but all of the network's programming.

After having aired only a handful of episodes, Walt received the annual Sylvania TV Award (a precursor to the Emmys) for "The Most Outstanding Television Show for All Ages." For Walt, the award brought both a blessing and a curse because theater owners saw the honor as confirmation that potential audience members were staying home on Wednesdays to watch *Disneyland* on TV as opposed to buying tickets to enjoy theater programs. After the award ceremony, Walt rebuffed critics who claimed he was undermining movie theaters. He was put in a position where he had to repeatedly affirm that his studio was "basically a motion picture producing organization" which found "working in co-operation with the world of television mutually advantageous." In the days that followed, he reminded reporters at the *Film Daily* and other industry journals that his TV show would also promote his movies, such as *20,000 Leagues Under the Sea*, and that these promotions would create a larger audience for American theaters, though these remarks were mostly met with skepticism.[52]

The success of the *Disneyland* TV show had one other unexpected consequence. Though not so much as one building had yet been finished at the Disneyland construction site, the public received a preview of the finished park through the show's extensive use of concept art and detailed models. Home viewers saw a beautifully constructed diorama of Main Street, as well as maps of the entire park and pencil drawings for Tomorrowland. These same viewers quickly understood the architecture of Disneyland: total control of the environment to create the illusion that one could enter the realm of TV and movies. Disneyland wasn't so much an amusement park but a series of elaborate movie sets. The design proved so appealing that Disneyland spawned imitation even before it opened.

The first of these imitations was an oceanfront shopping center in a touristy section of Long Beach, California, near the

Belmont pier. After learning about Disneyland on TV, Ruth Cameron, a local restaurateur, had the idea to theme a marketplace center as a fisherman's village, complete with a miniature harbor, a lighthouse façade, and dozens of small buildings fashioned after Cape Cod shops. Its centerpiece would be two restaurants: a 600-seat dinner theater with a revolving stage and, inside of an overturned ship, a 400-seat seafood bistro. In an early interview, Ruth Cameron told the press that her village would "make San Francisco's Fisherman's Wharf seem pale by comparison."[53]

To create the initial design, she quietly hired two principal WED designers who were still working to design Disneyland: Harper Goff, who was overseeing the development of Adventureland, and Herb Ryman, who had created the first aerial map of the park. As these men were consultants for WED—and not permanent employees—they were free to take outside work. Moreover, the culture of Hollywood encouraged art directors to work on multiple assignments simultaneously because of the project-to-project nature of their employment. Yet their work on this project would set an interesting precedent: it demonstrated how easy it might be for other WED designers to find subsequent work.

Late in 1954, Goff and Ryman began to develop the fisherman's village shopping center, relying on the principles of cinematic presentation to create a real-world environment that mimicked a Hollywood set. In other words, they used skills that they had developed while working for Walt Disney. Presumably Ryman and Goff completed the design work with the blessing of Walt—after all, how could a seaside shopping center compete with the world's most expensive amusement park—but even if they hadn't, Walt was so busy he scarcely would've noticed any such project.[54]

In addition to building his amusement park, Walt was producing movies, developing his TV show, and meeting with potential sponsors and lessees who might help underwrite the construction costs of Disneyland. Soon he would need to make room for one more responsibility. Because of ABC's success with the Disney show, executives at the network exercised their option to develop a second Disney series, one directed at children. A daily program called *The Mickey Mouse Club* was set to premiere in just eight months. But for the first time in years, Walt's schedule was stretched to the point where he was forced to delegate most aspects of this project to men he trusted.

As Christmas approached, Walt spent the majority of his time working with the WED art directors who were refining their renderings for Main Street buildings and closely supervising the men who were attempting to create rides for his unique park. One WED employee named Bob Gurr remembers working madly until 4 p.m. on Christmas Eve when Walt walked around the studio distributing small gifts. Gurr was at his desk, when he noticed Walt, dressed in a flannel shirt, by his office door. Though in years past Walt had handed out cash bonuses for the holidays, this Christmas he distributed large bottles of Old Forester whisky. Near the machine shop, he presented one to the young Gurr.

"Go home," Walt said. "It's Christmas Eve."[55]

Slowly the remaining men at the studio began to depart, leaving drawings on their desks and projects on their workbenches. They put on their jackets and hats then drove their cars slowly out of the lot. Only then did Walt leave the studio, deciding finally to spend at least this one night with his family. It wasn't so much a holiday, he understood, as a brief rest in preparation for the work ahead.

Six
CONFLICTS AND CONSTRUCTION

Despite growing concerns about the men from Texas and Oklahoma, Walt tried to work amicably with C. V. Wood as they both oversaw the day-to-day business of the developing amusement park. Around the studio most people perceived that Walt and Woody were friends—as they appeared to be most of the time—but Woody still felt that there was underlying tension in their relationship, though he attributed it mostly to Walt's enormous (and perhaps unrealistic) expectations for Disneyland. He also now understood that he and Walt were nothing alike in terms of managerial style. From Woody's perspective, Walt was a big dreamer who did not understand how to build something as complex as an amusement park. Walt was a man who lived inside of his animation studio. On the other hand, Woody believed himself to be a man who knew how to navigate the real world.

The real world, according to Woody, was about sales, impressions, and money.

As construction progressed, Woody moved his primary office from the studio over to the Disneyland site. Because Disneyland lacked the budget for a proper administrative building, he converted two old farmhouses into a makeshift executive complex behind Main Street. At the center of this complex was the Dominguez farmhouse, a two-story Spanish-style building, named after the family who had originally owned both the house and the ten acres of orange trees on which Frontierland would be built. Woody and many of his friends took offices on the top floor, while Walt took an office for himself down below.[1]

Each floor soon had its own orientation to the development of the park. On the top floor, in the original four bedrooms, was C. V. Wood and his hand-selected managerial team, all of whom were accustomed to the highly structured business culture of the 1950s, which included a management hierarchy, forecast reports, defined policies, and deadlines. They were called the Business Team or the Aircraft Team because so many of Woody's associates had also worked with him at Consolidated Vultee. On the bottom floor, in the living room, dining room, and den, was Walt along with studio artists. Studio employees were accustomed to greeting each other by first name, the informality of storyboard and gag meetings, and the job flexibility required to produce an animated feature. One member later explained, "Walt hated schedules. He said, 'I don't ever want to see an organizational chart.'"[2] Another explained that the Studio Team "was like a very small gang all moving really, really fast. You had to pay attention to what was going on because nothing was ever really written down."[3]

One member of Woody's team, Van France, remembers that the men from the studio repeatedly criticized his work style: "If I or somebody were to come up with some procedure, they'd say, Oh damnit, Van, that's aircraft thinking. You've got to learn show thinking."[4]

Few people moved easily between Woody's Aircraft Team and Walt's Studio Team. Among those who did was Admiral Joe Fowler. He was perhaps the only person to understand the fullness of Walt's vision as well as the financial and engineering difficulties of building such a park.

Aside from general management, Woody's most valuable asset was generating funds to complete the park's construction. Months earlier, Walt and Nat Winecoff had courted large American companies—such as Hallmark and Coca-Cola—to

lease space at Disneyland. When those contracts didn't mate-
rialize, Walt was hesitant to open his park to smaller and less
prestigious firms. During a series of tense discussions, Woody
finally convinced Walt that he had no other choice but to solicit
lease agreements from smaller companies: the park needed the
income. "Walt Disney had a bad time getting enough money
to build Disneyland," Woody later revealed in an interview.
"Bankers couldn't see such a park. For the good reason there'd
never been anything like it. [Walt] went in hock for his studios
and I went out and sold concessions. . . . That's how it started."[5]

At the end of 1954, one of Woody's largest duties was to lease
space inside the park and to arrange corporate sponsorships
for Disneyland attractions. Woody and his longtime friend
Fred Schumacher would pursue contracts with major American companies, but they were also free to enter talks with sec-
ond- or even third-tier outfits. They would also identify and
approach companies that had leased space at the 1939 World's
Fair in New York—that is, the fair where Shumacher himself
had once worked as a corporate representative—believing that
such companies might be more open to a Disney sponsorship.
Woody assured the Disney brothers that this plan would bring
in the money.

Together, Woody and Schumacher developed a new pitch
book that explained the concept of Disneyland to American
companies. Disneyland would be a family park, catering to the
middle class—families who might be more receptive to advertisements for new or existing products while on vacation than
while at home, listening to the radio, or watching TV. Their
goal was to convince these companies either to lease space
for a company showroom at Disneyland or underwrite an
attraction as an advertising sponsor. For weeks, they traveled
from city to city, speaking to junior executives because very
few senior executives would waste their time on such a hare-
brained scheme, despite the captive audience of middle-class

families the park promised to provide. Companies generally believed that advertisements and displays at fairs, carnivals, and amusement parks would do little to increase sales of their products. Moreover, many companies scoffed at the cost: sponsorship at a fair involved a financial commitment that would last a season or two, but this Disney sponsorship would drain advertising and promotion resources for years.

For the Santa Fe Railroad, Woody dreamed up a list of benefits the company would receive from institutional advertising and sponsorship of the Disneyland Railroad: the Santa Fe logo featured on the train and water towers, Santa Fe travel posters at Main Street Station, and a travel office to sell actual tickets on the Santa Fe Railroad.[6] But the initial meeting went so poorly that Woody was nearly thrown out after he explained that sponsorship of the Disneyland Railroad would cost forty or fifty thousand dollars for a single year. One executive told him: "Goddamn. Sometimes we furnish the paint to put our name on the trains at these kiddie parks. But that's all we've ever done."[7]

After being rejected by dozens of companies, Woody and Schumacher finally approached the Swift's Packing Company in Chicago, a company that had invested heavily in the 1939 World's Fair. Using this information, Woody and Schumacher were able to convince junior advertising executives to let them speak with senior executives, who eventually led them to the president's office.

"The economics were such that the entire project stood in jeopardy," Schumacher later explained. "It was an effective do-or-die day. . . . Not a single tenant or lessee had been signed up. We worked our way up through the entire Swift organization, trying to come to some kind of understanding so that we could at least have one major tenant in the park."

In the presidential suite, Woody removed his materials from his briefcase before setting it against the back wall. He handed a fresh copy of the pitch book to the company president and then explained the concept of Disneyland, referring to artwork and then forecast numbers completed by his old partner, Buzz Price. He focused on the projected attendance rate and per-capita expenditures, explaining that the park would offer advertising exposure more effective than magazines, radio, or even television. It was an environment where customers could see actual products—not just photos or televised images. Woody described how a Swift's company store or a Swift's-sponsored restaurant could bring thousands of new customers to their business, customers who would forever associate the good feelings of a vacation with products made by Swift's. At first, the president showed signs of interest, even enthusiasm for this crazy concept of Disneyland, but eventually he expressed concern, believing that a rational man would not invest in such an unproven concept. As the president revealed his doubts, Woody talked faster, hoping to monopolize the presentation, until, from behind his desk, the elderly man announced: "I've heard enough, gentlemen. Would you kindly leave the office?"

Fred Schumacher walked out with his head hung low, figuring that this would be the end of their sponsorship initiative. It might be the end of their jobs, as well. So far, all the two men had accomplished was to rack up travel expenses. As they made their way to the ground floor, Woody lifted his muddy eyes to Schumacher, his gaze oddly hopeful. "Just wait and see," he whispered. "Wait and see."

Once in the lobby, they took seats by the front windows, where Schumacher believed they would develop plans to revisit the junior marketing executives they had talked to that morning, hoping to somehow salvage this opportunity. But after five minutes, Woody simply stood, straightened his thin black tie, then brushed off the front of his jacket. With a theatrical air, he cleared his throat. "I'm going up again."

"How can you? You were thrown out of the office."

Woody's voice low, filled with gravel: "Wait and see," he said.

Together, the two men returned to the executive suite, though Schumacher hung back and let Woody lead the way. Woody talked his way past the secretaries and after knocking softly on the president's door, opened it without waiting for a response.

"What are you doing back here?" the president demanded.

"Oh," Woody began, before casually lifting a finger to the back wall. The president's gaze followed the gesture across the room and located a black leather bag. "I forgot my briefcase," Woody explained.

With that, the president released a skeptical chuckle, clearly entertained by Woody's opportunistic forgetfulness. More importantly, the laughter changed the emotional atmosphere in the room. To Schumacher, the office seemed softer now, more inviting. He sensed that the president had in fact been thinking about Disneyland since they'd left some twenty minutes ago. Most likely he'd been weighing the cost and the risk exposure against the possible benefits of signing up with Disneyland. Even before Woody brought up the subject of a Swift's-sponsored exhibit, Schumacher knew with absolute certainty that they would leave there with their first major contract. Swift's would develop a restaurant at Disneyland for which it would pay a lease of $110,000 per year. This contract would be the first real financial success for Woody as general manager of Disneyland.[8]

Woody phoned the studio later that day to report the tentative agreement, his voice casual, even flat, implying that the Swift's contract was nothing special, though, of course, it was.

The conversations with Swift's also gave Woody a new understanding on how to sell sponsorships and lessee contracts: initially, he'd suggested that American companies tie their business to Disneyland—and also to Disney's family-friendly reputation—but Swift's wanted Disneyland to tie the park's image to their company as well. For Swift's, specifically, this would mean that WED would design a special room in the Swift's exhibit on Main Street "to house a huge birthday cake, a cake that has 100 candles" to celebrate the centennial anniversary of their company.[9] In short, Woody adjusted the emphasis of his pitch, suggesting that Disney would find unique ways to integrate the identity of sponsors and lessees into the park as well.

With Swift's on board, Woody and Schumacher were now able to bring other sponsors into the project, including those that had earlier rejected their proposal. "Like the Santa Fe Railroad," Woody later explained, a deal eventually helped along because his father had worked for the railroad his entire life.[10] Among the best-known sponsors were Pepsi-Co, Richfield Oil, and Upjohn Pharmacy. Woody also signed many smaller companies, including Sunny View Farms, Yale & Towne Locks, and the National Lead Company.

By far the most unusual lease went to one of Woody's personal friends, a businessman named Hendron Norris, who owned the Hollywood-Maxwell Brassier Company in Los Angeles. Norris committed to developing a Victorian-style intimate apparel shop on Main Street, which would sell bras, corsets, petticoats, and "merry widow" torsolettes. The shop would also feature a historical exhibit on women's under-things—miniature displays that showcased the evolution of the bra, from the 1800s to the present.

For months, Woody met with executives of American companies in their offices, presenting his pitch materials and pushing company presidents to sign-up either as a ride sponsor or as a lessee at Disneyland. When office meetings didn't produce a contract, he changed tactics. He arranged sales meetings at restaurants and bars, as he believed that drinks helped men to see things his way. He told them that their kids would love that they were in business with Disneyland. He indicated that most of the space available for lease was already taken. More than once, he hired beautiful women to attend these outings as their flirtations, when applied just right, could help close a deal.

As the park developed in Anaheim, Woody also invited corporate executives out to view Disneyland under construction. He would walk them around the site then guide them back to his office. Upstairs, after the contract was signed, Woody would call for Milt Albright, the company accountant and notary. Woody would then open the top drawer of his desk. "He always had a bottle of Chivas Regal there," Albright recalls. "He would pull that bottle out and put it on the middle of his desk. . . . He would put about five or six water glasses up there, and he would pour each one about half full." After everyone had a glass, Woody would offer a toast.

"That," Woody explained, "was a Texas consummation."[11]

For its sponsorship of the Disneyland Railroad, the Santa Fe Railway Company paid Disneyland $50,000 per year; Eastman Kodak paid $28,000 to lease shop space; and Upjohn paid $29,600 to develop a factory showroom.[12] Each company to lease space at Disneyland paid their own construction costs to create an indoor exhibition area, their own staff salaries, and an annual rent of $20 per square foot.[13] In general, the term of each lease was for five years. But Woody insisted that payment for the first and fifth year was due upon signing, thereby doubling the money that the Disney brothers received upfront.

In addition to institutional lessees, Woody also sold the opportunity to sell food and merchandise at the park to outside companies because Disneyland could not afford to employ people to fill these jobs.

Though Woody had been excluded from most creative decisions concerning the park, he now entered the world of design through a side door: he helped sponsors and lessees design their shops, exhibition areas, and restaurants. In some cases, he offered straightforward suggestions as to how sponsors and lessees should used their space inside the park, but in other instances, he collaborated with his clients and park artists to develop an attractive shop, exhibition area, or restaurant that would not only suit the client's needs but also conform to the themed space of Disneyland.

Within a few months, over fifty such sponsorships and lessee contracts provided Disneyland, Inc., with millions of dollars to continue construction—much of it directly attributed to the salesmanship and resourcefulness of C. V. Wood. In many ways, this money saved Disneyland from going bankrupt during construction, as the park was now projected to cost more than anyone had predicted. In light of his efforts to successfully bring partner companies into Disneyland, Woody believed he deserved a higher salary. While drinking with his friends, he said, "What I'm making is an insult." But when he approached the Disney brothers to discuss a salary increase, Walt turned him down and was upset that he had brought up the matter at all.[14]

Without an actual raise in salary, Woody looked elsewhere to enhance his income, with his sights soon focused on a series of kickbacks and bribes received from the smaller companies who wanted to participate in the park. Though there is no record of Woody receiving kickbacks from major companies who leased space on Main Street—such as Bank of America, Carnation Ice Cream, or Upjohn Pharmacies—individuals recall Wood receiving kickbacks from small, relatively unknown companies through a scheme that employed another of Woody's longtime friends, Bob Burns, who was now the director of merchandising at Disneyland. In a variation of a "good cop, bad cop" routine, Woody graciously pulled in new lessees to fill smaller shops throughout the park and then Burns insisted that these lessees pay them additional funds directly. The two men split the money.

When I asked Buzz Price about the kickbacks Woody received, he told me, "I know of one. It was the Dickinson's

Jams and Jellies," which was a small specialty store on Main Street that sold homemade preserves. "There was a lady that I knew in Portland," Price continued, "who I thought would make a good Jams and Jellies addition to the park. I went to see her for [Wood]. . . . The next thing I know the bag man [i.e., Burns] is on his way."[15]

Their scheme was simple: individual lessees paid Disney $20 per foot per year for the space, and beyond that, they paid Bob Burns (and Woody) additional kickbacks to keep a successful business at Disneyland.

Though there is no record of how much money the two men made off this venture, the profits appear to have been substantial. In the late 1970s, Van Arsdale France set about writing "a candid autobiography" about his early experience at Disneyland. In the 1980s and early 1990s, there were many versions of this book that he privately printed, sold, and gave as gifts, before finding a traditional publisher. The longest version, weighing in at 268 pages, was edited down to the 118-page book that was eventually released by a traditional publisher in 1999. In one section not included in the final book, France discussed these kickbacks by explaining, "There was a merchandise promoter who had to borrow money from Fred Schumacher when he first landed in Santa Ana. After only six months, he owned an expensive, prestigious home. Kickbacks from lessees paid for it." Though France did not mention by name what he called the "kickback conman," the person is almost certainly Bob Burns, as the job description and supporting details fit him perfectly.[16]

In this story, Burn's share of the kickbacks was enough to buy a house.

Along with his increased wealth, C. V. Wood was also becoming a public figure of sorts.

For almost thirty years, Walt had consciously developed a studio culture in which no individual artist gained public notoriety or fame. Walt Disney was singled out as the man primarily responsible for his films—so much so that Disney promotional materials rarely included information about anyone aside from Walt. But Woody was either unaware of this policy or, more likely, ignored it.

From the start, Woody courted the press, posing beside models of the park. This was his opportunity to become a celebrity of sorts: though not a movie star, he was a public figure in the world of Hollywood. With his showman's background, he was extremely good at handling press events, speaking with such confidence and warmth that reporters were naturally drawn to him. In eight or nine months, Woody became the most visible employee on any current Disney project—far more so than highly trained animators or background painters who had worked at the studio for decades.

In photos from this era, Walt appeared happy beside C. V. Wood, both men smiling. Walt's facial expression was outgoing and expansive: he was most likely unaware that Woody was gaming the system for personal gain. But even in his current state of relative naïveté, one wonders why Walt—who had been hyper-conscious of the company's image for decades— would grant any public notoriety to a relative newcomer like Woody. The answer appears to be one of practicality: Walt was unable to simultaneously oversee both the studio and the park. At times, Walt needed someone other than himself to function as a public spokesman and ambassador for Disneyland.

In this role, Woody was a natural.

Woody regularly gave tours of the construction site to VIP guests and potential sponsors, effectively standing in for Walt. Though at times he would drive such guests through the site in a late-model Nash, he preferred to guide them around on foot so they could view the newly framed buildings up close while he slowly sold them on the revolutionary concept of Disneyland. His enthusiasm for the park came across as genuine and sincere as he, too, was in awe of the project, despite his ongoing troubles with Walt. Even after he injured his knee in a skiing accident, he continued to escort guests through the site on foot, relying on a pair of crutches to steady his gait. He would stagger along the dirt walkways, explaining to his guests that this building here would soon become a turn-of-the-century pharmacy and over there, that building would be an old-fashioned soda shop. Sponsor companies would bring something important to Disneyland, he said, and Disneyland would bring something important to sponsor companies as well.[17]

By now, Woody had an unusual relationship with the company that employed him. Despite his youth, he was used to being treated as a senior executive who oversaw the work of engineers and artists. Yet at Disneyland, Walt released the artists to do whatever they pleased. An effective company, according to Woody, should be directed by project managers and sales executives, whose work was supported by skilled employees and artists—not the other way around.

Despite these problems, Woody was drawn to the park. Walt might've stumbled onto a winning idea, an amusement park that looked like a movie, even if Walt himself was lousy with finance, economic projections, and budgeting. As Woody guided potential sponsors through the construction site, he observed how well they responded to the idea of Disneyland. In a way, Woody felt his injured knee and the crutches improved his presentations. He moved slower, forcing guests to linger, to imagine how this park might appear when finished.

As the park developed, the Disney brothers hired a new lawyer, Luther Marr, to review the deals Wood was making for the company, deals they didn't fully understand or manage. Marr sensed immediately that something wasn't right in Anaheim. "I do remember a problem arose rather quickly," Marr recalls. "[C. V. Wood] was a very impetuous, dishonest kind of a person. Devious, I'd say. So anyway, he didn't like it that I was hired. I could see that from the beginning. Because that meant that the establishment was going to get in his tent and look around and see what was going on."

One of Marr's initial assignments was to review and critique the current contracts that Disneyland was making with partner companies. After reviewing them, he was to report back to the Disney legal team and explain what, if anything, was wrong with them.

From the start, Marr sensed that Woody didn't want him anywhere near those deals. At first, Woody fed him harmless contracts, such as boilerplate lessee agreements. But, late one afternoon, Woody turned up the heat, delivering a forty-page document into Marr's hands a few minutes before quitting time. Leaning back on his heels, Woody said, "Look that over and give me your approval."

Marr glanced at the papers. "Well, yes," he began, "I'll take it home tonight."

"No," Woody said, "I mean, now."

"Well, there's no way. It would take hours and hours."

Believing that this request was unreasonable—and also socially aggressive—Marr decided to leave the office, stepping out the door with his hat in hand. He knew Woody's type: he was socially graceful and charming, yet his interest was probably directed more to the improvement of his own situation rather than to the profitable development of the company.

The next morning, all hell broke loose, as Marr discovered that Woody had asked Roy Disney to fire him. After Marr recovered from the initial shock, he understood what was going on: Marr was so close to the truth that Woody was uncomfortable.

There was something suspicious in those business deals, though Marr didn't yet know what it was.

Woody, Marr would later say, "was looking for any excuse to get rid of me."

That afternoon, Marr talked to Roy on the phone, explaining exactly what had happened—that Woody had dropped a long contract on him minutes before the end of the day. After considering the situation, Roy decided that he believed Marr's version of the events more than he believed those reported by Woody. Marr kept his job, but from that moment forward, he knew in his gut that Woody had deep secrets within the company—an opinion that others would soon share.[18]

For many months, each Wednesday night, as Walt watched his *Disneyland* TV show, he'd seen the Disneyland castle followed by introductions to each of the four themed lands, which included Tomorrowland. The decision to delay the opening of Tomorrowland still weighed heavily on his thoughts. So, in January 1955, six months before opening day, he reversed course. Even without the hanging monorail or a similar landmark icon to anchor the area, he now wanted to open Tomorrowland with the rest of the park. To open a half-finished Disneyland, he announced, would be a humiliation.[19] The following day, WED designers began to revise the old Tomorrowland plans, which now featured a fun-car highway as well as a silver rocket ship nearly eighty feet tall. Though Tomorrowland still did not yet have official sponsors or lessees, the designers finalized plans to include large exhibition halls in hopes that they would soon be filled. That Saturday, January 15, long before the working drawings were complete, a construction crew on overtime pay began to grade the site in preparation for new buildings.

At the studio, Walt revived efforts to design and build attractions for Tomorrowland. At one time, there had been artwork for a time-travel ride that would take guests back to the Jurassic era. Guests would witness dinosaurs rotate by on a massive 80' by 80' turntable.[20] There was also artwork for a dark ride in which guests journeyed across the surface of Mars, a ride that would be housed in a 6,000-square-foot show building. Guests would see the inhabitants of the red planet, their heads concealed inside glass space helmets. These inhabitants—identified in one drawing as "Interplanetary Penal Colonists"—would be watching an advanced version of TV and harvesting crops with a futuristic combine.[21] There were plans for an attraction called Space Station X-1, where guests would see Earth from the vantage point of outer space; a circular movie theater where guests were surrounded by moving images; also a you-drive-'em boat ride. But only two Tomorrowland attractions had received much attention in recent months: Flight to the Moon (a circular movie theater that simulated space flight) and Autopia (stylish gas-powered cars to be driven by young riders on an open road).

At one time, Walt had envisioned Autopia as a realistic recreation of an American highway, one filled with busses and trucks, and family sedans pulling vacation trailers. But that idea had narrowed to a two-lane highway filled with fun park cars. Walt felt hopeful about this attraction even though much of its development was presently overseen by a twenty-three year-old with limited mechanical training—a twenty-three-year-old named Bob Gurr.

Bob Gurr was by far the youngest member of the design team. A recent graduate of a local art school, he'd spent a year in Detroit as an automotive stylist before returning to California, homesick for familiar surroundings, where he found work as an hourly-wage industrial designer. His relationship with the WED team began in October of 1954, when Dick Irvine hired him to design the body of the Autopia car. The assignment quickly developed into a second job for Gurr—on evenings and weekends—but eventually he took over the development of the Autopia cars, even though he had hardly any experience as a mechanical engineer or as a machinist.

With the Tomorrowland attractions now scheduled for opening day, Gurr began to look for a location to turn his preliminary sketches into a full-size clay model—a model more accurately called a "clay buck"—that would become the basis for the fiberglass mold used to make the actual car bodies. But there was one caveat: Walt was running out of money. To produce the clay buck cheaply, Gurr returned to his alma mater, a nearby art school, and sought the help of an old teacher named Joe Thompson.

Thompson had a garage in North Hollywood that he had converted into a work studio. Using Gurr's drawings as a guide, the two men set sawhorses in the middle of the garage and then created a platform on which to build the heavy clay model. Because Gurr was also redesigning the car's chassis, he wasn't able to work on the project every day, leaving Thompson and his design students to complete most of the work on their own. That year Thompson "had students in a beginning class that could be taught how to do clay model work," Gurr later joked. "This would be a *practice* session."

When complete, the clay model would be too heavy and fragile to transport safely to the studio, so Walt would need to view it at the North Hollywood garage. On the afternoon it was finished, Bill Cottrell picked up Walt and Dick Irvine in his old Cadillac, a car the two men regularly joked about because its seats were ripped and its headliner loose. While being driven across town, Walt put his arm across the passenger seat, and, as usual, bits of white upholstery fluff stuck to his sleeve. "Bill, I pay you a lot of money," Walt said. "Fix your goddamn car."

As always, Cottrell silently nodded his head.

When they turned on to the street where Joe Thompson lived, they saw it there: the clay model, centered in his garage.

It resembled a cross between a Porsche and a Maserati. Again, Walt felt a surety in his chest. He had been right to pass on the large carnival vendors with their stock rides and to instead work with a local designer. Kids would love to drive this car.

He walked around the vehicle twice, before running his fingers along the fender. At Gurr's request, the clay buck had been outfitted with a steering wheel, a seat, and tires so Walt could sit in it. Once situated, he rested his hands across the steering wheel. He turned to Gurr, who stood beside the car in a white shirt and aviator sunglasses. He thoughtfully pursed his lips then smiled—or came as close to smiling as he did on most days—before finally saying, This will do fine, Bobby.

Walt was at the garage less than ten minutes, examining a clay buck that had cost him nothing, but as he stepped back into Bill Cottrell's ratty old Cadillac, one thought occupied his mind: he hoped that at least this Tomorrowland ride would be ready for the public on opening day.[22]

Walt repeatedly met with key designers to explain the realities of the Disneyland budget: cash was running short, and designers should save money wherever possible. The budget for plants and landscape materials, alone, was already at $386,000,[23] with many plants left to purchase. Following this edict of frugality, WED designers Bill Evans and Harper Goff scoured the streets of Los Angeles looking for mature trees with which to create the reasonable illusion of an established jungle in Adventureland.

As luck would have it, Evans knew the head of CalTrans' landscape architecture division, who informed him when the CalTrans crew was planning to remove mature trees from a local riverbed to extend the Santa Ana Freeway. The CalTrans team would normally bulldoze, crush, or burn the trees. But on the mornings when the CalTrans team began to clear new land, Evans and Goff showed up with a couple of trucks and offered to give the work crew up to $25 per mature tree. The money was not to purchase the trees, but a small incentive to encourage the road crew to work around desirable trees while the Disney men boxed and loaded the most attractive specimens.[24]

But the removal of mature palms from public land only solved a few of their horticultural needs, leaving Evans and Goff to search—of all places—the overgrown front yards at local estates.

Having a good knowledge of nearby neighborhoods, Evans drove his companion through the wealthier sections of Los Angeles, hoping to buy mature trees from homeowners. When they found a particularly desirable specimen, they'd ask the owner, "Any chance you're tired of that tree?" Most thought they weren't serious, not even when Evans produced a stack of twenty-dollar bills. For an especially desirable tree, he might offer as much as $200.

On one trip to Beverly Hills, Evans and Goff found an ancient Florida banyan outside a mansion—a tree that would easily cost them thousands of dollars if purchased from a nursery. After working up his nerve, Goff approached the house to ask the owner if he could buy the tree. "That big old son-of-a-bitch there?" the man said. "I'm so tired of that thing."

Goff smiled, sensing his advantage, then leaned forward to make his initial offer.

After some discussion, he was able to procure the giant banyan simply for the cost of its removal and a small replacement tree. The tree was so large it required special permits to transport it on public roads at night as Evans and Goff hauled it to Disneyland.[25]

Even with all these trees in place, the Jungle River appeared sparsely landscaped—more like the high desert than a tropical rain forest. To add basic greenery, Evans moved orange trees from the parking lot to the river area, paying special attention to plant them far from the water's edge. But for years after the park opened, "gardeners had to get out there early in the morning to make sure there was no orange fruit hanging on those trees out in the middle of . . . the Congo."[26]

Quickly running out of money, Walt asked Art Linkletter for a personal favor—to host the live telecast of Disneyland for scale wages, a mere $200 for what amounted to many days' work. In addition to hosting his own television series, Linkletter had experience as the master of ceremonies for the opening of the World's Fair. "I assured him that that amount would be perfectly satisfactory to me," Linkletter recalls, "if he would give me the concessions to sell all film and cameras in Disneyland for the first ten years."[27]

Happily, Walt agreed.

Though Joe Fowler repeatedly encouraged Walt to use more outside companies, Walt let very few of them, aside from Arrow, work in any way on the rides themselves. In practice, this meant that a growing number of the Fantasyland attractions were jointly developed by the WED design team and Arrow, which now functioned as a co-design and manufacturing unit. Arrow was given the contract to build the ride system for the Mad Tea Party and the Dumbo Flying Elephants, as well as vehicles for the Mr. Toad and Snow White attractions. Because Karl Bacon and Ed Morgan (of Arrow) had experience with carousels, they were also given the task of dismantling the carousel that Disney had bought from Toronto's Sunnyside Park and transporting it to California, where eventually they would reassemble it at the construction site.

On Friday, March 11, after work, Walt boarded an overnight train that took him from Los Angeles to Mountain View, California, along with Roger Broggie, Bruce Bushman, and Bill Martin. As the train traveled north, the four men reviewed progress reports on the park before getting some shut-eye in their sleeping compartments. The following morning, after the train pulled into the Mountain View station, Walt and his men traveled to the Arrow facility to inspect work recently completed.

Ed Morgan, one of the joint owners, showed them around the shop. Presumably it was on this trip that Walt and his men inspected a prototype for the Snow White car—a boxy fiberglass vehicle designed to hold two people—but to Walt, the car looked a little small. He sat in it, moved around, checked the space between his knees and the front of the car. Next, he asked Roger Broggie to sit in the car so he could see how the car looked when occupied by another adult. With Broggie, the car appeared a little small—but not *too* small.

As though the idea occurred to them at the same time, the two men turned to Bruce Bushman, a pear-shaped man so large he played Santa Claus each Christmas without padding. Walt simply raised one eyebrow, thereby directing Bushman to sit in the car. "If it fits you, Bruce," Walt joked, "it'll fit anybody."[28]

Bruce wedged himself into the Snow White vehicle. It was snug, but not uncomfortably so. Walt chuckled as Bushman crossed his arms then uncrossed them, a stiff smile etched into his face. From that day forward, Bushman provided a template of sorts, as Walt declared that every ride at Disneyland should be large enough to fit a full-sized adult, such as Bushman, and one child.

While inspecting a few components that had been developed for the engine on the Casey Jr. train, Walt smiled. He liked Bacon and Morgan's work for the most part. He made suggestions, asking them to alter a few details, but overall he was pleased with their progress because the men at Arrow knew how to make their rides look like *Disney* rides, as though the rides themselves belonged in an animated film, not at a carnival. Walt and his men left early in the afternoon, satisfied with their trip, and returned to Los Angeles by nightfall.

◆   ◆   ◆

Aside from Arrow, most work on the Fantasyland attractions remained in-house, an edict that forced studio animators to learn even more new skills to complete Disneyland.

Bruce Bushman oversaw the refurbishment of hand-carved horses for the park's carousel. By now, WED had received the antique Dentzel merry-go-round from Toronto, but Walt desired an elegant *carousel* (which featured only horses) as opposed to a *merry-go-round* (which included lions, tigers, and elephants). Bushman purchased additional horses acquired from Coney Island and from the amusement park owned by George Whitney's father to complete the stable of seventy-two necessary steeds. Also at Walt's request, Bushman surgically transformed the legs of a few standing horses into those of jumpers, so that the carousel's herd when finally assembled would appear in vigorous motion, the overhead cranks lifting each mount, as the ride performed its laps.[29]

Another studio artist, Claude Coats, built a three-dimensional tabletop model for Mr. Toad's Wild Ride because he had painted backgrounds for the movie a decade earlier. He spent days arranging the ride as a diorama, complete with scenery colored-up to match the palette of the film, which he assumed a manufacturing company would use as a guide for stage design. After Walt OK'd the model, Coats believed that he was finished with the project and could return to his regular work as a studio artist. But a few weeks later, Walt showed up in the background department, his bangs falling into his face, his eyes pinched with irritation. He explained that the damn company he had hired to paint the scenic backgrounds for the ride would not be able to do it because they didn't understand how to properly adapt the ride's color palette to work with new black light technology. He leveled his eyes at Coats and the other men in the office. "You guys do it," he said, leaving Coats to experiment with new colors that, once illuminated with black lights, would evoke the original color values used in the film. "After having painted cel-size backgrounds for years," Coats explains, "I went from a foot-high format to sets that were eighteen feet high!"[30]

The flat plywood characters and backgrounds for each dark ride were finished at the studio, after which the ride was mocked up on a sound stage. A quickly assembled vehicle was used to transport WED employees through the ride as the actual vehicles were not yet functional. These sets were visually impressive, admired by the entire WED team, as they had been painted in detail by the same background and layout artists who had worked on the corresponding films. Walt in particular loved these mock-ups because he could now visually take stock of the park's progress.

But George Whitney Jr., the only man on the development team with substantial amusement-park experience, saw the underlying problems. After viewing the mock-up of the Snow White ride, he understood that Walt intended to create a dark ride with many small, nearly enclosed rooms, all of them housed in a prefab metal building. The problem was one of air circulation. "The heat that builds up in the building," he wrote in a memo, "points to the fact that we must consider some sort of ventilation. This could be eliminated, however, if we changed the ride from 'Snow White' to 'A Trip through Hell,' in which the heat would then be a natural prop."[31]

As the mock-up of each ride was completed at the studio, the ride track, the painted background boards, and the plywood props were disassembled and trucked, piece by piece, to the construction site in Anaheim as the show buildings became available. The process was "somewhat akin to building a house of cards," remembers Ken Anderson, "with each card weighing five hundred pounds."[32]

The ride track and sets for both the Snow White ride and the Peter Pan ride transitioned easily from the studio to their new show buildings at the park. But on the day a team of construction workers attempted to reassemble the track for the Toad ride in its show building, Anderson learned that the track and sets would not fit. "It was too damn big for the building," Anderson later explained. After discussing the problem with Walt, he directed a construction crew to knock out one corner of the Toad show building, creating a small annex, to accommodate the ride.[33]

As far as the park itself was concerned, the early months of 1955 progressed without significant problems. Keith Murdoch, the city manager of Anaheim, supervised the annexation of the Disneyland property, making Disneyland officially part of the city. Following this, Murdoch saw that the site received various city utility services, including water and sewer—which was no small matter as the various farms previously on the land had existed without water or sewer hookups. Beyond this, he managed the development of roads and stoplights to accommodate the new traffic flow, which were two more land improvements billed directly to Disney.

The Disney creative team finally organized itself much like it did when making a movie—with one central director and many sub-directors developing individual segments. In this system, Dick Irvine was the central director, managing the day-to-day work of the creative team and personally signing off on each sketch, architectural drawing, and landscape plan. Though Disney employed many artists to design the park, five emerged as art sub-directors for the five lands: Harper Goff (Adventureland), Bill Martin (Fantasyland), George Patrick (Frontierland), Wade Rubuttom (Main Street), and Gabe Scognomillo (Tomorrowland), with Disney artist Marvin Davis overseeing the architects for the entire park.

Though Walt's amusement-park project finally looked like a business, it still lacked a viable financial plan. The mounting costs weighed heavily on many people, among them executives at ABC who had guaranteed a $4.5 million line of credit, a loan that they would have to repay if the park went bankrupt. In a secret meeting, the ABC execs met with Disneyland lawyers, where the concerns were immediately expressed. One exec said, "Can't you stop this madman? . . . This thing has gone way out-of-hand." But the Disneyland lawyers explained that all of the contracts had been signed—that Disney was delivering a TV show to ABC—and since Walt was president of Disneyland, Inc., he could spend the money on the park in such a way as he believed reasonable. The men from ABC, one lawyer noted, appeared "scared."[34]

Ed Ettinger, director of Disney's public relations team, would later reveal that, to his surprise, many local residents didn't want an amusement park in Anaheim. Despite the obvious benefit of jobs and increased land values, many residents were worried that an amusement park would bring drifters and seasonal ride operators to town. Ettinger assured residents that the park intended to employ primarily people who lived near the park and train them to work at Disneyland. He also promised that Disneyland would be a good neighbor—with Disney officials making appearances at city events and promising to participate in the town's Halloween festival for years to come. "The entire staff is taking an active part in community activities," he explained, "with the resultant improvements of community attitudes and feelings."[35]

Elsewhere in Anaheim, Walt experienced problems with another group of locals who sought to take advantage of his new amusement park. Real estate speculators and agents gathered listings and bought up properties intent on reselling them quickly at a high profit. The most brazen of the opportunists was Frank Cimral, manager of California Realty & Investment Co. To increase land sales, he advertised that the locations would be excellent sites for such new businesses as a "Disneyland Hotel" and even "Disneyland Liquor." Furthermore, Cimral told potential buyers that they could use the name "Disneyland" with whatever business they intended to open, in this way suggesting a relationship with the park that didn't exist.

Irritated, Walt brought suit against Cimral.[36] But Walt also learned an important lesson: the concept of Disneyland was taking hold in California in ways he hadn't imagined.

Though Walt had long employed the Evans brothers, Jack and Bill, to oversee landscape development at the park, early in 1955 it became clear that they were mainly experts in horticulture and plant procurement, not design. In February, Walt asked his friend, the architect Welton Becket for advice, and he, in turn, suggested the female landscape architect who'd created the outdoor space at Bullock's shopping plazas. Her name was Ruth Shellhorn, a stickler for details, a woman who regularly pointed out planning errors made by men ten or twenty years her senior.

Shellhorn first talked with the studio on March 7 and was hired the following week to create landscape designs for Main Street, Tomorrowland, and the castle courtyard—though her work soon included sections of Frontierland and the entrance plaza of Adventureland as well. Within days of being hired, she discovered that many of the grades were off at the construction site. She spent weeks drawing and redrawing plans, never understanding how the surveyors and foremen could produce and work with such faulty materials, with the construction crew fudging grades all over the site. Some of the grading problems were likely caused by sloppiness and the compressed work schedule, but others, no doubt, were caused by Disney art directors, such as Harper Goff, who, to save money, had eyeballed grades and replaced surveyor's stakes. On the male-dominated construction site, few people had time for Shellhorn's endless corrections. After presenting yet another set of grading inaccuracies, a construction manager said: "I'm very well aware of the constant problem, and I don't need a lesson on how to do our work."[37]

During these same months, Walt toured the park each Saturday to observe its progress, often accompanied by men central to the project, such as Bill Evans, Harper Goff, and Joe Fowler. He inspected the buildings, the landscaping, even the furniture that would be installed in leased stores and restaurants. Nothing was too small for his scrutiny. On one tour, Walt reviewed items in the prop warehouse, which consisted largely of antiques slated for Main Street. He stopped beside a turn-of-the-century music cabinet, a tall box with three sets of doors. He signaled for one of the workmen. "Don't you think it would look better," he began, "if the glass doors were on top instead of in the middle." The workman simply nodded, then went for his tools.[38]

For another Saturday tour, Walt was joined by Bob Thomas, a reporter for the *Los Angeles Examiner*, even though Walt was beginning to wonder if these press excursions into the half-finished park were a good idea. Thomas arrived early to find Walt wearing a Western-style hat and a white shirt. His outfit was complete with a red neckerchief in his pocket. He was sitting on a bench, pulling on his boots as Earl Shelton pulled the company jeep around for easy loading.

Walt greeted Thomas and talked with him for a while. But when Joe Fowler arrived, the conversation shifted to the park's construction: "How's it going?" Walt asked.

Fowler, turning to Thomas, understood this question was posed primarily for the benefit of the reporter. It was not the time to discuss that week's actual problems. "I took a look all around today," he explained. "And I think we'll make the opening all right. Just barely, but we'll make it."

After Walt put on his black coat, he stepped into the Jeep, motioning for the reporter to sit beside him. They visited Town Square, where Walt pointed out the future location of the bandstand. In Frontierland, they visited the dry riverbed and examined the steel hull of the Mark Twain steamboat, which awaited its ornate superstructure presently under construction at the studio. As they walked around the castle, Walt pointed to the future location of the carousel. In Adventureland, they drove along the dry riverbed, where no mechanical animals had yet been installed. At each stop, Walt carefully described the coming wonders so that, in his article, Thomas might focus on what Walt said rather than on what he actually saw.

At the end of the tour, standing beside the ad hoc administration complex, Thomas asked Walt a prophetic question: "Will Disneyland be duplicated elsewhere?"

Walt tilted down his hat to shade his eyes then looked off at the construction site. "I don't think so," he said. "You have to have a year-round business to make money from such a large investment. The only other place it would be possible is Florida. In the East, you could get only three or four profitable months."[39]

The article appeared days later as part of a public relations campaign to develop local interest in Disneyland, although in retrospect it seems clear that local residents were already curious about the new fun spot. Some eagerly awaited the opening of the mega-park, while others believed it would be just another Hollywood spectacular—that is, a spectacular failure. Regardless of their individual motives, "more than 15,000 autos filled with curious kids and their no less curious parents [drove] out from Los Angeles and surrounding cities for a preliminary peek every weekend," reported one local paper.

"Police and State Highway officials [were] already coping with traffic jams."[40]

The studio later reported that many of these families not only drove by, but also stopped to get a closer look. Over the course of a single weekend, 9,500 individuals arrived at the construction site to request information about the forthcoming amusement park.[41]

By mid-May, despite Wood and Fowler's best efforts, Disneyland was nowhere near finished. Its needs had quickly outgrown that of a typical amusement park. It was more of a self-contained city, and as such, it required improvements to make it work properly: green space and rest areas, parking lots and refuse collection. Further complicating the situation, the Orange County plumbers and asphalt workers went on strike, leaving the park without drinking fountains, adequate bathrooms, and paved streets. As the project neared bankruptcy, one of the landscape architects, Bill Evans, was forced to order seedlings instead of mature or even semi-mature plants. Attempting to sidestep the plumbers' strike, Walt hired a non-union company to install pay-toilets. "People can buy Pepsi-Cola," Walt told his staff. "But they can't pee in the streets."[42]

Walt could not, however, entirely fix the plumbing problem through a non-unionized pay-toilet company and soda fountains. If he hired scab plumbers, the construction crew would walk off the site in sympathy with the plumbers' strike. To make matters worse, other unions were eyeing Disneyland for their own greedy purposes. The inland boatmans' union wanted jurisdiction over the men who would operate the Mark Twain riverboat, even though the boat was fixed on a guide rail. The American Guild of Variety Artists demanded jurisdiction over those who would conduct guests along the Jungle River, categorizing their work as professional performance.[43]

One of the most persistent unions was the Teamsters, who made repeat visits to the construction site to demand union jobs at union wages. The manager of the Frontierland mule stables, Jack Montgomery, remembers two stubborn Teamster representatives visiting the site specifically to intimidate him. The men were wearing straw Stetson hats and blue jeans; each had one boot hitched up on the corral fence as they waited for Montgomery to join them. "Anytime you load a kid on a mule and take him off it again, that's Teamsters' work," one of the union men said, making the absurd comparison between assisting guests onto a pack animal and loading cargo onto a truck. "We mean to take over all the loading in this park, and the sooner you get that straight the better."

When the two men were finally finished, Montgomery stood there with his arms crossed in anger, waiting for them to walk away.[44]

But job demands were not the only union-related problem at the work site.

Union workers unaccustomed to taking orders from "artists" took advantage of their new studio bosses. Ken Anderson, one of the art directors, worked closely with construction men building the Fantasyland section of the park. Because Disneyland required far more skilled laborers than were available in Orange County, some workers commuted fifty or sixty miles to the park each day. On the first day that Anderson oversaw ironmongers from San Bernardino, they casually wandered in hours late, visibly unhappy to be reporting to a Disney artist. When Anderson explained the ironmonger's task, the lead man turned to his coworkers and chuckled before focusing his gaze on the artist. "Oh," he replied, "you want us to use *tools*?"

"Of course," Anderson said. "Didn't you bring tools?"

"Our tools are back in San Bernardino. We didn't know you wanted us to bring *tools*."[45]

To complicate matters, many Disney studio employees and contract workers at Disneyland were already unionized, belonging either to the Burbank or Orange County chapters of IATSE—that is, the union overseeing motion picture artists, craftsmen, and technicians. But the two branches of IATSE used Disneyland as the means to continue a longstanding feud in which the Burbank chapter claimed the Orange County chapter was taking away their jobs and vice versa. Men from the two chapters regularly fell into small scuffles at the worksite, disagreeing over the division of labor. When Arrow shipped the Casey Jr. Circus Train to southern California, the studio men in Burbank painted the train engine to match Bruce Bushman's color scheme, but after the engine was delivered to the construction site, the park men in Orange County sandblasted the enamel paint off its metal exterior, insisting that it was their responsibility to finalize and paint all ride vehicles.[46]

When studio members of IATSE visited the site to complete a project, the Orange County members would occasionally protest their visits by a project-specific work stoppage. Such was the case when Sam McKim, a WED studio man, went to the park to paint Native American pictographs inside Frontierland. "[The Orange County men] gave unofficial permission for me to come down," reported McKim. "They let me use their ladders, and they gave me the paint." But as was most always the case, the Orange County men would not help complete the project while studio men were working on it.[47]

But Disney's problem with unions wasn't even limited to the park and the surrounding areas. In a May 26 memo, Joe Fowler reported that the newly revised Mad Tea Party ride was still being developed by Arrow, though Arrow hoped to test it on June 11. The initial test, however, would occur at Arrow's facility in Mountain View, California—roughly 400 miles away from the Disneyland construction site. If successful, the ride would then be disassembled and shipped to Anaheim, assuming proper transportation could be found as union truck drivers were currently on strike in the northern part of the state.[48]

After reviewing the extensive problems with the park, C. V. Wood found Admiral Joe Fowler in his office. Fowler was a tall man, nearly bald, and wore thick glasses that magnified his determined, distant eyes. The construction team now viewed him as a stern father figure, seeking his approval, fearing his scorn. For a while, Wood discussed the problems with Fowler, listing them on his fingers, but he could not easily influence the old man. "We might as well postpone until September," Woody said. "We're not going to make it by July."

Fowler rose from his desk, his shoulders lifting with military starch, and set his hands on his hips. In Fowler's estimation, the Disney brothers might be able to overcome poor reviews of unfinished attractions and a partially completed showground. They might be able to overcome problems with the trade unions. Postponement beyond the lucrative summer season, however, would mean bankruptcy. He leaned close so Wood would not misunderstand him. "Woody," he said in a deep and measured voice, "we have to make it."[49]

In the weeks that followed, Fowler played hardball with the plumbers' union, by offering the plumbing work to the Teamsters union at higher wages. "The Teamsters," Fowler later explained, "said, 'Now, if the plumbers won't put this in, we're not going to have this park defeated. We'll put it in for you.'" News of the Teamsters' offer quickly worked its way back to the plumbers, who then sought out Fowler. In a hastily arranged meeting, Fowler promised to retroactively pay the plumbers post-strike wages if they immediately returned to finish the necessary pipe work. "Now, under those circumstances," Fowler concluded, "will you put it in?"

The plumbers reluctantly agreed.[50]

As for the asphalt, Fowler arranged for it to be trucked in from a plant in San Diego, flagrantly bypassing the Orange County strike zone. As truck drivers logged hundreds of miles and also interfered with a union strike, the maneuver was risky and expensive. "Jesus," Fowler later quipped, "what a cost!"[51]

Knowing that Fowler was right about the need to open by summer, Woody sold additional sponsorships in Tomorrowland to large American companies, offering exhibition space to showcase their products in exchange for a multi-year lease with some of the money paid upfront. Despite his ongoing troubles with Walt, Woody also felt a deep satisfaction in his job. He liked the work, and he also liked the visibility his position gave him. In his estimation, the park's success—assuming it would be a success—could be attributed primarily to Roy Disney (who somehow managed to arrange construction loans) and, of course, to himself (who brought in endless lessees and sponsors).

Under Woody's guidance, corporate partners in Tomorrowland soon included Kaiser Aluminum, sponsor of Hall of Aluminum Fame, for an annual rent of $37,500; National Lead Company, maker of Dutch Boy Paints, sponsor of the Color Gallery, for an annual rent of $9,000; Monsanto Chemical Company, sponsor of the Monsanto Hall of Chemistry, for an annual rent of $30,000; Transworld Airlines, sponsor of Rocket to the Moon, for an annual rent of $45,000; and Richfield Oil, sponsor of Autopia, for an annual rent of $45,000.[52] Woody also wrung additional money from existing lessees. For example, park designers now wanted to include an outdoor dining area at the far end of Frontierland, but they were careful not to mention this area on any park planning materials so that Woody and his team could sell the idea to Swift's, with Swift's then picking up the tab for its construction.[53]

While Woody focused on the finances, other members of his team handled publicity, worked with the local Highway Patrol to create a traffic plan, and develop training materials.

But the problems associated with opening Disneyland weighed heavily on Walt because the decision to build Disneyland, from the start, had been his. At home, his wife, Lilly, feared that he was working toward a breakdown. At the studio, men noticed a change in their boss. "I don't think he was that sure of himself on a lot of his decisions at that point," animator Frank Thomas said during a 1997 interview. "I can remember the way he said things to us, and the way he acted, and the way he squirmed in his chair. I felt that he wasn't sure, but he didn't want to admit that he wasn't sure, because he was our leader."[54]

Repeatedly, Walt argued with his brother about money, as construction costs continued to spiral out of control. One afternoon he told him simply: "I've got to have more money, or I can't open the park."

Roy crossed his arms. His eyes narrowed and focused intently on Walt. "Well," he said, "I'm just not going to give it to you. You've spent enough. And enough is enough."

Walt raised both of his eyebrows. It was the expression he adopted whenever he was about to make a threat. "Okay," he intoned, "I'll sell my name to some banks I know, and I will raise my own money."

The threat worked. The following day, Roy was able to find more money, though not nearly as much as Walt needed.[55]

But money could not solve all of Walt's problems.

In this atmosphere, further difficulties developed between Walt, who demanded high quality shows and rides, and C. V. Wood, who understood the near-impossibility of delivering these things by the park's grand opening. At times, Walt would complain to the Studio Team about the inflexibility and self-centered ambitions of Wood, and likewise, Wood would complain to his management team about the unrealistic expectations of Disney. Months earlier, when Ron Miller, Walt's son-in-law, shuttled blueprints between the park's designers in Burbank and the construction site in Anaheim, he'd repeatedly heard Wood complaining about Walt. "Woody at the time had Ron thinking [Walt was] some kind of crackpot," Walt's daughter, Diane Disney, revealed in an interview, "that [Walt] can't do all these wild things he wanted to do at Disneyland."[56]

When tensions rose, the responsibility fell to Roy to keep Walt and Woody apart, each focused on his own tasks toward the construction of Disneyland.

Yet Woody's version of these events differs significantly from those of the Disney brothers. According to Woody, there were days when his "biggest function was keeping Walt and Roy from each other's throats," mostly over ongoing disagreements about the park's finances.[57] Though it is possible that Woody both exaggerated the problems between the Disney brothers and his own role as peacemaker, it is also possible that over time both Walt and Roy downplayed tensions inside their family.

Regardless of how these tensions were parsed, Walt finally agreed to the arrangements made by Roy—namely, to let Woody work as the park's general manager without unnecessarily butting heads with him at the studio. But to close friends, Walt expressed a desire to restructure Disneyland's management team immediately after the park was open. Specifically, he wanted to limit Woody's authority by creating a committee to manage Disneyland. Walt's first idea—a poor one—was to hire managers to run each area of the park as its own town. One morning, after learning of this plan, Woody found Fred Schumacher and Van France to talk over the issue. "The boss has a crazy idea about park organization," Woody began. "He wants to have guys in complete charge of the areas . . . those guys would be like the mayor of a town . . . to find guys like that, we'd have to pay forty thousand dollars a year."

To shoot down this plan, Woody decided the best strategy was to develop actual job descriptions for these "mayor-like" positions, individuals who had the capability to run a town like Chicago. He used these descriptions as a means to demonstrate to Walt that, even if such individuals were willing to work at Disneyland, the company wouldn't have the money to employ them. Van France, who was privy to this conversation, felt that Woody was motivated by both the desire to preserve his power and also by cronyism: "My educated guess is that at the time Wood wanted to have his own team in positions of responsibility, and none of them had the necessary qualifications."[58]

Walt's next plan was better developed. The heads of finance, show, and operations, Walt reasoned, could jointly make decisions concerning the park. This would spread power out over more people and, more importantly, downgrade Wood's role to that of park spokesman and fiscal manager.

In late May, Walt approached Joe Fowler, offering him a permanent position at the park. "Joe," Walt began, "I want you to stay on [after construction] and organize the operation." Putting his hand on Fowler's shoulder, he brought the tall man closer, explaining that he especially wanted him to oversee all future construction. "Now we're not going to call you a manager. We're going to run the park by committee."

Fowler considered the request before replying. "If I sit on a committee, I want to be Chairman."

Walt smiled and lifted his eyes to meet Fowler's. Though he could not offer Fowler the title of park manager—that was Woody's title—he could promise him the position unofficially: "You run the park, Joe. Don't make any mistake about that."[59]

Though Fowler didn't address the matter directly, he must have understood that Walt was designing a system of management that would purposefully diminish the authority of C. V. Wood.

As a secondary benefit, an operations committee comprised of WED and Disneyland employees would also shift the park's overall power structure, removing some power from Roy's financial team (which included Woody) and giving it back to Walt.

There was simply no other way to interpret such a comment.

Across town, in Burbank, a producer at ABC named Sherman Marks was gearing up for the largest show in the history of TV: a live telecast showcasing the grand opening of Disneyland.

Described as both anxious and quietly nervous, Marks was slowly coming to understand the enormity of this project. Already he had hired a central director to assist him in the control booth, and now he was hiring segment directors, all of whom worked with ABC. One director would oversee the parade on Main Street. Another would direct the work in Frontierland. And so on. Each segment director would have an assistant director, again pulled from ABC. But beyond this, Marks now understood that he would need to borrow personnel from other networks, such as NBC, to fully staff the event.

The telecast would involve over twenty cameras; most accounts place the number at twenty-four, but some place it as high as twenty-nine.[60] Some of these cameras, as well, would be borrowed from stations in San Francisco, Chicago, and Detroit.[61] Following Walt's wish to create a TV spectacle, Marks planned to mount one of these cameras atop the castle. Three mobile cameras would be stationed on construction cranes. And another with a high-power zoom lens would be situated atop a 100-foot observation tower. In all, the ninety-minute production would employ a producer, a central director, four segment directors, four assistant directors, a musical director, a choreographer, various floor managers, and a crew of sixty-three technical and support personnel. According to the central director, Harold Eisenstein, it would be "the biggest engineering feat on television up to that time."[62]

But as May came to a close, Marks was unsure exactly how he would pull together this "engineering feat" by opening day.

Across the street from Disneyland, in an abandoned farmhouse, Van France was frantically developing the last of his training materials for future Disneyland employees. Already, a maintenance crew had knocked down a few bedroom walls to create a makeshift training space in the old farmhouse and France himself had crafted a preliminary set of presentation cards. The theme for his program was simple: "Employees at Disneyland would create happiness for others." But even at this late date, he had no idea if his program would be approved by Disneyland executives.

"I didn't know a damn thing about show business. I didn't even know that much about Disney," France would later admit. "And here we were, assigned to go from zero to 600 people [in just a few weeks]. And I was scared to death."[63]

Because a motivated workforce was central to the Disneyland concept, many top executives insisted on viewing the orientation program firsthand before it was presented to employees. On the afternoon of May 26, studio executives drove down to Anaheim, including Roy Disney, where they were joined by the vice president of Bank of America and executives from Eastman Kodak and Swift's. "C. V. Wood was there," France recalls. "And he was worried to death because he had recommended me to Walt. He thought that if I flopped it was going to be bad [for him]."

The training presentation was straightforward—if somewhat corny—with Van France asking each executive to introduce himself and name his hometown. He explained the history and traditions of the Disney studio, and then to help his audience better understand the concept of Disneyland, he produced slides of artists' renderings, as the current park was nowhere near finished. "I had to get up and say, 'Our theme, the purpose of Disneyland was to create happiness for others' . . . at a time when there wasn't much happiness [or much money]." But slowly the executives were able to see through the corniness of the slogans to the larger concept France was nervously attempting to explain: that employees at Disneyland shouldn't focus on a paycheck or performing a job, but rather on presenting an attitude of cordiality. "Instead of employees, we [would call] everyone hosts and hostesses [as though] we have invited people here [to Disneyland]."

For the most part, the executives and lessees liked the training program—or, at least, they liked it enough to allow Van France to start training actual employees the following day. "Now, Van," Roy Disney commented before leaving, "we are going to create a lot of happiness, but we're also going to have to make money to get Walt's life insurance out of hock." Before stepping out the door, Woody shook France's hand, visibly relieved. As the executives left the farmhouse, most of them had only one thought in mind: hopefully France and his team would be able to hire and train enough employees before the July 17 deadline.

With the presentation over, France and his assistant retired to the back office, which was simply a converted bedroom. He took out a bottle of good booze and filled two glasses. "I sat there with some scotch, smelling the fragrance of the orange trees," France later wrote. Through the window he watched a small group of chickens scratching at the ground for their evening meal. Beyond them, he could see half-finished buildings rising from the muddy foundation of Disneyland.[64]

At Walt's request, C. V. Wood sent an inter-office memo on June 2, enumerating the major projects not yet complete at the park. "The following represents the best estimate that can be obtained at this time," Woody wrote, "regarding the status of the individual sections of the Park on opening day." The list included major attractions from each of the five themed areas, highlighting the obvious: the park was nowhere near finished. Large sections of Main Street were not paved. The plaza and central hub lacked landscaping. About them, Wood optimistically wrote, "If all goes according to plan, I think we can be fairly certain that both [the plaza and hub] will be green for opening."

He indicated that the moving sidewalks (or "speed ramps"), originally designated for Tomorrowland, could not be installed before the opening. Neither the exterior nor the interior of the Rocket to the Moon attraction was yet finished, but, he added, "the big question is how much time will be required to perfect the operation [of its show components]," thereby placing blame on studio electricians supervised by WED, not by those employees managed by Wood. In Fantasyland, neither the castle nor its courtyard was complete. In Adventureland, the mechanical animals were not yet installed on the Jungle River. More significantly, the attraction's waterway had not yet been filled with water. In Frontierland, many shops remained empty.

Along with the construction problems, Wood explained that the park had only been able to hire 100 employees. Rather optimistically, he added, "we expect to have approximately 550 at opening."[65]

In a separate memo, also dated June 2, Joe Fowler reported to Walt construction problems associated with Tomorrowland. An entire wing of shops and exhibits, he explained, would need to be roped off. Likewise, he doubted if the Richfield Show, the Kaiser Aluminum exhibit, or even the Yacht Club snack bar would be finished. Roughly half of the Tomorrowland area, he estimated, would not be ready for the public on July 17.[66]

The problems at the park, however, were larger than Wood and Fowler estimated, though the one that gained the most attention was not in Tomorrowland. It was in Frontierland.

◆   ◆   ◆

The showpiece of Frontierland was to be the Rivers of America and the Mark Twain paddleboat. In short, the river would be a manmade canal that circled a wooded island, a body of water wide enough and deep enough to house a full-scale Mississippi sternwheel steamship.

Months earlier, Bruce McNeil's land-preparation team had carved out a deep channel, using the excavated dirt, in part, to create decorative mounds and foothills around the river's edge. A loading dock had been constructed at the top of the river, as well as a dry dock for the boat's maintenance and repair. Initially, Joe Fowler believed that amending the soil with a synthetic sealant would create a watertight basin for the river. A crew, under his direction, applied the sealant to a test section and once it had dried, Fowler ordered the same men to flood the section with water. He watched the water level rise but soon noticed that the level was no longer rising. In fact, it was starting to fall. He looked at the walls of the riverbed and observed that moist dirt existed a few inches above the waterline. He shut off the hoses, stood on a small mound so that he could better observe the area.

Over the course of many hours, he watched water in the test section disappear, leaving only puddles and mud. He knew the problem: the ground was too coarse to hold water, even with the sealant. "It was almost ball-bearing sand," one designer later explained. "You could have used this stuff for a good grade of concrete."[67]

After discussing the problem with Walt Disney, who was visibly upset, Fowler experimented with other methods of sealing the bed. He tried plastic liners as well as other soil stabilizers—all of which failed to create a watertight basin. "We had a hell of a time with the design of the river so that it would hold water," Fowler reported.[68] He eventually applied clay to a small test area, which, it seemed, solidified the section. With this tentative success he ordered truckloads of clay, hoping that a mixture of clay and liquid cement sprayed gunite-style (through high-pressure nozzles) would create an effective riverbed. As an added measure, Fowler's crew laid a thin metal grid over the open sand, much like rebar, to ensure that the mixture of clay and cement would unify into a continuous surface, one strong enough to hold tons of water.

Fowler understood the importance of this task. No river, no steamboat, no centerpiece for Frontierland. There was only one problem: he would not be able to completely fill the river until July. The Rivers of America and the Jungle River were connected beneath a walkway as one continuous water system, with parts of the connecting route hidden from public view. Months ago, this had seemed like a good idea—to connect the river systems at the park in a way that would help with filtration and limit stagnation. But now this "good idea" was causing unexpected problems. Fowler needed to test the big river—the Rivers of America—to see if the channel would remain watertight once filled to capacity, but he was unable to do this without flooding the Jungle River, where a team was still setting and adjusting track, finishing rockwork, and establishing platforms for mechanical animals.

In the second week of June, Fowler raised the big river to roughly the halfway mark—just below the point where the big river would feed the connecting channel that led to the jungle.[69] The water level appeared stable, but the river was nowhere near full. In fact, the riverbed was only carrying a small fraction of the water weight it would eventually need to support. Realistically, Fowler would only have one chance to fill the big river before opening day. The cement-and-clay mixture, despite the coarse substrate, needed to create a continuous watertight bed. There would be no time to drain the river and fix a problem before the park opened on July 17.[70]

During the final weeks of construction, the total size of the work crew, previously 800 individuals, tripled to include 2,500 men who often muscled through two shifts to complete a seventeen-hour workday.[71] As hourly union employees, the construction workers were entitled to overtime and double overtime as well as additional pay for work on the sixth and seventh day of a workweek. Men earned over $1,000 per week as the grand opening of Disneyland approached—a figure slightly more than twelve times the average weekly paycheck of an American worker in 1955.[72]

To better oversee the two construction shifts, Joe Fowler converted one room of the Dominguez farmhouse back into a bedroom. He brought sheets for the bed. He filled its closet with fresh clothes. "Work was so strenuous during that time," he explained, "I had to have an apartment here at the park where I could stay at least three or four times a week."[73]

But some members of the construction crews stayed at Disneyland most every night. "I was on the job 24 hours a day," recalls one truck driver. "I'd sleep in my truck, and I only went home on Sundays."[74]

Herb Ryman would simply say: "It was frantic, frantic work."[75]

For the Disney brothers, activity was measured not only in effort and a lack of sleep, but also in dollars.

"We were still talking eleven million dollars in April," recalls Joe Fowler, "when I was walking down Main Street with Roy and a representative from Bank of America, who scanned the project and said it looked closer to fifteen million."[76]

Overtime wages weren't the only factor in the skyrocketing costs to complete the park. There was, among many unplanned expenditures, asphalt trucked in from San Diego at expedited rates. On Main Street, Walt demanded many buildings be repainted to better establish the opening scenery of Disneyland. He insisted that storefronts have more elaborate—and more costly—gingerbread trim. At the Train Station, in a fit that approached irrationality, he ordered workmen to re-crush the ballast rock alongside the track so that it matched the 5/8th scale of his railroad. "That's not to scale," he quipped to a group of workmen as he held a large rock in his open hand. "It gives the wrong appearance."[77]

In moments such as these, Woody found Walt's attention to minor adornments infuriating. Woody understood that the park needed to offer a reasonable illusion to guests—such as the illusion of a frontier town and of a turn-of-the-century street—but he believed an American audience would easily accept a lower level of detail. He repeatedly looked for ways to scale back on the park's ornamentation, scenic touches he felt utterly frivolous. Woody told himself he wasn't cutting corners so much as trying to live within the park's budget. "I wanted to put plastic railing up on top of the houses on Main Street," Woody later explained, "and [Walt] wanted real wrought iron. Forty feet in the air—nobody could tell the difference."[78]

To keep the park managers focused, Woody held nightly meetings in his office. "Happy Hours," they were called. The gatherings started with a review of construction progress. As anxiety increased—with discussions of unfinished projects—to help the men, Woody almost always served alcohol. His invitation to drink was another of his Texas sayings: "Let's get out the old Loud Mouth." According to one attendee, people didn't have a single cocktail; they had "a few."[79]

The escalating expenditures weighed heavily on Roy, who began to wonder if he had done the right thing in supporting the park through a series of loans. In part, these loans were provided by banks and in part they were provided by Walt Disney Productions. By spring of 1955, Walt Disney Productions had loaned Disneyland, Inc., a total of $2,383,000, with the notes coming due in seven years.[80] "Roy was very candid," studio employee, Donn Tatum remembers, "in saying that at the time he couldn't see how anything that was going to cost that much could be successful."[81]

By now, the tremendous financial pressure also ate at Walt. Though he was good at masking his anxiety, once, while on his way to lunch, a television director from ABC told him that Disneyland "is a wonderful thing you're doing for the children of the world."

Walt stopped walking and turned to him, his eyes bleary, betraying exhaustion. "What did you say?" he asked.

"This park," the director repeated, "what you're doing here—is so great for children."

In an uncharacteristic manner, Walt's expression reddened to incredulity, briefly revealing his own apprehension. "Don't you know anything?" he said. "Kids don't have any money."[82]

In Adventureland, work progressed slowly on the Jungle River. Unsure exactly how to lay out the track, Harper Goff created a plywood template in the precise shape of a Jungle River boat and strapped it to the top of a Jeep. As he inched along the dry riverbed, checking the plywood template for adequate clearance, his assistants used wooden stakes to mark projected placement of the track. "It worked pretty well," Goff recalls. "We had to correct some of the curves. That was all."[83]

Once the boats were added to the attraction, George Whitney noticed a significant problem with the ride design in terms of hourly capacity: the boats contained only a single entrance for guests, which meant that the boat would stop alongside the dock, allow guests to disembark before other guests entered. The single entrance and the lengthy stop to load and unload passengers would cause the attraction to loose thousands of dollars on peak days. To fix this problem, Whitney proposed an entrance at the back of the boat and a separate exit at the front. "The attendant would in essence push people out the front," Whitney later explained. "The boarding guy would push them in from the back."

After the economics of this problem were explained to Walt, he ordered the striped canopies (cut with a single center opening) removed from each boat and then authorized the creation of new canopies cut with both an entrance and an exit. "I forget how many boats we had on that Adventureland ride," Whitney continued. "But we spent quite a bit of money redoing all of the canopies in order to do the on-and-off."[84]

Without their canopies, the boats continued through their circuit as divers made minor adjustments to the track. Along the banks special-effects men from the studio worked double shifts in hopes of populating the riverbanks with mechanical animals before opening day, some of the animals so large that they needed to be assembled on-site.

Toward the end of June, Karl Bacon and Ed Morgan of Arrow Development arrived at Disneyland to oversee implementation of the last of their rides, only to find that some ride systems and vehicles did not function properly once they were installed at the park. Though the Arrow-built arm-and-lift system for the Flying Elephant ride had worked at their Mountain View plant, once the ten studio-designed elephants (each weighing 700 pounds) were attached to the Arrow lift system, the ride no longer operated properly. During lengthy tests, the pistons did not correctly elevate each elephant into the air, mainly due to a problem with an experimental hydraulic system. On the recommendation of a NASA consultant, Bacon and Morgan had used a combination of oil and nitrogen in the hydraulic system for added power, though with the rapid and sometimes jerky movement of the ride the mixture now produced foam, effectively disabling the lift system. Likewise, each elephant's huge ears were supposed to flap but failed to do so because the ears were too heavy, the motors too small. Once on the rail, the Arrow-designed vehicles for the Snow White ride jumped the

WED-designed track when passengers moved around in their seats or when ride operators stepped on the bumper while loading guests. But the most serious problems concerned the Casey Jr. Circus Train. The Arrow-designed engine could not safely climb the 45 percent grade on the WED-designed track.[85]

On the first day of testing, Roger Broggie manned the controls attempting to engineer the train around its course—a course that was filled with hills and many turns. As his son recalls, while the train was climbing an incline suitably named "Impossible Hill," the engine became unbalanced: "The front end of the engine started to lift up off the track and was coming back over the top of my father. And a worker who saw what was going to happen ran over and jumped on the front of the engine and pulled it back down on the track and kept it from rolling over onto my father, who would've been pinned underneath."[86]

Shortly after the test run, Joe Fowler went to Walt Disney's on-site office to explain the difficulties. In Fowler's estimation, the problem was a combination of the train's speed, the track's steep grade, and the angling of the rails at important turns. There was no way to fix these problems quickly. After laying out the situation, he offered his assessment: the cars, designed as big cages, were top heavy and liable to tip over without special shoes to attach the cars to the track: "Walt," he said, "I'm just as sorry as can be, but we can't, in safety, let the public operate that railroad until I've devised some means to prevent it from capsizing."

He expected Walt to be angry, rattling off a litany of goddamns, but he just sat there, slowly folding his hands into his lap. Fowler would later say that he could see that his boss "was awfully disturbed." Walt looked briefly out the window, his eyes becoming heavy, before turning back to Fowler, his voice soft and resigned. "Well, all right, Joe," he said, "do it as soon as you can."[87]

◆   ◆   ◆

Two weeks before the park's grand opening, Walt decided to display movie sets from 20,000 *Leagues Under the Sea* in an empty Tomorrowland exhibition hall to create a last-minute attraction. Because the studio could not redo entire sets in such a short time, Walt was forced to rent nautical props at great expense from Marine Props and Rentals in Culver City.[88] The attraction's centerpiece, though, absolutely had to be the giant squid—a massive puppet that the studio effects expert, Bob Mattey, would have to reassemble because it had been hacked to pieces during the filming of the motion picture.[89] Mattey received the call on Monday, and though he was still working on the Jungle River creatures, he was able to load the squid, newly repaired, onto a flatbed truck that Friday. The squid was enormous with twenty-foot tentacles and a body as big as three men. A special shed annex, made mostly of tin, was quickly constructed to house the rubbery animal, an area that employees soon called "squid row."

To lure Kaiser Aluminum into a multi-year lease at the park, C. V. Wood had promised company officials that he would purchase and use aluminum prominently in Tomorrowland. Kaiser would build a company exhibit called the Hall of Aluminum Fame, which included both an aluminum telescope and a three-foot tall cartoon mascot, an aluminum pig named Kap.[90] Beyond the exhibit, however, Disney agreed to use aluminum in the construction of other attractions. "If [Kaiser] were to sponsor Disneyland," Bob Gurr remembers, "they were going to shove as many pounds of aluminum as they could into Disneyland."[91]

Outside of the Hall of Aluminum Fame, the largest single use of aluminum was in the construction of the seventy-six-foot tall Moonliner rocket, which marked the entrance to the Rocket to the Moon attraction. With its sixty-foot body and sixteen-foot nose cone, the rocket required hundreds of square feet of aluminum skin, which turned out to be a poor choice of materials for such a large object.[92] Each morning, as the air warmed and the massive aluminum structure expanded over its steel skeleton, the rocket would emit thunderous groans, resonating in its hollow body, and each evening, as the air cooled, the same occurred. Though the Moonliner was the largest use of aluminum, it was not the poorest conceived use of the metal. That dubious honor went to the bumpers on the Autopia cars.

Unlike later models, the first Autopia cars made use of wraparound bumpers that encircled the entire vehicle so early visitors could safely navigate the "open road." The concept for Autopia was to allow young drivers to experience realistic freeway conditions: no rails and no lane dividers, only an endless road. With this layout, collisions would be inevitable. On the first day of full testing, Bob Gurr took a few cars to a section of smooth dirt outside the park where he tried them out with other employees. "I confirmed that the bumpers indeed were going to be a disaster," Gurr later wrote. The "material deforms and does not return to its original position. . . . Now what [were] we going to do?"[93]

Aluminum was used in the construction of many attractions outside Tomorrowland as well, such as to ornament Sleeping Beauty's castle and to create the seventy-foot canopy covering the carousel. It was so widely displayed at the park that, on opening day, Kaiser took out a full-page ad in the *Wall Street Journal* to highlight the aluminum features of Disneyland. "At Disneyland, which opens today," the text began, "you'll see shining objects made of Kaiser Aluminum almost everywhere you look. . . . We believe that the exciting uses of aluminum at Disneyland indicate how aluminum can improve many familiar products and make possible new ones. We are eager to work closely with any manufacturer who wishes to hitch his wagon to 'the brightest star in the world of metals.'"[94]

Similarly, Southern Counties Gas Company strong-armed Disneyland into piping natural gas throughout the park. (In the mid-1950s, gas companies were promoting natural gas as a viable alternative to manufactured gas.) The street lamps on Main Street would use natural gas. Dozens of fast-food restaurants and snack counters would use it, too, as would Swift's Red Wagon Inn. Promotional brochures (distributed at the park) would tout that "Gas will be on hand in Tomorrowland, too, as a fuel for cooking and heating. For gas will be a part of the actual world of tomorrow." But the most unique use of natural gas would be with one of the steam engines: "The train will be drawn by a Diesel-fired steam engine, and natural gas will be used every morning to fire the engines for the day's first run."[95]

Many of the gas lines were installed quickly, toward the end of construction. The problems with these gas lines would not become apparent until opening day.

Most mornings, the construction team was met by rain, as 1955 was the wettest year in over a decade. Truck drivers transported mechanical rhinos and crocodiles from the Burbank studio to Anaheim—a trip that before the expansion of the Santa Ana Freeway took two-and-a-half hours each way. Animators and artists, still employed by the studio arm of Disney, pitched in with the painting and final staging of Fantasyland dark rides. Even Eyvind Earle, who was in effect the lead production designer for the studio's next animated feature, *Sleeping Beauty*, was asked to work on the park. "Along with [layout artist] Don Da Gradi," Earle remembers, "we designed and created the Art Store at Disneyland, and I painted the mural for [the] Welch's Grape Juice [stand] and one for the pirate ship [room in the] Peter Pan [ride]."[96]

Milt Albright, a Disneyland accountant, explains that by this point in the park's construction many bills were left unpaid: "We owed everybody in Orange County that had concrete, steel and anything to sell of consequence."[97] After hearing rumors about the park's financial status, some suppliers refused to deliver additional goods to Disneyland unless they were paid on the spot in cash. Other suppliers considered placing a lien on Disneyland, Inc., for money that they were already owed. A series of liens would've been devastating, perhaps even forcing Disneyland, Inc., into bankruptcy. Albright did his best to keep creditors at bay: "Trust us," he told them, "and after we open on July 17, 1955, you will get paid."[98] But promises from a young accountant were not enough.

Eventually, a lead studio accountant, Larry Tryon, came down to Anaheim to help solve these problems. Tryon determined that payroll must be paid; McNeil Construction must be paid; and suppliers of new construction materials insisting on cash must be paid. But for other bills, Tryon delayed payment as long as possible. He met with many suppliers individually: "I want you to drive to Burbank and talk to Roy," he told them, "because we are going to make it. If we make it, you are going to be our vendor for umpteen years." But surely he must have sensed that such promises for future contracts could only stave off creditors for a little while.[99]

Burdened by the tension at the construction site, Joe Fowler began to have bad dreams. One night he dreamt that the Disneyland river had lost its water yet again. In his dream, the riverbed was nothing more than dry sand and an exposed metal track designed to guide the steamboat. "I think I was the most relieved man in the world," Fowler recalls, "when I got up that morning and found that we had the river."[100]

Unsure how his horses and burros would react to a park filled with guests, Owen Pope, manager of the Disneyland stables, assembled a loudspeaker system to amplify the recorded sounds of a crowd. Each afternoon, as his horses pulled empty stagecoaches and his burros practiced their journey through the Frontierland desert, he played the recording at a high volume to acclimate his animals to a busy environment. "It's a little unusual and eerie," one newspaper reporter wrote, "in the vacant open spaces of the Disney corrals, to listen to a playback that sounds like the halftime noises at a SC-UCLA football game."[101]

But the actual sound recording was creepier than the reporter guessed: not only did it include crowd noise, but also the sound of guns being fired at a shooting gallery to accustom the animals to arcade games that would soon inhabit the area.[102]

By now, the ornamental entrances to three of the four lands were mostly complete. Fantasyland had its castle. Frontierland had a partially finished fort. Adventureland had its tribal-themed archway and jungle foliage. And now the gateway to Tomorrowland received an ornamental icon as well—the Clock of the World. Appearing as a giant tumbler, the clock accurately reported local time anywhere on the planet. And just inside Tomorrowland, the central courtyard also received an ornamental flourish, a collection of forty-nine flagpoles: one to hold a flag from each of the forty-eight states and one for Old Glory as well. But as a crew began work, C. V. Wood made a quick deal with a construction foreman to better honor his home state. "Woody made the Texas flagpole slightly higher than all the others," one of his associates recalls, "hoping Walt wouldn't notice."

With this, the pole for the Texas flag was set a few inches higher—a secret tribute not only to the Lone Star State but to Woody as well.[103]

Due to financial and time constraints, Walt Disney began to prioritize the unfinished projects at Disneyland. The Dumbo attraction would be left without the planned Timothy the Mouse figure, guiding the elephants' circular flight, at the center of the ride. The Casey Jr. train track would be regraded from a 45 percent to a 25 percent slope for daily use after the park opened. Disney abandoned plans to create their own walk-around costumes for Mickey Mouse and other animated characters, instead opting to borrow similar (though lower-quality) costumes used by a touring Ice Capades show.[104] "Captain Hook's Galley, the big pirate ship was only half completed by opening day," explains Bill Martin, a lead art director at Disneyland. "It was no more than an empty shell, and we only had time to paint half of it, the half facing the public. The rest remained bare wood."[105]

On July 2, Walt personally met with Ruth Shellhorn, the landscape architect, to examine the western road station in Frontierland—an area so undeveloped no one had even drawn up plans for basic paving and walkways, let alone for landscaping. According to Shellhorn, Walt "went all over things for quite a while" then left her to get a tape measure and sketch out loose plans.[106]

The team overseeing personnel continued interviewing and hiring the 550 employees necessary to sell tickets and operate rides. Some of these new hires were close personal friends of C. V. Wood, most of whom were given supervisory jobs overseeing the ride operators. Each employee received a one-day orientation to Disneyland, a training program that in addition to "creating happiness" now emphasized cleanliness, courtesy, and safety as well. Afterwards, those hired as ride operators were sent over to the site to learn their trade—only to find that most rides were neither finished nor functional.[107]

Another young man hired shortly before the opening of Disneyland was Ron Dominguez. As a boy, Dominguez had grown up on ten acres of orange groves now converted into the frontier section of Disneyland. Over the previous year, he'd attended the University of Arizona, but as he returned to Anaheim he found his family house now located behind Main Street, hundreds of yards from its original location, and strangely converted to administrative office space. Walt kept an office in what was once his family room. Upstairs, C. V. Wood and his managers kept offices in rooms where he had once lived with his mother and brother. On opening day, Dominguez would be assigned the strange task of taking admission tickets from guests so that they could enter what had once been the neighborhood of his youth.[108]

But the largest unfinished area was not inside the park; it was, instead, the land earmarked for the parking lot. The area still held houses and sheds as well as a few chicken coops. One of the abandoned houses had been used as a construction office, while another was simply empty. Regardless, they all needed to be moved or torn down before the park could open. But rather than use a bulldozer or wrecking ball to tear down the unwanted structures, a crew member suggested that they have a "house-wrecking party." As one Disneyland employee recalls, "Woody approved, with the thought that it might be a good way to release some tensions before the final pre-opening push."[109]

But Woody's motivation was larger than that. He quickly seized on this opportunity to solve a problem much more complicated than the unfinished parking lot.

After a fourteen-hour workday, an exhausted C. V. Wood and Earl Shelton took about fifty men from the construction crew to the area just outside Disneyland. In the dim light of evening, the land looked nothing like a parking lot: the unpaved ground was still dotted with orange trees and farm structures. As promised, Woody bought the men beer and whisky, which arrived with ice in the back of an open-bed truck. While the men were getting liquored up, Woody told Shelton that it wouldn't be the end of the world if one of the farmhouses "accidentally" caught on fire, knowing that the Anaheim fire department was too far from the construction site to save any burning structures. The land needed to be completely cleared, he repeated, and this might be an easy way to accomplish it.

Besides, at least one house still had a homeowner's insurance policy—a house that he then pointed out to Shelton. It sat at the edge of the parking lot and was still owned—according to Woody's letters—by the Claussen family, who had been willing to sell their farmland but not their house.

Woody dipped his head in a knowing way to let Shelton know the importance of this task. With dark eyes that betrayed confusion, Shelton nodded back at Woody, happy to complete any task, no matter how unusual, for his old friend.

After an hour's break, the construction crew began to tear down the first farmhouse, using crowbars and sledgehammers. This house—according to Van France—had once been owned by the Peltzer family. One worker remembers the demolition in detail: "The bolder of our group—of which I was not one—started on the second floor, wrested staircase newels out of their sockets and used them to hammer down the interior walls. Some clambered on the roof to rip off the shingles. Others went to work breaking up studs, cross-beams and disemboweling interior fixtures."[110] Another participant recalls "tearing up the banisters and throwing the plumbing out the windows."[111] Many men actually found the demolition a good way to let off steam.

Around ten o'clock, the structure "accidentally" caught fire.

Van France, who was present, but didn't see the fire actually start, described the incident as such: "Somebody dropped a match."[112]

As the house was burning, the men stood around watching the flames, drinking the last of the beer, and throwing empty bottles into the blaze. The old house, composed of dry wood, burned bright, crackling and tossing embers into the ink-hued sky. Earl Shelton stayed with the men for five or ten minutes before slipping away. Alone, he drove back to the main office where he telephoned Woody with his update.

"Woodsy, I've got something to tell you. One of those houses is on fire."

Woody simply acknowledged this by saying, "Oh, it is," then asked how everything else was down at the construction site. They talked for a few minutes before Woody finally asked, "Have you phoned the fire department yet?"

"No," said Shelton.

"Don't you think you ought to phone the firehouse?"

"I guess I will in a minute."

To be sure that Shelton had accomplished the task correctly, Woody asked: "Which house is it?"

Shelton described the white house that had, until twenty minutes ago, stood in the dirt parking lot, only to be cut short by Woody's excited voice: "Oh my God, you idiot, that's the wrong one! There's no insurance on it," an announcement that sent Shelton quickly back to the parking lot.[113]

The house that Shelton's team had set ablaze was not the intended house, but rather one of the other structures on the site.

To remedy this problem, Woody and Charlie Thompson soon arrived on the scene, and after discussing the matter, they eventually decided to "burn everything down so it was just an act of God."[114]

In a letter, Woody later explained how he accounted to city officials for the supposedly "accidental" demolition of two houses and some sheds, though some of the details in his letter were no doubt pure invention: "that the contractor had bull-dozed the [remaining] orange trees into piles and when dry, set them on fire," following a customary land-clearing practice of the day. "To the dismay and chagrin of the Disney people," Woody continued, "sudden changes in the wind currents blew embers on the house," thereby igniting it. The letter then identifies the site, "the northwest corner of Harbor Boulevard and

Cerritos Road," which was roughly the entrance to the parking lot. The letter further explains that one of the two burned houses was intended to be reoccupied by the owner's daughters, "who wished to continue living there," once the park opened, revealing that the fire not only removed unwanted structures from the land but might have solved other problems as well.[115]

Despite these troubles—or rather, because of them—Shelton managed to clear the area quickly, leaving only burnt lumber and a few household fixtures, such as a bathtub and a sink, as well as some confused firemen inspecting the remains.

The drunken demolition of the first house left some workers bruised and injured. The following day, one manager recalls, "our infirmary was busy, passing out Alka Seltzer, aspirin, and band aids for those individuals suffering from oversize hangovers and bruised appendages."[116]

Van France later wrote: "How and why nobody was hurt amazes me."[117]

Around this incident there are some important ancillary details. First, the city block that contained the Disneyland parking lot was not wholly owned by Disney: there were two cut-outs, toward the back, privately held by families. In 1955, this acreage was simply not needed by Disney. Second, though Woody—in one of his letters—indicated that the Claussen daughters intended to reoccupy the house at its current location, it's possible that the family, after seeing the park's construction, might have considered moving the house to another location. At least two of the farmhouses Disney purchased were later moved to new neighborhoods and reused as residential homes, including one given to Disneyland's lead accountant, Milt Albright. Finally, adding to the problems, not long after selling his land, the patriarch of the Claussen family died, perhaps leaving the remaining family members unsure or in disagreement as to how to repurpose this house.

In this matter, Woody and his Bombers acted utterly alone—and in secret. The primary problem, it seems in retrospect, was that the unoccupied house remained at the edge of the Disney property, without firm or reasonable plans for its future use. There is no evidence whatsoever that the Disney brothers had any foreknowledge of Woody's plans, though it is possible that Walt was able to ascribe motivation to the fire after the fact. Throughout the construction process, Walt was extremely attentive to small details concerning both construction and the land—so much so that more than once he corrected engineers about the grade and elevation in certain areas of the park. It's possible—in fact, likely—that Walt would've known the arrangements of the purchase contracts, especially one that allowed the Claussen family to retain their house. If Walt was aware of this detail—which seems likely—he might've also understood Woody's motivation for burning the house. This observation—if correctly assembled by Walt—might've created a window through which he could more clearly see the personality of the man who would soon manage Disneyland.

Though in public, Woody claimed that the fire was accidental, much later in life, when he was with his friends and a little drunk, he would tell the story more directly. One close friend remembers exactly how Woody used to launch into this particular tale: "[Disneyland] had one guy who was not willing to sell his property," Woody would say before beginning in about the fire.[118]

The details of this barroom story match those of a letter Woody once sent to Earne Moeller, in which, adopting a more business-like tone, he explained that he had purchased for Disneyland "fourteen parcels and all the houses but one," meaning, of course, that there was one owner who didn't wish to sell part of his holdings.[119]

One can only speculate if this event contributed to the escalating problems between Walt and Woody.

◆   ◆   ◆

On Monday morning, July 4, Walt invited several dozen studio employees to preview Disneyland—more aptly, those few areas that could be previewed. Walt specifically invited employees with young children, as he wanted to see how kids would react to his new wonder world, to assure himself that the park would prove a success. "Fantasyland and Tomorrowland were completely off limits," one guest, Alan Coats, remembers. "They were boarded up, with sawhorses and planks and Do-Not-Enter signs." Frontierland was somewhat complete—with its Calvary fort made of logs and a street lined with old-time western shops—though workmen were still applying signs and paint to many buildings and the ground, in places, was nothing more than hard mounds of dirt. In Adventureland, Walt personally skippered families down the Jungle River ride, only the river was still missing most of its animals. "The striped canopies weren't on the boats . . . and . . . the only foliage were mostly orange trees." The families were offered rides on the stagecoaches, the Conestoga wagons, and the pack mules, all of which toured the back corner of the park, an open area with sagebrush made to resemble the desert. But aside from these few attractions—and perhaps also the train—the other rides remained unfinished.

"And this," Coats concludes, "was a week-and-a-half before the park opened."[120]

During the final days of construction, work escalated to a frenzied pace.

On July 6, Dick Irvine was so overburdened that he told at least one designer to simply "sign his name" to "surveyor's plans" if he could not be found so that construction could continue.[121]

On July 8, Walt and his art directors again met with Ruth Shellhorn, a landscape architect, to walk through the New Orleans section of Frontierland—yet another area without any landscape or hardscape plans whatsoever.[122]

On July 9 a public fight broke out between Shellhorn and Wade Rubuttom, the art director overseeing the park entrance, with the two of them yelling at each other over how to install the gigantic floral pattern of Mickey Mouse on the slope leading to the train station. The fight was so serious that Dick Irvine had to be called in to break it up.[123]

On July 11, Irvine left the project for at least one day due to the death of a parent. Also on this day, the planting crew decided to use whatever flowers and seedlings were available to fill in empty spaces at the park, as the material they had ordered had not yet—and probably never would—arrive.[124]

In this chaotic environment, the American Broadcasting Company (ABC) attempted to stage technical rehearsals for the ninety-minute live telecast of the park's opening. Though ABC producer Sherman Marks had intended to begin work at the park in May, he was not able to move cameras and other equipment onto the site until the end of June. "When I arrived," one of the four segment directors, John Rich recalls, "Main Street was still an unpaved stretch of California dirt." Unable to conduct technical rehearsals, the directors spent much of their time eyeballing camera positions that could be occupied once certain buildings were finished.[125]

Along with celebrities, the telecast would feature a large team of dancers. In the parade, the dancers would dress up as famous Disney characters, such as Snow White and Cinderella, and afterwards, they would perform dance numbers in Frontierland. They rehearsed at a Hollywood dance hall, but then, shortly before the park was set to open, they arrived at

Disneyland to find that large sections were unfinished. On Main Street, there was no possible way to rehearse any aspect of the parade because the street was *still* not fully paved. Main Street existed, in part, as a long trough of dry dirt zippered down the center with a pair of trolley tracks. In Frontierland, the show's choreographer, Miriam Nelson asked construction men to clear space beside the burro stables so that they could rehearse their first big dance number, "Bang! Goes Old Betsy," a number that would feature Fess Parker as Davy Crockett. They danced for hours on the uneven ground—dressed in halter tops and T-shirts, with the men twirling the women into a hoedown-style finale. Some construction workers watched and whistled, a few even applauded. Before leaving the park that night, Miriam Nelson received a note from Walt Disney: "Please have your dancers cover up a little more because the workmen are all stopping to watch them."[126]

In other areas of the park, ABC segment directors directed men to roll cameras over loose gravel to practice tracking shots, hoping that the areas would be paved before opening day. Just in case they weren't, one of the directors decided to mount additional cameras to the elevating arms of hydraulic forklifts to more reliably capture footage above the crowds. In some areas that were paved, the wheels of these forklifts sank through the newly poured asphalt. To make matters worse, the construction crew constantly moved or removed TV cable to complete work on the rides and show buildings, creating a feeling of general animosity between the ABC crew and the construction team.

When one of the segment directors vented his frustration, a construction worker told him, "Don't worry. You'll have plenty of action to shoot. We'll be pouring cement!"[127]

The ABC producer, Sherman Marks, saw the situation spin out of control. In this environment, he'd made one significant and perhaps fatal error: he had not communicated to his segment directors how each segment would contribute to the overall telecast. Having never produced a show of this magnitude, he believed he could orchestrate the live production from his control booth, stitching together segments as they happened. But as he witnessed the technical rehearsals, he started to second-guess his directors, asking them to reconsider their shots and ordering them to reposition cameras.

Within days, the working relationship between Marks and his team of segment directors deteriorated to the point where Marks was unable or unwilling to trust his directors and the directors openly resented him. "[Marks] was obviously a madman," recalls one segment director, John Rich. "He had no business to be in that position. [He] was nominally in control. And I say nominally because he was a madman who refused to share any information with his sub-directors. . . . It was bizarre."

At one point, the segment directors—or at least some of them—threatened to quit. In response, ABC sent network executive Bob Lewine down to the park to sort the matter out in person. Together, the segment directors explained that they were not getting adequate information to properly plan their shots and that Marks was running roughshod over their authority to direct. "It was an ugly moment," one director recalls.[128]

During the final days of rehearsals, the musical director, Walter Schumann, suffered a heart attack. "The pressure had taken its toll," one employee recalls. Disney management received word late in the afternoon that the show would be produced without him because, with only a couple days remaining, no replacement could be found. Ironically, during the grand opening, the musical director would recover "sufficiently to watch [the show] on TV from his bed in a local hospital" with his mattress angled up so he could better see the screen.[129]

Aside from the ABC television special, Disneyland's public relations director, Ed Ettinger, was forced to rely primarily on newspaper inserts to advertise Disneyland in local markets, as the company could not afford radio and TV spots, nor could it afford space on more than a few billboards. "Our chief adver-tising medium," Ettinger remembers, "was a special 4-color supplement in *the Los Angeles Times, Examiner,* the *Santa Ana Register,* and the *Anaheim Bulletin.*" But even at this late date, Disneyland was still in such disarray that Ettinger was unable to use photographs of the park. Photographs would only reveal that the park was an unfinished construction site. To overcome this problem, Ettinger adds, "I made do with various art direc-tor renderings" to create his newspaper insert, offering readers the illusory vision of a finished Disneyland.[130]

Throughout the park, Walt scaled back on show items: One order was even cancelled for live birds—specifically, crown her-ons and exotic waterfowl—that Walt initially wanted to place on the Jungle River alongside mechanical animals, thereby mixing the real and the artificial.[131]

Now completely out of money, Bill Evans transplanted large weeds from the parking lot into the park, attaching to each a Latinate nursery tag, while other workmen spray-painted patches of dead grass with green paint.[132] "Toward the open-ing," Evans explains, "we did a lot of irrigating to get the weeds to grow on the barren areas, particularly on the dirt berm that surrounded the Park."[133]

Though I've been unable to find an official Disney source to corroborate the following story, three of Woody's friends told me that during the final days of construction Woody used his personal connections at the Pepsi Corporation to secure a last-minute loan for the park—one that Bank of America refused to carry. "Just before the opening, Woody went to New York to borrow another $2 million," one of his friends explained.[134] Another added that it was upper level execs at Pepsi who arranged the loan.[135] Woody borrowed enough money to cover payroll and other expenses for the first week of operation.

Along with this, Walt likely made one final loan against what remained of his life insurance.[136]

But these weren't the only last-minute loans Walt received to stabilize Disneyland. There was one more—a loan that originated not with a corporation, but rather with an individual. "Joe Fowler loaned Walt Disney some of his own personal money to keep Disneyland afloat," recalls Fowler's longtime assistant, Patricia Branham. "He did that on a personal level for [Walt]." Fowler himself never publicly talked about this loan, most likely out of a sense of propriety. Neither did Walt Disney. But this gesture, in all likelihood, furthered Walt's resolve to minimize Wood's influence at the park and to increase that of Fowler.[137]

Now officially broke—with no further lines of credit available—Walt directed his staff to order thousands of balloons and reams of festive bunting to "decorate" the park. It needs to "cover up what isn't finished," he told Joe Fowler.[138] On the day before the park opened, a team of workers began to ornament the park with these decorations—adding them liberally throughout Tomorrowland. The most obvious problems in Tomorrowland were two enormous show buildings: tall structures fronted with wide windows—windows that revealed exhibit space mostly empty.

At about this same time, Harper Goff reviewed the menu that would be served in the pressroom—a smorgasbord of sandwiches and snacks. Only with Anaheim's longstanding liquor laws, he was unsure if the park would be able to serve drinks to the press without a special license. He expressed his concerns to Walt—namely, that the press would expect mixed drinks in the pressroom. But Walt decided that if the press wanted to bring their own liquor, they could, but Disneyland was not going to serve them liquor nor have it for sale.[139]

Before a quick dinner, Walt dealt with yet another pressing concern. Over the previous day he'd heard about the trouble that existed between the ABC segment directors and Sherman

Marks—specifically, that some segment directors and their assistants were still threatening to quit. Walt walked over to the ABC production center, where he said: "So I hear we have a little problem. Anybody who wants to do the show, be in my office in a half-hour. If you don't want to do it, then leave."[140]

Amongst themselves, the segment directors decided that it would be unprofessional to walk off the production at this point. But they also decided that, for the sake of the show, they would utterly ignore any new direction given by Sherman Marks during the actual telecast. Having arrived at this secret agreement, they walked down the muddy trail of Main Street to talk with Walt in his office.

That night, though exhausted, Walt pitched in to work on the park, hoping that his efforts would help ready at least one more attraction. He was supposed to be with his wife, Lillian, to entertain VIPs, but instead, dressed in an old work shirt and jeans, he walked to the 20,000 *Leagues* exhibition hall. The hall should have been dressed and propped to resemble the interior of a submarine, but most rooms were far from finished.

Toward the entrance were displayed two twelve-foot special-effects miniatures: the Nautilus submarine hung before a matte painting of a volcanic island and, on the other side of the entrance doors, the Golden Arrow schooner hung before a seascape. Around them were cans of paint, a bucket of ship rivets, and lengths of steel piping used to make the hallways appear as nautical passageways. The adjoining rooms featured movie sets from the Nautilus itself, including the wheel room and the chart room, though not all furnishings were in place, not even in Captain Nemo's salon. The salon was essential to the attraction because it provided guests a wide circular window to view the giant squid. The squid itself was accommodated in a special annex on the other side of the glass.

Walt spent the final hours of July 16 in the squid room. Despite the heat, he put on a protective face mask and spray-painted the backdrop with fluorescent paints, as machinists calibrated the Hudson 8-cylinder engine and guide wires used to animate the animal's rubbery arms. An animator from the studio, Ken Anderson, also wearing a facemask, adjusted a motor that controlled the squid's beak, causing it to snap open and shut.[141] Walt left the exhibition hall at least once to check on other last-minute projects.

Inside the Rocket to the Moon theater he found John Hench and a group of electricians still working on the projection system. Walt stood at the entrance, regarding the tall cylindrical room ringed with stadium-style seats. Because of its shape, some men called the theater "the big washing machine." He remained at the entrance, his hands on his hips, before inquiring about their progress. As expected, the answer was not positive. "We had difficulty with the electricians," Hench explained. He didn't estimate how long it would take to fix the projection system, but the message was clear: the attraction most likely would not be ready by morning.[142]

On the other side of the park, Walt visited the Jungle River to learn if the final 900-pound mechanical elephant was now functioning. Earlier that evening, as a crew attempted to install it, it had begun to sink into a mound of fill dirt.[143] A handful of men were still working with the animal, propping up its base, adjusting its movements and arranging the foliage, but at least it was in place. After they promised that all would be good in the morning, he moved onto Fantasyland.

In Fantasyland, Walt saw that the three dark rides were now working—vehicles were cycling through each show building, as newly hired operators learned how to use the controls—but individual show rooms were still not fully assembled. Props were missing from some attractions, and on the Peter Pan ride even its centerpiece, Captain Hook's pirate ship, was not fully painted.[144]

In the courtyard, he watched workmen paint the deck, skirt, and supports for the carousel—yet another job expected to take all night. Under Walt's judicious gaze, the workmen became nervous, their labor slowing. But he hurried them along by pointing out the following: "My insurance money is paying for painting that carousel."[145]

Satisfied that work was progressing as fast as could be expected throughout the park, he began his trip back to the *20,000 Leagues* exhibit, which he found was still not finished. After putting on his protective facemask, he continued painting his murky seascape until it appeared to be a realistic sub-aquatic view of the sea at dusk.

Sometime after midnight, Walt and Ken Anderson decided to call it quits. As they walked through hallways only half-ornamented with riveted pipe, they realized that the attraction would not open the following day. They continued out of the gallery and into the outer exhibition hall, where they saw electricians gathered around a breaker box. Walt simply pushed through the glass doors and stepped outside. The summer air was sticky and warm. A few areas of the park were lit by construction lights, some of them so large they must have reminded Walt of lights they used inside a soundstage.

He tapped a cigarette out of its pack and offered one to Anderson, who waved it away. Tired and frustrated, they moved toward Main Street, finding that small portions of it, up by the castle, were still unpaved. In places, the track system for the streetcar—the rails and railroad ties—were exposed, presenting themselves like a long scar rising from the bare earth. Even some shops weren't finished; in the Main Street music store, the manager was still papering the walls with old sheet music covers, quick decorations to cover large empty spaces.[146]

Overwhelmed, Walt and Anderson rested on the curb beside Town Hall. It was their first break in many hours. Around them, recently rehired plumbers moved from building to building and painters touched up the Main Street facades. After only a few moments of rest, they were greeted by a workman who told them, "There's no power on the Toad ride! Somebody cut the wires!"

Ken turned to Walt. "Don't worry. I'll take care of it."

Walt stayed there a moment more, gathering his strength. He made one final tour of the park, inspecting last-minute changes. The problem with the Toad ride, he learned, extended to the Snow White and Peter Pan attractions as well. But the power cables weren't cut, only disconnected. Both Walt and Ken assumed this was the result of infighting between the Burbank and Orange County chapters of IATSE. Satisfied the rides would open, Walt returned to his personal apartment on Main Street.[147]

Built into the second story of the Main Street firehouse, the living space was essentially a large sitting room that included two sleeper sofas, a kitchenette, a bathroom, and a patio. Before going to sleep, Walt parted the lace curtains to observe the activity below. A man dressed in overalls was hanging red-white-and-blue bunting from the guardrails around the train station. An ABC technician secured rooftop camera equipment. Another technician tightened lines of video cable that sagged, like clotheslines, across Main Street. Lastly, two members of the construction crew carried tools to prepare gravel beds for the final truckloads of asphalt. Those would be poured at 6:30 the following morning—just hours before guests arrived.

Later, Walt would talk about the emotions he felt that night: excitement, doubt, exhaustion, and a touch of loneliness. Earlier that week, he had asked his wife and daughters to stay at home during the grand opening. He did not want them here with all the crowds and the mess—or so he had told them. Perhaps he did not want them there in case the park failed.[148]

Before falling asleep, he lifted his head above the sleeper sofa so he could see his park one last time. Walt would've found the street mostly empty, except for a few men clearing cut lumber from Town Square. When the lumber was removed, the men roped off an area around the flagpole for the opening ceremony. Walt liked to see his park like this, empty and peaceful, a city waiting for its citizens. This was the last time he saw the park as his exclusive playground.

In a few hours it would belong to the world.

A few miles away, C. V. Wood was putting his father to bed. They were most likely in Fullerton, where Woody kept a house during the construction of the park.[149] No doubt they would've been talking about the festivities the following day. Unlike Walt Disney, who feared Disneyland would fail, Woody assumed the opening would be a success, as he believed that the American public generally enjoyed spectacles. He, therefore, had invited the Bombers and his father to the event. As a lifelong railroad conductor, his father, Hunky Wood, had been so enamored with the Disneyland steam trains that he wanted to experience them firsthand. Knowing this, Woody had asked his father to bring his own Santa Fe uniform with him so he could help captain the Disneyland Railroad through its inaugural circuits.

If all went as planned, the following day millions of people across America—including thousands of people in Woody's hometown of Amarillo—would see Hunky Wood on TV, as the first train pulled into Main Street station. Its cab would carry Walt Disney and the president of the Santa Fe Railroad, Fred Gurley, but just behind them, at the entrance to the combine would be Hunky, a slender man with large glasses and a pressed conductor's uniform. He would step from the car, look briefly out at the impressive park his son had helped build, then return to his position as the train began to pull away.

Seven
GRAND OPENINGS

Even a casual history of American entertainment would note the significance of July 17, 1955. Far more than just the day Disneyland first opened its gates, it was the day on which America's relationship to Hollywood entertainment changed forever.

In the early 1950s, the average American watched numerous pieces of filmed entertainment each week both on the large and small screen. But there was always a distance between the audience and the entertainment. The audience sat in its chairs while the performance remained on screen. But in Disneyland, Walt created a cinematic environment in which people visited themed lands arranged like Hollywood sets. For most Americans, Disneyland was far more than another amusement park. It was an opportunity to step through to the other side of the looking glass, to exist for a day inside the world of Hollywood entertainment.

One of Woody's friends, Fred Schumacher, would later describe the experience of attending a Disneyland-style park as one of immersion. In such a park, he told a reporter, "the spectator truly steps behind the footlights and becomes part of the cast. It is not like *presenting* a show . . . it is more like creating a whole new world into which the visitor is transported for many hours at a time."[1]

Walt's big gamble boiled down to this: Did the American public really want to spend their vacation inside the fantasy world of the movies? Or to put this another way: How strongly did the American public identify with characters and stories they watched on the screen?

For most Disneyland employees, opening day started early. Hours before dawn, members of the publicity department placed illegal street signs at major highway intersections in and around Anaheim directing guests to the park. Walt woke in his Main Street apartment around 6 a.m. to the noise of last-minute construction, only to find himself locked in: the door was sealed shut with new paint recently dried. He had to call his own security people to be let out.[2]

C. V. Wood woke early as well and headed to the park. Though he'd given over twenty tickets to his family and to the Bombers, he would have little or no time to spend with them. He would spend most of his day entertaining VIPs—such as the president of Swift's and the marketing manager of Pepsi—and making sure the park was in excellent condition for the TV cameras.

By 7 a.m., the first employees had reported to the park. Disneyland was able to provide most with uniforms, though some were asked to wear street clothes because of a shortage. One girl remembers that a wardrobe supervisor advised that "the not-so-well-endowed wear falsies."[3] All employees wore paper nametags on which they handwrote their names, as their official nametags had not yet arrived.[4] One worker recalls that the starting wage for a ride operator that day was $1.65 per hour.[5] Staff shortages were covered by last-minute replacements, including secretaries from Arrow Development who volunteered to work the front gate.[6]

Inside the park, a work crew poured the last of the asphalt—with park managers assisting to rake down the hot top and roll it smooth. Dick Nunis recalls: "We had literally paved Main Street with asphalt down and opened the gate."[7] Beside the work crew were dozens of ABC cameramen, most of them dressed in black-and-white striped referee shirts so as to easily identify one another. And with the cameramen, another eighty employees of ABC were assigned the task of keeping the crowd away from the cameras. "Another thing I remember about Opening Day were the [TV] cables everywhere on the ground," Roger Broggie said in an interview. "They had all this heavy cable laid everywhere and big arc lights which created a lot of additional heat. Everything was live, and there was no margin for error anywhere."[8]

Construction crews cleared their work materials from the show areas. Painters did their best to touch up a few damaged buildings on Main Street. Just outside the park, a newly hired college student named Marty Sklar helped local ABC news anchor Hank Weaver and his cameramen settle into the public relations office, where they were soon joined by journalists writing for magazines and newspapers from across the country. With the exception of the ABC news crew, most members of the press expressed open skepticism about Disneyland's ability to stay in business beyond its initial summer season.[9]

At 8 a.m., Van Arsdale France enjoyed a quick breakfast with a special Highway Patrol unit assigned to manage traffic, a unit that even had temporary workspace given to them in the Disneyland training building. Over biscuits and coffee, France discussed contingency plans with the officers in case attendance exceeded the company's expectations. By 10 a.m., he was riding in the Goodyear Blimp with Police Chief Mark Stephenson, high above the city, to identify road congestion before it became a problem. From their vantage point, they could see the partially completed Santa Ana Freeway, which would take guests from Los Angeles to Orange County. But the freeway ended just eight miles shy of Disneyland, forcing guests to finish the trip on regular city streets. The guests had been invited to arrive in staggered intervals throughout the day, with the park officially opening early in the afternoon. At 11 a.m., the streets were empty. At noon, the same. France wondered if the critics had been right, that Disneyland would be an instant failure. But in the early afternoon, once church let out and Sunday brunch ended, he saw that traffic was beginning to increase. At first, small groupings of cars, all of them moving together. Fifteen minutes later, a solid line of vehicles. And then there was Traffic—Traffic with a capital T—car after car after car.[10]

"Halfway to L.A. were automobiles, solid all the way from [Disneyland to the freeway]," remembers the police chief who rode with Van France. Though the two men had set up a radio system to talk to the ground officers, the city streets were now so busy they could do nothing to improve traffic flow. All around Disneyland—for at least fifteen miles—cars choked every available roadway. It would later be described as the worst traffic jam in the county's history. Feeling frustrated and helpless, the police chief finally turned to France and admitted defeat. "Well," he said, "it was a nice day for an air ride, anyway."[11]

During the morning, Walt met with lessees and corporate sponsors. But as the park opened its gates for early arrivals and dignitaries, Walt returned to his firehouse apartment, where he stood by the window, looking out lace curtains as the public ventured into Main Street. He had waited many years for this moment, to see how individual guests responded to his park of wonders. He watched their expressions, noting what aspects of the street most captured their interest. For Walt, it was a perfect moment, one full of hope and not yet tainted by the later problems associated with that day. Also in his apartment were a few of the Mouseketeers from the forthcoming *Mickey Mouse Club* TV series who would perform in the opening day ceremonies. "When I looked up at him," recalls Mouseketeer Sharon Baird, "he had his hands behind his back, a grin from ear to ear, and I could see a lump in his throat and a tear streaming down his cheek."[12]

With guests in the park, Walt left his firehouse apartment still wearing his work clothes and walked up to the train station, where he boarded the cab of the E. P. Ripley steam engine. As the day warmed, he conducted the train—or, more likely, assisted in its operation—giving distinguished guests a preview tour of the park from the benefit of the elevated tracks. During one trip, as the train pulled into Main Street Station, a guest threw Walt a Hawaiian floral lei, which he immediately looped with a showman's flourish around his neck. Photos show that Woody's father, Hunky, was there for this event as well, standing beside the train and helping with its operation.

At about the same time, Roy Disney and his wife, Edna, drove to the park in their Cadillac sedan, both of them nervous. The traffic began at the Orange County border and increased as they approached Anaheim. The sight of so many cars pleased Roy, who had been concerned with the studio's investment in Disneyland. After traveling surface streets, he pulled into an open spot, where he and Edna watched in amazement as hundreds of people surged toward the Disneyland gates. The kids, it seemed, were pulling their parents toward the park.

Roy remained in his car, drinking coffee and eating the homemade cake Edna had packed, until one of the new Disneyland employees spotted him. "Mr. Disney," he gasped, "I'm glad I found you. A lot of these people have been stuck in traffic for hours, and the kids need to go to the bathroom. Now they're peeing all over the lot."

Roy stepped from his car to better survey the area. He folded his hands over the top of his car door as he realized it wasn't hundreds of people he saw moving toward the main gate. It was *thousands*. He felt their enthusiasm, an energy that for him suggested that this strange little park might someday turn a profit. A smile widened across his face. "God bless 'em," he replied. "Let 'em pee."[13]

◆   ◆   ◆

By early afternoon, it was clear that there were too many people arriving at the park. The Disney brothers had distributed roughly 11,000 invitations to friends, employees, dignitaries, and members of the press for the private opening, known to park officials as Press Preview Day, but thousands of additional guests arrived, some of them presenting well-crafted counterfeit tickets. The newly hired ticket-takers were not able to distinguish between the real and the counterfeit, so they admitted anyone holding an invitation. "We would open for twenty minutes," recalls one ticket-taker, "then close for twenty minutes," in an attempt to slow the progress of the crowd surging into the park.[14] The tickets were pre-stamped with staggered entrance times, with some as late as 5:30 p.m., but, as another employee remembers, "[the staggered entrance times] didn't really work because nobody wanted to miss a thing."[15] Still another first day employee recalls that the wording on some tickets allowed a guest "and party" to enter Disneyland. "One person got off his huge bus with his *party*. With one ticket."[16]

To complicate matters, Walt's promotion of Disneyland on his TV show proved so successful that it attracted gate-crashers who didn't even possess a counterfeit ticket. Scores of people scaled the eight-foot perimeter fence with wooden ladders—at least one of which was built by neighborhood farm children.[17] Another ladder positioned behind the Frontierland stables belonged to a man who charged the general public $5 apiece admission.[18] This homemade ladder was so elaborate, recalls C. V. Wood, that it didn't look like a ladder: it looked more like a set of wooden stairs, painted green, a magical walkway leading into the park.[19]

Beyond this, hundreds more arrived at the Disneyland gate to see celebrity guests as they entered, all of them hoping that somehow they might be admitted to the park as well. "My mother was pretty much an autograph hound," explains Tom

Nabbe. "My mother asked [Danny Thomas] for his autograph, and he was more than happy to give it to her. He said, 'Have you been in the park?'" Nabbe's mother shook her head, then Danny Thomas handed her two tickets.[20]

All preview tickets informed guests that the day's events would feature "a television program originating from Disneyland . . . from 4:30 to 6:00 PDT." In thick red ink, it warned, "If you wish to be present during this telecast, please plan to arrive before 4:15 p.m." because "Disneyland's gates will be closed from 4:20 p.m. to 5:30 p.m."[21] Due to traffic congestion, many invited guests missed the 4:20 deadline. During the telecast, thousands of people impatiently crowded the entrance gates waiting for Disneyland to reopen.

"It took us over two hours getting into the park," remembers studio veteran, Harry Tytle. "Except for the fact that we can say we were at the opening, it was most disappointing in that neither [of our] children nor ourselves could get near any rides, nor places to eat."[22]

Disneyland placed the final attendance at 28,154—counting at least 17,000 extra guests—but the actual number was probably much higher because park management had no way to count the people who entered by scaling the fence.

During the early afternoon, some members of the ABC crew attempted to stage a quick walk-through of the opening ceremonies now that all of the principle speakers were inside the park. The ABC crew was able to clear the crowds from Town Square, holding them at the train station. The speakers approached a single microphone in the order of their presentation: Walt Disney, who would later deliver his park dedication speech; Walt and Roy's nephew (by marriage), Glenn Puder, who would lead park guests in a silent prayer; and, finally, California governor Goodwin Knight, who would oversee the flag-raising ceremony. Though this section of the park was beginning to fill with invited guests and members of the press,

Walt was still dressed in his casual morning clothes, a wrinkled blue jacket and patterned shirt he had worn while inspecting the park. Even his black shoes were covered with a patina of cement dust.

Once the Town Square rehearsals concluded, Walt and Art Linkletter walked to an open space before the castle to practice the live commercials. While Walt was taking a break, one of the reporters wanted to ask questions about the park, but decided not to because Walt appeared "so nervous you couldn't believe it." He kept "flubbing lines and running his fingers through his hair."[23]

After Walt had taken a couple practice runs at each commercial, he returned to his firehouse apartment where he planned to lie down for a few minutes so he would appear rested on TV, but the noise and his anxiousness proved too much for him. Unable to relax, he changed in to a crisp shirt and tie, along with the new suit he had purchased for the occasion. He checked his appearance in the mirror. This was how he wanted to look on the day his park opened to the world.

Another of Woody's jobs was to manage the park and also the crowd—a task that turned out to be more difficult than expected. The initial plan was to sequester all 10,000 guests on Main Street. As each area opened, employees would send a couple thousand guests in through the gates—Adventureland, Frontierland, and so on—but as attendance swelled to 15,000 then 20,000, Woody found it increasingly difficult to manage the crowd. "Christ, we had them packed on Main Street like sardines," he recalls. "They were bitching. They were mad." Tones of anxiety moved through the crowd, edging toward rowdiness. It was Woody's job to make sure none of the problems appeared on TV and that the crowd radiated only optimism and joy for the cameras.[24]

◆　◆　◆

According to Miriam Nelson, most ABC segment directors did in fact ignore last-minute orders given by Sherman Marks concerning the telecast. The show included a few obvious mistakes, with images occasionally mismatched with narration, but the errors appeared whimsical, overshadowed by excited commentary, as though these flubs were an essential part of live TV. Much to the credit of ABC—and despite ongoing tensions among the production crew—Disneyland's grand opening appeared as one continuous dream to roughly 70 million viewers across the country: dressed in his buckskin jacket Fess Parker (appearing as Davy Crockett) rode his horse into the western village of Frontierland; Frank Sinatra and Sammy Davis Jr. motored Autopia cars down the open road of Tomorrowland; Alan Young happily flew a pirate ship with Peter Pan above London; the Disneyland Railroad steamed into a Midwestern, turn-of-the-century depot; and Art Linkletter ad-libbed his way through various miscues and unplanned cutaways. "I was on the balcony of one of the shops," Linkletter later revealed. "I was watching a T.V. monitor and describing what I saw there. All of a sudden the sun came out and was shining right on my monitor and I couldn't see what shot was being shown, so I just started to describe what I saw in front of me in the street. I figured that if the director was smart he would have the cameraman follow whatever part of the parade I was talking about."[25]

There were problems and numerous close calls: because of the crowd, the show's two co-hosts had trouble moving from one location to the next. Cohost Ronald Regan climbed over an eight-foot fence in Frontierland to make his live appearance on schedule, and cohost Bob Cummings pushed his way through a security closure when a guard didn't believe that he was a member of the production crew. The show's producer had to cut away from a shot of the Main Street Station because Walt Disney, who prided himself on his ability as an engineer, was having difficulty maneuvering the steam train up a slight grade. Shortly before airtime, the show's choreographer was told that the location for one number, the Plantation House, had been repainted that morning so that dancers could no longer slide down the balcony poles as part of their performance. In the five control booths, dry ice was used to cool video monitors simply so that they would continue to function in the heat. Yet, throughout the park, the ABC crew carefully maneuvered around these difficulties to somehow present a show filled with enthusiasm and spontaneity.[26]

One of the most memorable scenes from the telecast was the opening of Fantasyland: hundreds of young children running hand-in-hand with Disney characters across the drawbridge and into Sleeping Beauty's castle. But unbeknownst to home viewers, the parade of children was a carefully choreographed event intended to appeal to viewers' emotions. Earlier that day, fourteen school busses had collected 500 children from local churches and brought them to Disneyland. To ensure a festive atmosphere, hundreds of happy children were positioned in various areas of the park.[27] Robb Fischle, who was seven years old in 1955, remembers that Disney officials "herded us into position and we made our 'mad dash' across the drawbridge, through the Castle, and into Fantasyland. Once inside, we were divided into groups to be filmed boarding the different attractions. . . . I went on Mr. Toad. I remember being really impressed when Art Linkletter slapped me on the back as I passed him. He was big stuff in those days. After our ride, we were given a box lunch then it was back on the bus."[28]

Likewise, the park was also stocked with studio employees masquerading as guests. Along with complimentary tickets, studio employees also received a typed memo requesting them to "report to the New Orleans section of Frontierland at 4:00 p.m." From there, attendants would guide them to key sections of the park showcased in the telecast, a strategy that, the memo claimed, would "aid greatly in the success of the show."[29]

"My group was assigned to the Mark Twain riverboat," animator Jack Kinney remembers. "We were ready to mutiny when at last Art Linkletter and Walt came aboard. The television cameras and crew moved in, and we were all on live television, waving happily at the cameras."[30]

At the front of the boat stood Linkletter, who introduced Irene Dunne, an actress who had once starred in the film *Show Boat*. She appeared in a white dress, holding a bottle to christen the ship, but before dousing the deck, she offered a line that would prove nearly prophetic. "My, it's listing," she said, referring to the way the ship tipped slightly toward the dock.

Garrulous and happy, Linkletter placed his hand on Dunne's arm. "It's listing a little because it will be shoving off in a moment."[31]

Another group of studio employees waited on the train, exposed to the summer sun, for the cameras to finally pull into place. "My assistant was stuck on that freight train for two hours," studio artist, Blaine Gibson recalls.[32] One of the WED designers, also stuck on the train, remembers: "We were sweating it out, literally, standing in the cattle cars."[33]

There were other problems the TV audience did not see.

To start with, the popular comic actor Jerry Colonna was scheduled to captain the Casey Jr. Circus Train around its circuit. Colonna had worked repeatedly as a voice actor for the Disney studio, most recently providing the voice of the Marsh Hare for *Alice in Wonderland*, but after seeing the ride's rickety tracks and unusually steep grade, he began to have doubts about the safety of such an exhibition. "Colonna just chickened out," Ed Morgan (from Arrow) later explained. "He looked at that hill and said, 'No!'"[34]

Park managers explained that ballast weight had been added to the engine, specifically to pin the vehicle to the track, but the actor simply shook his head.[35]

Unable to change Colonna's mind, the ABC crew quickly searched for a suitable replacement. First their gaze fell on Ed Morgan, one of the train's architects, but the engineer's outfit wouldn't easily fit him. Next, their attention settled on Karl Bacon, a quiet, slender man, also from Arrow. "Karl looked at me," Morgan remembers, "and I said, 'Yes, you can do it.'" The ABC crew put Colonna's engineering clothes on Karl just in time to seat them both on the train—with Karl, not Colonna, operating the train's controls—as the cameras zoomed in to capture Casey Jr. powering its way over the manmade hills.[36]

Elsewhere in the park, wet paint ended up on guests' clothes, and women's high-heel shoes got stuck in the fresh asphalt—including those worn by Frank Sinatra's wife as she ventured toward the castle.[37] "When I looked down Main Street," one employee remembers, "I saw nothing but high heels being stuck in that new asphalt," though this memory might have overstated the actual problem.[38] Rocket to the Moon, expected to be operational, experienced problems with the electrical control system, so ABC showed clips from the rocket's theatrical film, suggesting the attraction was open to the public. Likewise, the Dumbo attraction was simply parked in a stationary position, with each of the elephants slightly elevated to create the illusion of flight.[39] Individual cars derailed in the Snow White ride, slowing its operation, while other rides shut down completely. One guest recalls seeing his five-year-old son leave on the canal boat ride, and forty-five minutes later, long after the ride should've concluded, watching as "four guys with hip boots on came trudging through the water, pulling the broken boat" back to the dock.[40]

But far more troubling, workmen discovered that guests were climbing up into the castle.

In Fantasyland, the construction crew had forgotten to lock the side doors to Sleeping Beauty's Castle, and guests, believing it an attraction, surged into its interior where they found an empty shell along with ladders that led to a second story.[41] The second story was no more than a false floor made of plywood set across ceiling joists. After learning of the problem, C. V. Wood sent his friend, Van Arsdale France, to manage the situation. "There are people up in that castle," Wood yelled. "Get them out before they kill themselves." Upon arriving, France found the work doors open and park guests standing on unsecured construction platforms "at the top of the castle enjoying the show."[42]

In Tomorrowland, the heat caused the Autopia cars to lock up, and when the cars were working, kids gleefully crashed them together, further denting their aluminum bumpers. Minutes after Sammy Davis Jr. was filmed riding an Autopia car for the ABC telecast, he was forced off the road, his car bouncing over a short curb, as a pair of teenage drivers sped past him. Some cars possessed faulty fuel governors, allowing them to spin out at high speeds. The cars also contained only two foot-pedals—one accelerator positioned for adults, one for children, but no manual brake. Brakes were applied whenever a driver released the accelerator, a design flaw that contributed to many rear-end collisions. As cars broke down, the line for the ride increased, causing some guests to jump the perimeter fence and commandeer moving vehicles. "Several super head-on collisions took place while the ride operators were trying to hold back the crowd at the gate," recalls Bob Gurr, who oversaw the attraction on opening day. "I took a couple of kids to first aid, one with his hand full of teeth!"[43]

On Main Street, guests were confused by the arrangement of shops: some were open while others remained closed. They pressed their hands to the windows of the closed shops, only to find the buildings empty. "Some ground floor shops still had interior construction underway after the park was opened to the public," recalls Harper Goff. In jest, studio employees had taken to hanging paper signs with their own names to disguise the empty windows. "We would put up a serious looking sign that might say 'Harper Goff will be opening his shoe store here soon' . . . but there was nothing inside the store," only lumber and empty shelves.[44]

The most famous problem of that first season was the partial sinking of the Mark Twain steamboat due to new employees overloading its main deck.[45] A teenager named Terry O'Brien was given the job of loading guests into the queue holding pen for the boat ride. Since the park had not tested any ride for guest or weight limits, O'Brien was given a clicker and instructed to load between 200 and 300 guests per trip—a number range that was merely an educated guess at the ship's actual capacity. For most of the day, O'Brien kept to the rough load estimate, but as the crowds grew heavy, he began to pay more attention to the long line that snaked down the riverbank than to counting guests in the load area.

Late in the day, while the steamboat was cruising on the other side of the island, he heard the distinctive double-blast of the boat's horn, a distress call. Workers on a maintenance boat motored around the island to find that the sternwheeler had either come off its track or was stuck on the rail, positioned in such a way that the water washed over the deck. One alarmist yelled, "The boat is sunk," though the boat was not actually sinking. It simply wouldn't move, with the deck tipped to one side. Some guests were offloaded into two feet of water, with their shoes hooked on their fingers, and asked to wade over to the dry bank. It took a half-hour to unload enough guests to properly float the boat over the rail. At least one man with a dive mask examined the wheel-and-rail system underwater, giving the vessel the all clear to move forward. When the pilot finally brought the paddle-wheeler back to dock, he found a group of angry guests, still wet, waiting for the rest of their parties to arrive.

When O'Brien's boss asked how many guests he'd loaded, he told him about 250.

"Well, better keep it at about 200," he was told.

After his boss left, O'Brien remembered the clicker in his pocket. He was shocked to see that he'd put 508 people on the boat.[46]

He was so embarrassed by his error he didn't tell anyone the actual number for over fifty years.

The most serious problem never was reported in the news.

Shortly after the cameras concluded the telecast, Joe Fowler was signaled over to the phone: "I got a call that we had a problem," recalls Fowler. "You could smell gas coming up through the courtyard (in Tomorrowland). The question was: What the hell do we do?"

Fowler arrived in Tomorrowland to find the ominous smell of natural gas everywhere, an odor that reminded him of rotting cabbage. Fowler's immediate impulse was to close a large section of the park, but after talking to the fire chief, he decided that the problem could be handled by simply roping off a section of the courtyard, unearthing the pipe and letting plumbers replace the broken line. The problem took hours to fix, but as there was construction equipment and scaffolding elsewhere, Fowler was fairly sure that no more than five or six guests understood that a gas leak had erupted beneath Tomorrowland.[47]

From an operational standpoint, the most obvious problem was overcrowding. The food service at Disneyland didn't have enough food for the extra 17,000 people. Lines for all of the rides proved impossibly long and poorly organized. "There were no lines," one reporter later noted, "just mob scenes in front of each attraction."[48] One employee remembers that "there were so many people [in Fantasyland] that they had to close the carrousel a few times because guests climbed over the chains and we couldn't control them."[49] After completing his segment of the live broadcast, Fess Parker quickly found a young Disneyland publicist to help guide his horse through the crowd. "Get me out of here," Parker demanded, "before this horse kills somebody!"[50]

Trash piled up. One longtime employee recalls, "It was probably the trashiest I'd ever seen Disneyland."[51] The refuse was moved in loads behind Main Street, mounds so high that the Health Department later told Walt: "This is either gone, or you're not open!"[52]

To mediate the problem of no drinking fountains, Disneyland asked a couple men to move through the park with pressurized canisters of water on their back—canisters attached to small hoses. These men, then, distributed cups of water.[53]

Even employees had problems. Unable to build dressing rooms for both men and women, park managers created a ladies' locker room out of canvass curtains—like a tent with no top. There were no lockers: "we just hung our clothes on poles with our names on them."[54] Later, one manager would recall the unusual roof-less dressing rooms that Disneyland used that first summer by explaining, "planes used to dive down to see the women dress."[55]

Guests who arrived after 6 p.m. saw only an endless expanse of people. "Everything was broken down," one guest recalls. "They were out of food. The place looked like a cyclone had hit it."[56]

In the pressroom, Harper Goff noticed that a few reporters were growing angry. Accustomed to receiving alcoholic drinks at publicity events, a small group complained that Walt Disney was cheap. "Dumb bastard!" one said. "Where's the liquor?"

Attempting to appease them, Goff explained that a local law would've required Walt apply for a special injunction to serve alcohol at this event, but they could bring their own alcohol into the press areas.

"Where's the nearest liquor store?" another asked.

Goff explained that unfortunately he knew of no liquor stores in Anaheim.

Crossing his arms, the first reporter fell back into his chair, visibly upset. Even though all attractions were "free" for the press during the grand opening celebration, the reporter explained that in a few days he would tell the world that Disneyland was overpriced: "I'm going to sit down here and say that a father and mother with two kids came and left and it cost them two hundred dollars. Everything is *so* expensive."

"Well, I'll make it worse than that," the other reporter countered. "[Walt] always thinks he's had good press, but he'll learn."[57]

Every ride—except for the Jungle River—broke down at one point during the day. The pistons on the Dumbo ride continually malfunctioned; one of the railroad coach cars derailed in the station; dark rides repeatedly shorted out. Years later, Bob Gurr would explain the specific problems with the Autopia cars: "It was hotter 'n hell and these cars were suffering from the typical gasoline vapor lock," meaning, of course, that their engines would no longer run.[58]

The developing crisis was so serious that the machinists from Arrow had to race to a local war surplus store in search of spare parts to immediately repair rides while guests waited in line.[59]

Even after the food was gone, the park ran short on drinks. Long lines formed at the pay toilets. According to a Disney in-house publication, "Walt himself was seen running toilet paper to some of [the units]."[60]

None of this was lost on reporters and dignitaries. Even the city manager of Anaheim, Keith Murdoch, left before the 4:30 dedication ceremony because of overcrowding. The park was such a "mess that I went home and watched it on TV," Murdoch recalls.[61] As evening darkened into night, reporters began to question Walt about the problems of opening day. He did not discuss the most serious problems, but pointed to minor ones, such as the mechanical elephant (presently working) that was still sinking into a section of fill dirt in Adventureland. He explained that the Rocket to the Moon attraction would open in a few days. To one reporter, he admitted "that the Peter Pan Flight swayed too much and must be altered." To a few others, he explained, "The men worked all last night and we still don't have all of the rides ready."[62] To his nephew, Glenn Puder, he simply said, "Things weren't going so well."[63]

"Children were probably the most disappointed," one local reporter observed, "because of the inability to get near the rides. Tears were evident on many tykes' faces because they couldn't take a ride in a covered wagon or enter the magic realm of Fantasyland. . . . Many of the rides in Fantasyland, designed primarily for children, operated only a short time and were occupied mostly by adults."[64]

Retreating from the crowd, Dick Irvine and other WED designers slunk back to the administration building. "We sat up in Joe's office and looked at [the opening] on television," Irvine recalls. "We didn't bother to go down and fight the mob."[65]

Even Disneyland's own publicity team was disappointed. The director of public relations, Ed Ettinger, remembers collapsing "on a park bench at the entrance to Tomorrowland" with Disneyland publicity manager, Eddie Meck. The two men surveyed the crowd, noticing that people appeared hot, tired, and frustrated. From their vantage point, they could see the 20,000 *Leagues* exhibit (closed to the public), Flight to the Moon (closed to the public), and a show pavilion large enough

for three or four exhibits that presently only held the Circar-
ama theater. "Both of us," Ettinger recalls, were "exhausted and
depressed." He later coined the term "Black Sunday" to describe
the day, a term that would be embraced by many employees at
the park.[66]

Though the Disney Company would later portray Walt as
confident and exuberant on opening day, men working closely
with him would recall him as a "nervous" man, "running around
with his celebrity guests, trying to schmooze away the technical delays and long lines."[67]

Sensing that his theme park might soon close because of
bad reviews, Walt needed someone to blame. He had placed his
professional reputation on the line—along with the money he
had raised with personal loans and by selling personal property.
And who was the park's general manager? It was C. V. Wood.

According to Buzz Price, Walt found Woody in the old
Dominguez farmhouse. Following the completion of the live
telecast, an exhausted Wood had retreated to his office. In its
cool interior, he fixed a congratulatory round of mint juleps for
his staff, while outside, in the sticky 80-degree heat, Disneyland literally fell apart. Walt stood in the wooden doorway, his
lips thin, his face pale and furious, waiting for Wood to notice
him.

Wood had just finished building the world's first fully
themed amusement park, asking his crew to pull many all-
nighters to complete attractions on time. Moreover, he had
made the park look good for TV, a park that even by optimistic
estimates shouldn't have opened for many more months. From
his perspective, congratulations were in order.

But across the room was Walt Disney who, unlike Wood,
was able to see this park through the critical eyes of the public.
This was the primary difference between the two men: Wood
courted lavish spectacle while Walt courted the steady approval
of the middle-class.

There were other issues: Wood had a salesman's ethics, occasionally cutting corners to finish a difficult job in a timely fashion; he told racy jokes of which Walt, a Midwesterner, disapproved.[68] Perhaps most significantly, Wood, a good-looking man with raven's hair and genuine charm, had begun to receive media recognition for the construction of Disneyland, thereby drawing some of the attention away from Walt. According to Dick Irvine, "Walt always said that Woody was a great salesman, but he was a lousy administrator, and terribly ambitious," by which he most likely meant self-serving.[69]

In newspapers the following morning, the reviews were decidedly mixed. But the bad reviews were terrible. Sample headlines read: "Walt's Dream a Nightmare," "Park Can't Handle Opening Day Crush," "Disneyland Opens Amid Traffic Jams, Confusion," and "Disneyland: Dream or Nightmare?" A columnist for the *Los Angeles Times* described the day as a "mob" scene, complaining that "there were lines for everything" with the park so crowded children could only see "a forest of baggy pants and summer skirts."[70] Members of the press pieced together bitter sentences to express their discontent. "Everyone agreed," one journalist later wrote, "it had been one of the most unpleasant days of his life. . . . One reporter announced he was billing Disney for extra pay for his unwilling role as a TV show prop."[71]

One of the worst reviews, titled "Chaos in Disneyland," described the park as "The 17-Million-Dollar Trap That Mickey Mouse Built." The reporter went on to note that "it was nearly impossible to beg, buy or steal anything to eat or drink." The crowding was so severe that "irate adults cursed Mickey, Minnie, Pluto, Snow White and all Seven Dwarfs," and guests tried to escape the park but were told they "couldn't leave while the TV show was on the air." One such confrontation ended with a guest punching a security guard.[72] But the most damaging critique didn't concern the overcrowding, it concerned the cost.

Though all rides and refreshments were offered without charge on July 17, some members of the press—holding good to their threat—observed ticket prices and calculated (or, rather, *over*-calculated) the cost of a family visit to Disneyland. The "Chaos" article quoted one father retreating with his disenchanted family as saying: "I figure [this terrible experience] saved me $500 in never being pestered to go back." A reporter for the *Los Angeles Mirror*, Dick Williams, claimed that adults would spend at least $8.75 each for a day's entertainment and that, for a family of four, "the total outlay would be $32 if they went on every ride and ate and drank for a dollar apiece." In an era of twenty-five- and fifty-cent movie tickets, $32 was an astronomical figure for a day's entertainment—especially considering Disney's internal numbers suggested that a family of four would spend roughly $9 to $10 overall.[73]

The articles were a blow to Woody, who arrived at Disneyland early that morning, determined to make the park a success on its second day of business. He checked the park for cleanliness. He made sure that the ABC production materials had been removed from Main Street. He introduced himself to a few photographers who were there to cover Disneyland's second day of operation.

Though many local citizens had snuck into Disneyland the previous day, July 18 marked Disneyland's official opening to the general public. As with the day before, Walt stood in his firehouse apartment and watched guests enter the park. One employee saw Walt standing there, his hands laced behind his back, observing people pass on the street below. A breeze inflated the sheer curtains, causing him to step closer to the window. "Paying guests," he cooed. "I love you." Then, with a gesture of pantomime, he threw them all a kiss.[74]

Walt spent much of the morning participating in a second set of opening day ceremonies. These ceremonies included the welcoming of the first "official" children to the park and a partial repeat of the previous day's dedication speeches. (The marketing and press team at Disneyland had earlier suggested that Walt pose for staged "opening day" photographs after the press event, once the TV cameras, along with their arc lights and cables, had been removed from Main Street.)

The bad news arrived mid-morning, when Woody received a call that yet another gas line had burst. This time, the broken pipe was located inside the castle courtyard, a place already occupied by press photographers wishing to capture the first wave of paying guests as they entered Fantasyland. Woody arrived to discover flames licking up through the recently poured asphalt. One witness recalls: "There were little blue flames all around the base of the castle."[75] As best Woody understood, a workman had thrown down a cigarette, which caused a small section of the ground to boil with fire.

Aside from the workmen, park employees and a few members of the press, Fantasyland itself was still empty: it was not yet open to the public. The public opening of Fantasyland would take place in a few minutes, with thousands of curious guests streaming into this section of the park. No one knew if the leak was confined to one small area or if it ran beneath the entire castle. A gas leak under the castle, Woody knew, would be a public relations disaster.[76]

With his publicists, Woody asked the press photographers not to photograph the flames. "Ben Meister, who was the fire chief at the time, was running around in circles," recalls Bill Martin. "He was really worried."[77] And then with Joe Fowler and some workmen, Woody began to dig through the asphalt, working down to the gravel and sand. The leak—as far as they could tell—was confined to a connection between two pipes, a single damaged joint.[78] While Meister's crew capped the broken line, Woody and his team began to throw matches down on the ground, checking for other leaks. Woody ventured into the castle and all neighboring buildings. Unwilling to take any more chances, he entered each room alone, holding a lit match to ensure that the structure was safe for guests.[79]

Woody knew that he had an important decision to make. He asked his men to keep testing the ground with matches. When no flames appeared, Woody was confident that the area was safe for guests. He directed two workmen to cover the hole with plywood. He looked at the area once more. Just a few minutes before Fantasyland's scheduled opening, Woody gave the word that it was OK to let guests enter this section of the park.[80]

In a public relations maneuver that was nothing less than miraculous, Woody ensured that no photographs existed of the flames or even of the repair work. Furthermore, he charmed the reporters so thoroughly none of them mentioned the event in their articles—none of them, that is, except one journalist from the *Los Angeles Times*: "A gas main leak broke out in Fantasyland," he wrote, "and the area was cleared of all spectators for nearly an hour." But even here the reporter framed the event to make it seem not particularly serious.[81]

With the problem averted, Woody did his best to ensure that the public opening went better than the grand opening. He walked through the park. He talked to ride operators and ticket-takers. He tried to get a handle on how much business the park was doing. Woody labored under the belief that financial success at Disneyland would mend his relationship with Walt.

But by then, Woody should've known that Walt was rarely swayed by money.

Eight
WALT AND WOOD

For its first week, Disneyland attracted strong crowds. On July 18, Disneyland received 26,007 paying guests—a number far higher than the "mile-long lines" of "15,000 persons" initially reported in the local paper.[1] For each of the next four days, Disneyland received roughly 20,000 guests, but then, on Saturday, the crowds began to taper off, with only 13,910 people entering the gates. Still, even this lower number was impressive, with Disneyland receiving 135,133 guests for its first week of business.[2]

But these numbers did not change Walt's feelings for Wood.

Walt might've also sensed that these initial numbers—these crowds who were curious about Disneyland—would not sustain the park all summer. Lean times were coming—and coming soon.

A few days after the park opened, Walt stormed into Woody's office and angrily waited for Woody to hang up the phone. Once Woody was free, Walt leaned over his desk and icily asked, "C. V., do you know there are *pay* toilets in *all* the park's restrooms?" The question implied that even though the pay toilets had been Walt's idea, Woody should've had the foresight to use some of the post-strike plumbers to outfit Disneyland with public restrooms.

Woody admitted that due to the strike, he wasn't entirely sure what types of toilets had been installed throughout the park.

"C. V.," Walt continued, "I want you to see that they're removed before tomorrow. It's terrible—like inviting someone into your home and then having them pay to use the bathroom."

Later, as Woody told this story to his friends, he admitted, "I knew that I was in big trouble because he'd never called me C. V. before."[3]

Though the Walt Disney Company regularly presents Walt's initial reaction to the problems of opening day as one of optimism, the edges of that experience rounded out over time. Card Walker, the man who would later become the company's president, vividly remembers Walt's initial response to the lousy reviews in newspapers and magazines: he "wanted to shoot himself," Walker later revealed.[4]

Walt's anxiety was no doubt tied to the disappointing reviews, but in all likelihood it was also connected to a new wave of Disneyland-spurred losses at the studio. Though Walt Disney Productions had seen its stock price rise to almost $60 before the opening of Disneyland, immediately after its debut, the stock plummeted, losing 15 percent of its value during the park's first week, 10 percent more during the second, with analysts predicting continued downward movement.

In those early days, critics accused Walt of a bare capitalist drive and of marketing his park with an air of hucksterism. Members of the press focused on the park's pricing structure—an entrance fee plus ride tickets—even though the average guest would end up spending just over two dollars on entertainment. To one interviewer, Walt later said that these reviews were malicious, utterly without foundation. There was no other way to look at it.[5] But the image of overpriced entertainment stayed with Disneyland like an unfortunate scar that wouldn't fade.

These troubles weighed heavy on studio accountants. One executive, Jack Lindquist, later put it bluntly: "If Disneyland had sunk, the company would have gone down with it."[6]

In light of these problems, Walt developed a threefold plan to save his park and also to stem further losses in the value of Disney stock. First, construction crews and maintenance men would work long hours to finish all of the pending rides and ensure that the existing rides stayed operational. Second, the Disneyland public relations staff would launch an energetic campaign to convince media representatives that on opening day Disneyland simply hadn't been ready for its grand premiere. Lastly, though Disneyland remained in substantial debt, Walt would use all available funds in a vigorous reinvestment strategy to expand the park. His long-term goal was to channel 16 percent of Disneyland's income into new attractions—though in that first year, Walt earmarked far more than 16 percent for various improvements, which irritated his brother and executives at ABC.

The men from Arrow remained in Anaheim for many weeks, repairing rides and helping the WED team regrade the Casey Jr. track. The most serious problem, though, was the Dumbo attraction, which never worked properly once the heavy elephant cars were attached to the Arrow-designed lift system. Using new hydraulic pumps from local stores, the Arrow team was able to get the ride in reasonable working order in just a few days. But even with modifications, the combination of nitrogen and oil in the hydraulic system still produced foam that was nearly as thick as shaving cream, thereby disabling the lift mechanism. One Arrow employee named Paul Harvey stayed with the ride, changing the fluid and removing the foam at least a dozen times each day, while Ed Morgan and Karl Bacon returned to their workshop to build a completely new ride system. "We just left [Paul] there," Ed Morgan explains. "It was a mean thing to do . . . he was in the inner enclosure. He was draining fluid and putting fluid back" while the ride operators moved guests on and off the attraction. In jest, the Arrow men referred to the process of removing the foam as "milking Dumbo."

But not all of Arrow's four joint owners were rolling with the punches. Arrow had already lost money on the Disney contract due to their fixed bid agreement to build the Fantasyland rides. With these problems, they would lose even more. After the Dumbo fiasco, Bill Hardiman, who had helped bring Disney to Arrow, decided to leave. "He said that he was ashamed of our company," Ed Morgan recalls, "so he exercised a buy-and-sell agreement that we had with him." But Hardiman did not leave alone. He took with him another of Arrow's joint owners, Andy Anderson, their chief electrician, and formed a new construction company that had nothing to do with the amusements industry. Without Anderson and Hardiman, Arrow was now a company owned by just two men, Ed Morgan and Karl Bacon. Through their work on Disneyland, they had learned how to build unique ride systems for a unique amusement park. But what would this specialized knowledge mean for them in terms of future contracts now that Disneyland was finished? Would they be able to build these types of rides elsewhere?

Bacon and Morgan spent months repairing the Fantasyland dark rides, overseeing improvements to the Casey Jr. track, and building a replacement manifold and hydraulic system for the Dumbo attraction. Some weeks after the park opened, Walt asked Karl Bacon, "How did you boys come out on the rides?"

Bacon's eyes sheepishly dropped to his feet before rising to meet Walt's gaze. We lost money, he admitted.

After a brief discussion about the losses, Walt moved closer, his voice low, almost conspiratorial. "I don't want you to lose any money on my work," he said, as though he understood he'd need these men from Arrow yet again. "I'll cover your costs."[7]

Now that the park was open, many key designers, such as Wade Rubottom, were leaving the company. Some left for jobs at rival studios. Others were nudged out. The art director who had designed much of Tomorrowland, Gabe Scognomillo, was fired over various disagreements he'd had with Walt. But Walt kept a few art directors on his WED payroll, such as Sam McKim and Herb Ryman. Walt didn't always retain the most talented men, though in some cases he did. Rather, Walt retained those men who were team players. By now, Walt was tired of art directors with big egos, as well as other individuals with personal agendas that interfered with his own vision for Disneyland.

Expecting that he, too, would be asked to leave now that the project was finished, Bill Martin was surprised when Dick Irvine asked him to stay on as part of a permanent design staff. "I was given a pass," Martin explains, meaning he wasn't forced to leave with the others.[8] These remaining men—along with individuals such as Roger Broggie and John Hench—formed the new WED design team, a group whose job it was to help Walt expand and improve his park.

Together, they expanded the Indian village at the edge of Frontierland into an entire encampment. For Fantasyland, they built storybook villages that they would place alongside an existing canal. But to Walt the most important expansion project was Tom Sawyer Island, a western fort and playground out on the river. Though Walt initially gave the design assignment to Marvin Davis, he ended up creating the land-use map himself, paying particular attention to the placement of the fort and an interconnected system of caves. The playground was loosely based on a cardboard fort that Walt had built as a kid.[9] Walt's childhood fort had been built on a sandbar island near his house; now as an adult he created a full-size version of it, the cardboard transformed and enlarged into a structure of logs.[10] The remaining WED designers understood immediately that this project was unusually important, that it was another example of how Walt's own memories were expressed as physical objects and controlled experiences inside the park.

There was, however, a cost to reducing the number of art directors and designers at WED: these artists that Walt let go understood the process of building Disneyland. Many returned to film, but a few continued to flirt with the world of outdoor amusements. As luck would have it, some of these men would get a chance to design a second Disneyland—a park just thirty miles from Anaheim.

Charles Strub—the man who once offered to build Walt's park down at the beach—carefully watched the public's reaction to Disneyland. Despite the bad press and unfinished rides, the public was drawn to the park, curious about this strange land of movies. Quietly, Strub approached CBS—one of the networks who'd turned down Roy—and convinced executives there to co-invest in a new cinematic theme park, one that would be built beside one of the largest tourist beaches in the country.

Weeks after Disneyland opened, in secret, Strub began negotiations to acquire a rundown seaside amusement park that occupied multiple interlocking piers in Santa Monica, California. He then commissioned the architectural firm of Pereira and Luckman to prepare a site plan that would transform the old park into a new nautically themed showpiece, one he planned to call Pacific Ocean Park. The next step was to hire an art director. Though Strub considered men from three architectural firms, he settled on an ex-Disney artist named Fred Harpman, an artist who'd helped design Frontierland and Main Street.[11]

With Harpman on board, Strub now had most of the talent necessary to replicate the efforts of Walt Disney: a major TV network for exposure and backing; the site planning efforts of Pereira and Luckman; and Fred Harpman to head up art direction. Strub would still need a managerial staff, ride designers, and effects men, but that was something he could work on in the coming months.

In the weeks after Black Sunday, Joe Fowler worked with the WED team to organize fixes, however temporary, for Disneyland. The list included the Fantasyland dark rides (which needed alterations to prevent derailments) and the teacup attraction (which needed improvements to better balance the large, spinning platform). For Autopia, one of Fowler's team members sent around a memo in early August requesting that workmen sufficiently pad the steering wheel of each car to avert subsequent face and mouth injuries.[12]

During these same months, C. V. Wood worked closely with his public relations team to rehabilitate Disneyland's image. In August and September, Woody escorted dozens of reporters down Main Street, pointing out recent improvements. He arranged celebrity appearances as a means of courting new interest from the press. He oversaw the developments in Tomorrowland, insuring showrooms and attractions there opened as quickly as possible.

For reporters, Walt and Wood played friendly, though there was a coolness between them, a visible stiffness in their limbs and hands. When Vice President Richard Nixon visited the park, Wood, not Walt, stood on the steps of City Hall and placed the key to Disneyland into Nixon's hands.[13] At Walt's request, in the second week of October, Disneyland sponsored Newspaper Week, which offered newspaper carriers free admission to the park. Though Walt himself had spent his childhood as a paperboy, Wood greeted the boys at a publicity event on Main Street.

To most reporters, it appeared as though Walt and Wood were friends.[14]

But this image was only an illusion.

That fall, Woody felt Walt's favor continue to turn against him. Though he had previously aroused Walt's anger, he understood that this new tension was more substantial—a force he could no longer control. To others, Woody glossed over the true source of the problems attributing them to Walt's fickleness and uncertain moods. "Oh, hell, you know Walt," Woody once said in an attempt to explain away these problems. "He'd throw his arms around you and kiss you one day, and he'd look right through you the next."[15]

Even at home, Woody rarely—if ever—discussed the specific problems he faced at work. "My dad never talked much about those days," Woody's son told me in an email. "He would just say that he and Walt did not agree on how things should be done after the park opened. He never had anything derogatory to say about Walt, and he had a great deal of respect for Roy. He felt Roy was the real business man of the two."[16]

Like Walt, Woody was a private man, who had great trouble facing his own weaknesses and limitations. He wanted people to see him as a success, that miraculous man from Texas, who came from nothing and now mingled with Hollywood celebrities. Once C. V. Wood said that Walt was "a big-time crap shooter" when describing his gamble to build Disneyland— only in Woody's mind, he saw himself as one of the people who stepped in to save that crazy bet, right before the park went bust during the final stage of its construction.[17]

To close friends, it must have appeared that Woody's life had come full circle. As a boy, he'd so loved the movies that he'd learned to twirl a rope, thereby imagining his thin, boyish frame up on the silver screen. As an adult, he again fell into the world of movies. He managed Disneyland. He was regularly introduced to top-level stars. He attended exclusive social events. His office was filled with assistants, people seeking favors, and underlings trying to cozy up to the boss. And through it all, he remained close to his childhood friends.

At the park, he sanctioned after-work parties on Saturday nights, most of which were held on the Fantasyland pirate ship—festivities that were in many ways an extension of his own personality, his boyish exuberance, and his carefree love of drinking and companionship. In attendance were Woody, his friends, and other Disneyland employees. "These parties would start right around midnight," one of the Bombers recalls. "Everybody could stay as long as they liked. And I'm pretty sure that some stayed so long they just left the party and went back to work" the following morning.[18]

"It was the wildest place to work," explains another original employee. "I don't know if it was the morality of the times or the spirit of being involved in this brand new venture that was so much fun. But it was a nonstop party. There was something going on everyday."[19]

Yet on dry autumn afternoons, when feelings of melancholy touched him, Woody spent his time wandering through the park. He noticed how guests responded to the architecture and the rides, how they pleasurably lost themselves inside certain themed areas. Many ride supervisors were old friends, some dating back to his college years. Often he would greet them with hugs and handshakes, but other times he would examine the park from a distance. In his best moments, he believed he had contributed to a project that would be remembered for years to come—perhaps even beyond his own life.

Woody now felt more stress at work than he had while Disneyland was under construction. Most visitors, he observed, loved the park, but attendance was sporadic, with turnstiles clicking through less than a thousand guests on particularly slow days. One employee recalls that on such days "you could shoot a cannon through most areas and not hit anybody."[20] Further proof of these problems was in the studio's stock price. By mid-October, Walt Disney Productions was down to $36 a share, a 40 percent devaluation since July.

Analysts blamed the loss on Disneyland.

Stress from Woody's job spilled over into his home life, where he found his marriage falling apart. By now, Margo had turned to drink as a way of managing the sense of isolation and failure she felt in her marriage. Unable to deal with his wife's sharp emotions, Woody responded to the problem by avoiding it. He would spend days at a time, if not weeks, away from the house. "One time [Margo] got mad because [Woody] came back into town [from a business trip], went into the office, piddled around, and got back on the plane and left again without even calling her."[21]

Outside the home, Woody and Margo attempted to keep up the appearance of a functioning marriage, though their friends clearly understood their problems, as did members of their extended family. The stress of their marital life would occasionally leak into public conversations. While Woody walked to catch a plane one relative saw him turn to Margo and say: "I'm going to miss you, but you know I *can* live without you."[22]

With the problems at home and at work, Woody spent a great deal of time with his old Bomber friends. Around them, he could just be himself, telling jokes and complaining with humorous exaggeration about the unrealistic expectations of his crazy boss, that eccentric movie mogul, Walt Disney. He rarely, if ever, talked about his troubles at home, and though he joked about Walt, these conversations never led to a deep examination of the problems he experienced at the park.

In many ways, Woody's greatest weakness had been with him since childhood: he loved to be seen as a success, as a maverick, as a man smarter than those around him. It was an image he worked tirelessly to uphold.

Woody still enjoyed aspects of his job as well as the status it afforded him. His name regularly appeared in the paper, often in conjunction with celebrity guests he'd help bring to the park. He was respected by local businessmen. He liked that the park was admired by many people. He also understood that his connection to Disneyland would open many doors.

His hometown newspaper, the *Amarillo Globe*, ran a front-page feature story about his work on Disneyland titled "Bombers from Amarillo Patrol New Disneyland." The article included a large photo of Woody, surrounded by three fellow Bombers, and led with a joke about the sheer number of Texans Woody had employed at the park: "When C. V. Wood . . . escorts a new staff member into meet the boss, Disney is likely to greet him with: 'I'll be pleased to know your name, but I [already] know where you are from.'"[23]

That fall, the largest disagreement between Walt and Woody focused on something called the Mickey Mouse Club Circus.

Immediately after opening day, Walt looked for quick ways to expand the entertainment offerings at his park as a means of attracting more guests. At first, Walt considered adding a Wild West stunt show, but then returned to a concept for live entertainment he'd previously enjoyed—an area devoted to an actual circus. Years ago, in its original incarnation, Walt had imagined a "Circusland" branching off from the park's central hub, a lane filled with sideshow performers that led to a big top. Walt no longer liked the original name. Also the real estate long ago considered for the circus was now reserved for an outdoor bandstand. Still, he wanted a circus, one complete with trapeze artists, clowns, and trained animals. Furthermore, he thought that he could alter this show to feature the Mouseke-teers, a group of performing children featured on *The Mickey Mouse Club*.

In short, Walt wanted to book a real circus to perform at Dis-neyland—an attraction he hoped to debut before Christmas.

Walt assigned WED artists Bruce Bushman and Dick Irvine the task of arranging the show. George Whitney Jr. was given the job of figuring out how to promote a ticketed show within Disneyland—as the circus would be an additional charge above general admission. The problems came when Walt approached Woody with the idea to host the circus for the holidays—a circus that, according to Woody, would cost at least $600,000.

Woody explained that, with attendance shrinking for the school year, he had no idea how the park would fare for the Christmas season. Woody again explained that the park needed to produce a profit, that it actually needed to make money, which, from Woody's perspective, was an idea com-pletely foreign to Walt. Woody crossed his arms. He felt his face wrinkle with frustration. The argument, as far as Woody was concerned, wasn't just about the circus: it was about some-thing larger than that, what the American public wanted and what they would pay for. It was also about running Disneyland as an actual business. "No, Walt," Woody finally said. "There ain't no way." He studied his boss who stood only a few inches away, the redness of his face, the determination in his eyes. "We don't need no six-hundred-thousand-dollar fucking circus right now. Period."

Walt, infuriated, narrowed his eyes but eventually walked away.

Later that day, Woody picked up his phone and talked to Roy, hoping that Walt's brother would fix the situation. Woody explained that the park still owed money to various suppliers. They were barely meeting payroll. On weekdays, the park was so empty it was easier to find an employee than a guest. And then there was the marketing pitch for Disneyland: guests can see a circus any old time; out here, they expect unique rides. "Jesus Christ, Roy, if you tell me to do it I guess I don't have any choice," Woody said. "But I got to tell you, don't ever ask me to lie to the banks. Because if they ask me if I think it's a wise thing to do, I'm going to tell them 'no.'" And then Woody heard a tone of understanding in Roy's voice, a tone he had heard many times before.

The conversation ended with Roy agreeing that Woody, as general manager, shouldn't allow the park to be dragged into this circus enterprise if he felt that it would fail. Woody was, after all, responsible for the fiscal health of the park.

That same week, Walt explained to his brother that the two big top tents (with a purchase price of $48,000) could also be used in a live-action circus movie called *Toby Tyler* that he wanted to make. Likewise, the circus wagons (with a yet-unknown purchase price) could be used as well. The circus at Disneyland was a way to utilize and monetize film props, Walt explained, as well as a way to increase the popularity of the Mouseketeers.

Roy now found himself stuck in the middle. The resulting compromise speaks largely to how much power Woody had amassed within the company.

The compromise was arranged as follows: Disneyland, Inc., under the guidance of C. V. Wood, would not absorb the cost of the circus. Rather, Disneyland, Inc., would lease a large plot of unused land at the back of the park to Walt Disney Productions for $1. Walt Disney Productions, then, would develop the circus, hire the performers, purchase the tents, and restore the circus wagons using funds from the studio's budget—with all money derived going back to the studio's coffers. The ninety-minute show opened on Thanksgiving weekend, with Fess Parker serving as a guest ringmaster. As Woody noted with an ironic smile, the circus tent was nowhere near full.

In subsequent days, the tent remained empty—both for the midday and the late afternoon show. Walt moved a large sign to advertise the circus out to the parking lot, allowing guests to buy tickets for the show even before they bought admission to the park. Walt arranged for a special Disneyland circus package: for three dollars, an adult would receive admission to the park, admission to the circus, and tickets for eight rides. Nonetheless, the tent bleachers were mostly empty.

One afternoon, by the big top, Woody told Walt that the circus might make more money if it were shorter—maybe forty-five minutes—as most guests didn't want to take ninety minutes out of their visit to Disneyland to see a show. Walt erupted with anger: "Goddamn you, this is my circus and get out of here." Walt stepped up to the edge of the circus grounds, where a red banner advertised the big top. He pointed to the pavement, an invisible line that separated the rented circus property from the rest of Disneyland. "Get out," he growled, then waited for Wood to leave.

Years later, Woody would admit that was the "biggest fight we ever had," but back then he simply walked away in frustration.[24]

By December, Woody sensed he was on his way out of Disneyland.[25] "I never knew after that whether [Walt] was going to be mad at me, or happy with me," Woody later explained.[26]

By the end of the year, everyone knew. "Walt didn't like Woody," Buzz Price recalls. "He was too fast-moving for Walt. C. V. was capable of making a fast deal. He wasn't corrupt; he was just fast-moving. Walt didn't trust him."[27]

Van France first heard about Woody's problems from other employees: "The rumor was that Walt and Wood were not getting along, and Wood's job was in danger."[28] France described the situation in terms of Woody's managerial style: "Walt demanded loyalty from his key people. Here was the problem:

Wood had developed his team within the Disney framework," which Walt perceived as a threat.[29] But other people believed the problems stemmed from a personality conflict, with Walt overseeing "every tiny decision." Under such a system, "C. V. Wood left because there were two geniuses [at Disneyland], and that doesn't work well."[30]

But neither of these explanations fully account for the deeper struggles that had already formed between these two men—individuals who had very different ways of perceiving value in the world.

While on a business trip in New York, Walt and Woody once again argued over a Disneyland restaurant, the Maxwell Coffee House that had not opened on schedule. Dick Irvine, who witnessed part of the disagreement, recalls that "they had a knock-down, drag-out fight," just like the one they'd had about the circus.[31] Walt blamed Wood entirely for the delays in finishing the restaurant, but this, most likely, was just another excuse to get rid of Woody. Dozens of shops and attractions had not opened at Disneyland on time, leaving one to wonder how rational this explanation would appear to other executives.

When Walt returned to California, he asked Irvine to look into the matter: "I want all the information you have on why that shop wasn't opened." The information pointed to the relationship between Maxwell House officials and the people in charge of food service at the park—which, in a very general manner, fell under the jurisdiction of C. V. Wood.

Even though the problems didn't directly implicate Woody and even though the Maxwell Coffee House was now scheduled to soon open, Walt approached Roy with the intention of using this information as a reasonable justification to end his association with C. V. Wood. In all likelihood, Roy had seen this moment coming, a confrontation that he had tried to put off as long as possible. Walt sucked in a breath. "Fire him," he said.[32]

◆   ◆   ◆

It is not known—nor will it ever be—exactly how much Walt knew of Wood's shadier deals, but according to Buzz Price, the decision to fire Wood had far more to do with Walt's intuitive sense about Woody than with problems arising from the Coffee House or even the circus: "Walt blamed the mess [of Disneyland's opening] on C. V. By that time he had decided he didn't like him and didn't want him there."[33] Yet, in a separate interview, Price later confided that "when it was over, [Wood's dismissal] had something to do with [Walt and his associates'] feeling that they had identified kickbacks [received by Wood] . . . They felt he had to go because he was connected with some kind of monkey business. . . . They were sure they didn't want him running the park for that kind of stuff."[34]

Ex-Disney employee Michael Broggie (son of a WED designer, Roger Broggie) adds: "C. V. was not only devious. He was also very bright. He could keep a lot of what he was doing secret. Because of his personality I think people were intimidated. This was a person you didn't want to cross. . . . He was somebody to reckon with."[35]

Woody was given many weeks notice to vacate his office. Though he never learned the underlying cause of his dismissal, he correctly sensed that Walt was behind it. He also sensed that one or two close associates in management had betrayed him, though he never knew which men to blame.

In typical fashion, C. V. again became "Foggy," exuding warmth and expansiveness as a way of concealing feelings of injury. One of Woody's friends later said that the final troubles between Woody and Walt was a subject "that was unapproachable." He added, almost as an afterthought: "Woody would never admit defeat."[36] Another park employee explained the situation more directly: "There were rumors. But with C. V. Wood, you never talked about it."[37]

As with his experience at the University of Oklahoma, he covered up the actual events. He told friends that he was now free to do whatever he liked, masking his frustration with optimism. Most of the Bombers didn't know he had been fired and instead believed that he was choosing to end his contract with Disneyland six months early to pursue more lucrative opportunities.[38]

Inside the park, Wood appeared happy and jovial. He strolled around casually as though he would forever be its general manager. His greetings were loud and boisterous. He called out: "Howdy" and "Hey there, fella"; his voice was easily identified by its northern Texas drawl. In general, his friends remember that even during these months, Woody was warm and hospitable, often embracing them in public and patting them on the shoulder.

At first, he worked out his frustration through long lunches and by leaving Anaheim for days at a time. Art director Bill Martin remembers that, during those days, "we didn't see much of Woody."[39] Still, Wood felt cheated. He had been asked to oversee the nearly impossible task of opening Disneyland in less than a year. He'd raised the money; he'd organized the park as a business; he'd even assisted with the design work—or at least the design work of some leased stores on Main Street. Once the park was finished, he was forced out because Walt no longer valued his "management style." He felt used—a reaction that was not entirely unwarranted.

Walt Disney's son-in-law, Ron Miller, explained to me how people at Disney viewed Woody's dismissal after the fact: "Woody served a purpose," by which he meant that the Disney brothers needed a highly driven person like C. V. Wood to ride herd over the Disneyland project simply to open the park on time. "But Woody was not Walt's type of person. . . . He was an opportunist and a manipulator. . . . And he took credit for lots of things he shouldn't have taken credit for."

I then asked Miller if any of the following events contributed to Woody's dismissal: the sale of the souvenir rights to one of Woody's friends, the hiring of the Bombers, the kickbacks Woody received from businesses on Main Street, or the houses he burned down while clearing the parking lot. Miller was quiet for a moment and then said, "I'm not going to comment on individual items, but you're fairly accurate on all of them," which indicated that at some point the Disney family had learned of many, if not all, of Woody's shady deals while at Disneyland.

During the same conversation, Miller also complimented Woody, saying that "he was a damn good salesman," which suggested that his ability to sell contracts had, in part, saved Disneyland.[40]

Around the park word spread quickly that Wood was leaving. "He got too big for his britches," one employee remembers, "and Walt fired him. Walt gave him a $10,000 bonus. And in 1956, that was a lot of money."[41] The rumored $10,000 bonus, however, was more likely a payment to satisfy Woody's yearlong contract. But Woody probably didn't represent it that way.

To park executives, Woody explained that after leaving Disneyland he would "organize a new company in research, planning and marketing of television productions," which he would call Telesearch, Inc.[42] But this idea didn't last long. Wood most likely sensed, even then, that his future would somehow be tied to Disneyland. At the end of some workdays, he took a few files from his office, most likely concealing them inside his briefcase. At home he placed them into a new filing cabinet he installed in a spare bedroom. He didn't know specifically how he would use this information, but sensed it would help him. He took copies of land-use reports, attendance figures, requisition forms, and work orders. He procured financial records for the construction of many attractions, as well as detailed reports documenting how construction costs were allocated. He gradually assembled an accurate record of the materials and personnel needed to build Disneyland—as well as a long list of companies and individuals whose services had been used to complete its construction.

A few days before Christmas, Woody told his immediate staff to buy every employee a Christmas turkey. A nice Christmas turkey, he explained, because he wanted to endear himself to the Disneyland staff, most of whom were working on a reduced schedule now that park attendance had tapered off. On the following day, frozen turkeys were distributed to enthusiastic employees from the back of a truck, but even this gesture had its cost. "Walt got pissed," one employee recalls, because the park "didn't have the money."[43]

Yet Walt didn't express his anger beyond a few words murmured to his staff. There was no need: Woody would soon be gone, allowing Walt space to reorganize his park. In the coming months, Walt planned to pump two million dollars into Disneyland—a figure that far exceeded his initial goal of 16 percent of net proceeds. This plan would not be popular with Roy, nor with executives at ABC—especially when they found out that some of the money was earmarked to improve *existing* attractions. But Walt would find the money somewhere—perhaps from the sale of his two TV shows to the United Kingdom and maybe even to Canada, both of them expanding television markets.

About his park, Walt once explained, "I want to keep adding, keep *plussing*," even if these improvements don't directly translate into immediate ticket sales. During the same interview, he explained that he wanted to give the public anything he could give them. In other words, Walt was focused on quality for its own merits and, perhaps, a personal sense of satisfaction, with the belief that high standards and a strong reputation would eventually translate into revenue.[44]

That January, at an early morning meeting held at Disneyland, Walt further explained his philosophy to those in attendance: "The Park was not set up to 'make a quick buck,' he
began, "but is a long range development." He looked at those
seated around him—committee members and merchants, all of
them gathered in a restaurant on Main Street: "We must build
Disneyland into an attraction that will never be in competition with anything else. It must be impossible to duplicate." He
then listed off attractions he hoped to build in the coming year:
a playground on Tom Sawyer Island, a sky ride that worked like
a Swiss ski lift, a new train that took people through the great
outdoors, and even Paul Bunyan's boot, a twenty-five-foot tall
marquee structure slotted for Frontierland.[45]

Leonard Goldenson at ABC hated this plan, once going so
far as to claim that Walt and Roy "turned out to be terrible
business partners . . . Disney kept plowing his profits back into
park expansion."[46]

In the days leading up to Woody's departure, his friends understood they needed to give up "aircraft thinking" and embrace
"show thinking"; if they did not, they, too, might be out of a
job. Likewise, the late-night employee parties were over, as was
the controlled rowdiness that had so animated the staff during the park's early months. "While Wood was in power," Van
France recalls, "having a Texas accent was 'in.'" But the Bombers all understood that a Texas accent was now a liability.[47]

On January 1, 1956, Jack Sayers began performing the
duties of chairman of the Park Operations Committee, a
position that in practice had once been held by Wood, with
management of ongoing construction, expansion, and maintenance now falling to Admiral Joe Fowler. Sayers had a history in entertainment. Once the West Coast editor for *Look*
magazine, he had worked for Gallup Polls and had conducted
research for Walt, years ago, to help best direct his movies

at an audience.[48] He understood people and popular tastes; moreover, he knew how to get along with bosses. In operations memos, Wood was no longer included in the CC list of recipients. Even though Wood still kept his office, he was a powerless vice president, a man merely collecting the last of his contract money. A January 14 memo from Walt's office discussed the reorganization of Disneyland management and specifically the operations committee, most likely alluding to the dismissal of Wood. Five days later, on Thursday the 19th, Walt sent a memo to Disneyland management announcing Wood's departure from the park. In it, Walt politely disguised the true circumstances surrounding Wood's removal, instead claiming that C. V. Wood had resigned—an arrangement that most likely had been previously discussed with Woody.[49] The following week, in a meeting with the park's merchants, Walt echoed these statements, claiming that Woody's efforts with "planning, promotion and construction were of great help to all concerned."[50] The effective date of Wood's departure was February 1, 1956.[51]

That same week, the park announced its attendance figures for the first five months of operation. Since July 18, two million people had passed through the main gate. They had spent, on average, $2.20 per person on amusements, which was slightly lower than Buzz Price's initial projections but still within the range of profitability. Sixty-five percent of park guests were from California. Amazingly, 21 percent were already repeat customers. For Woody, these numbers were a slap in the face: he was being fired despite the growing success of Disneyland.[52]

On a Sunday shortly after that—most likely February 5—Walt would call Jack Sayers at home and ask him to take over Wood's job as the de facto general manager of the park,[53] but a week or so earlier, on Wood's final day, Sayers did not yet realize he would be Wood's permanent replacement.

Late in the afternoon, as Woody prepared to leave, Sayers and Van France came to visit him in his office.[54] It was misting that day, with low, doughy clouds hanging over Main Street and a patina of rain glistening on the ground. By the time Sayers and France reached the Dominguez farmhouse, the managers' parking lot was mostly empty, with only a few cars pulled up beside the building. Among them was the car Woody drove.

Together, they walked up the wooden stairs, passing from Walt's area of the farmhouse into that of Wood's team. Though once Woody's office was filled with favor-seekers and people trying to climb the corporate ladder, today it was empty. The glass tumblers on a portable bar had been washed and stacked, the ashtrays emptied, his large metal desk cleared of paper. Usually enthusiastic and talkative, Woody stood at his window, staring at the park. From his vantage point, he could see employees dressed in costume venturing out onto the damp asphalt of Town Square and beyond that the green foliage rising above Adventureland.

Wood shook his friends' hands, but they didn't talk much. Instead, France and Sayers took Wood out for a farewell cocktail. They ended up staying late, reminiscing, and finishing several drinks before any of them decided to go home.[55]

That night, Woody was the last to leave, stumbling out into the cold night air, a cigarette in his mouth. Out of habit, he walked with a quick, determined pace, avoiding puddles, as though he had some place to go. He passed a few buildings. Then he saw his car. He stopped for a second, perhaps noticing his reflection in the glass. He was still a young man—a little pudgy in the cheeks but good-looking nonetheless, with dark hair and determined eyes. He understood the image he projected far more than he understood the youthful ambitions that bristled under his skin—namely, the need to avoid poverty at all costs and an attraction to fame. He must have felt that these desires, if fulfilled, would heal childhood scars.

He took one last drag off his cigarette then stubbed it out with his shoe. He drove slowly, shadows crawling through the interior of his car, his radio most likely tuned to the type of big band music he'd loved in college. He headed toward Los Angeles, as the big city felt more like his home than Anaheim. Once settled into the rhythms of the road, he lulled himself into a protective bubble of thought, far from his troubles with work and marriage, a place where his self-confidence bloomed once again.

He did not yet know that one day he'd build Disneyland-style fun spots across the United States: massive parks in California, Colorado, Massachusetts, New York, and Texas. In Walt's vision for a cinematic park, the fantasy realm was always bordered off from the real world through the use of a raised earthen berm, a manmade screen separating the fanciful from the actual. But in Woody's vision there would be no such berm: the imaginary and the authentic mingled together. In many ways, C. V. Wood would be the grandfather of themed space throughout America. At first, he built cinematic theme parks; later, themed residential communities and shopping centers; lastly, through employees he trained, these techniques were applied to elaborate hotels in Las Vegas, Los Angeles, and abroad, each as grand as a movie.

But on that drizzly January night, he knew none of these things. He only felt the murky pain of the present moment. He was working his way through a troubled marriage. He was presently unemployed. He thought maybe he could find some new business, one where he could again bring the Bombers together under a common roof. Through friends, he'd heard that CBS and Charlie Strub were going to build their own Disneyland-style park over in Santa Monica, a massive fun spot down by the sea. He thought maybe he could get in on that. He knew a few things about amusement parks. After all, he'd spent nearly three years with the Disney brothers.

Woody drove quickly now, his high beams sending dimes of light onto the asphalt ahead. The injury and emptiness of the current day grew faint, replaced by vague ambition. In his rearview mirror, the radiance of Anaheim faded into the night. Around him was farmland, the silhouettes of trees rising against a darker sky. The only sound came from pistons cycling through his engine and tires thrumming over a damp road.

In the distance, the lights of Los Angeles rose up like a luminous cloud, a city filled with millions of people—parents and children, most with vast amounts of newly acquired leisure time. Woody felt he understood American appetites better than Walt Disney—better than a dozen Walt Disneys: what people wanted and how the cinematic images of childhood flickered inside their hearts. All of America wanted to step into the splendor of a movie, the beauty of Hollywood rising up around them. Parks like this could produce a profit, he believed, perhaps a very good profit if the parks themselves were made with a little less gingerbread trim and ornate ironwork than the one Walt Disney had just produced. Woody felt it then, that old sensation, the finger of providence pushing him along. He told himself what he always did during moments of professional crisis, that everything would turn out fine.

He thought about that for a moment, then corrected himself.

No, he added, everything wouldn't be just fine. Someday, it would all be great.

Acknowledgments

First and foremost, I would like to thank my mother, who supported me in all of my interests as I was growing up. I would also like to thank my grandmother, who worked for the Walt Disney Company, believed in the wonders of constructed cinematic fantasies, and provided me with boxes of company newsletters and other materials collected over the years of her employment.

This book would not be possible without the dozens and dozens of art directors, architects, executives, early employees of Disneyland, and friends of C. V. Wood who allowed me to interview them—often multiple times. I'm indebted to countless individuals who shared their memories, their photos, and even their diaries so that I could better understand the events described in this book. In particular, I'd like to thank X Atencio, Jerry Blakeley, Patricia Branham, Michael Broggie, Harriet Burns, Alan Coats, Rolly Crump, Bud Dreager, Ron Dominguez, Don Edgren, Blaine Gibson, Bob Gurr, Don Iwerks, Gene Johnson, Stan Jolley, Doc Lemmon, Quentin Lewis, Jack Lindquist, Art Linkletter, Bill Martin, Ron Miller, Bob Minick, Keith Murdoch, Tom Nabbe, Miriam Nelson, Terry O'Brien, Marijess Parsons, Anita Porterfield, Buzz Price, John Rich, Charlie Ridgway, Rolf Roth, Paul Skillman, Bill "Sully" Sullivan, and Cliff Walker. To Jim House, a special note of thanks for allowing me to use the reel-to-reel recorded interviews conducted in 1970. I am grateful to the special collections and archives at UCLA, USC, UCF, the Presidio, the Margaret Herrick Library, the city of Burbank, the Anaheim Heritage Center, and to the work of Becky

Cline and Bob McLaughlin. I have relied on the efforts of other historians, particularly in their published interviews; without their work this book could not have been written. Among them are: Michael Barrier, Greg Brown, John Canemaker, Richard Hubler, Jim Korkis, Dave Smith, and Bob Thomas. I'd like to thank my compatriots, Paul Anderson and Didier Ghez, in this endeavor for their boundless support, friendship, and excellent advice.

To Cal Poly University, especially the College of Liberal Arts and the Department of English, my deepest thanks.

This book would not exist without the patience and enduring efforts of my agent, the amazing Victoria Sanders. Nor would it exist without Leila Salisbury and the superb team at the University Press of Mississippi.

To Brad Campbell, Kevin Clark, Jerry Compton, John Hampsey, Adam Johnson, Jarret Keene, Ryan Van Cleave, and Kevin Winard, a lifetime of friendship, for their encouragement and for tolerating the moods and obsessions of a writer.

Lastly, but most importantly, to my family—Kerry, Owen, and Ellery, who have (and continue) to put up with my endless trips to archives and to record interviews with those who worked in the studio during the 1940s, 1950s, and 1960s—my endless love.

Author's Note on the Construction of This Book

In writing this book, my primary goal was to chronicle the creation of the American theme park. To accomplish this, I spent nine years researching the topic, with much of the work accomplished on-site in various American cities. I interviewed over 150 individuals who designed, managed, and operated these parks in the 1950s; I reviewed countless documents at historical, corporate, and academic archives and libraries; I carefully worked through the holdings of major American newspapers and magazines; and I spent weeks driving around the Southwest to gather information on the man responsible for many of these parks, C. V. Wood. A great deal of information included in this book is unique and has not been previously published. This book includes hundreds of quotes, many from new interviews, to create a multi-vocal presentation of history. It is my belief that this book contains the fullest and most complete picture of the creation of the American theme park industry, Disneyland in particular, ever committed to print.

My secondary goal was to fashion language in such a way as to create a narrative history, allowing readers to better understand the time period of the 1950s, the growth of the amusements industry, and the individuals associated with the first wave of American theme parks. The majority of information in this book comes from eyewitness accounts. But to more fully explain the book's construction, I would like to include the following notes: (1) to better establish a sense of place, I often used period photographs to solidify visual details; (2) likewise, in places I have used period photographs and other sources to define an individual's wardrobe, appearance, habitual gestures, and daily routines; (3) all of the dialogue rendered in quotation marks (i.e., "dialogue") is presented exactly as eyewitnesses remember it. In a few places, I have included dialogue without quotation marks to indicate that it is an approximation of the historic conversation, though the information in the conversation is tied to an eyewitness account; (4) lastly, at times, this book assumes the perspectives of the historic individuals. I allowed the information in interviews and documents to guide me as I crafted these sections of interior thought and emotion, even as I recognized that presentations of interiority are always subjective.

With this, I have done my best to present a fully realized and historically accurate account of the men and women whose lives are honored in this book.

—Todd James Pierce
January 2015

Notes

CHAPTER ONE

1. "Rotarians Hear Story of CC&F Pleasure Island." *Wakefield Daily Item.* Nov. 19, 1958. 1.

2. Blakeley, Jerry. Interview with author. Dec. 15, 2005.

3. Disneyland, Inc., and Walt Disney Productions. Petition to Perpetuate Testimony. Los Angeles Superior Court. Apr. 27, 1959.

4. Author's note: notice of exclusion from *Disney A-Z* first made by Jim Hill in his column on the website, LaughingPlace.com.

5. Tieman, Robert. Correspondence with author. Aug. 10, 2005.

6. Smith, Dave. Correspondence with author. Oct. 3, 2006.

7. Albright, Milt. Discussion with author. May 7, 2008.

CHAPTER TWO

1. In Oklahoma, the request of vital records, such as birth certificates, are issued only to next of kin, leaving no reliable means to confirm his legal name. The name Commodore Vanderbilt Wood does not appear in known public records for C. V. Wood in California. In fact, after years of searching documents, I've only been able to find it listed once on a single travel itinerary: "Commodore V. Wood." A marriage announcement in the *Woods County Enterprise (Oklahoma)* dated Jul. 20, 1917, confirms that his father's name was "Mr. Commodore V. Wood."

2. Wood, C. V. Interview with Jim House. Nov. 1970.

3. "Aunt B." Interview with Jim House. Nov. 1970.

4. Mrs. Dickerson (C. V. Wood's aunt). Interview with Jim House. Nov. 1970.

5. Hunky is a later derivation of C. V. Sr.'s earlier nickname, Honky. As a young man, C. V. Sr. regularly produced a strange honking to wake railroad employees who were asleep before their shift, thus earning him the name "Honky." Later in life, his name morphed from Honky to Hunky. C. V. Wood's

friends, the Bombers tended to call him Hunky, while his family tended to call him Honky.

6. Bryson, John. Interview with Jim House. Nov. 1970.

7. Olson, Susan. "Born in Waynoka: C. V. Wood, Jr., Disneyland Masterplanner." *Waynoka Chronicles*. Fall 2005. 1–2.

8. Lemmon, Eugene. Quoted in Price, Harrison "Buzz." *Walt's Revolution! By the Numbers*. Orlando, FL: Ripley Entertainment, 2004. 132.

9. Slick, Tom, II. Interview with Jim House. Nov. 1970.

10. House, Jim. Quoted in Price. *Walt's Revolution!* 133.

11. Skillman, Paul. Interview with author. Jun. 21, 2007.

12. Skillman, Paul. Correspondence with author. Jul. 2, 2007.

13. Skillman, Paul. Interview with author. Jun. 21, 2007.

14. Price, Harrison "Buzz." Interview with author. Feb. 9, 2006.

15. Group interview of the Bombers. Interview with Jim House, conducted for C. V. Wood's fiftieth birthday party. Nov. 1970.

16. Thompson, Charlie. Interview with Jim House. Nov. 1970.

17. Lewis, Quentin. Personal notes. Approx. 1992.

18. Bryson, John. Interview with Jim House. Nov. 1970.

19. Group interview of the Bombers. Interview with Jim House, conducted for C. V. Wood's fiftieth birthday party. Nov. 1970.

20. Skillman, Paul. Interview with author. Jun. 21, 2007.

21. Bryson, John. Interview with Jim House. Nov. 1970.

22. Lemmon, Eugene "Doc." Interview with author. Jul. 26, 2006.

23. Combined source: Olson. "Born in Waynoka." 1; Thomas, Bob. *Building a Company: Roy O. Disney and the Creation of an Entertainment Empire*. New York: Hyperion, 1998. 188.

24. Combined source: Price. *Walt's Revolution!* 132; France, Van Arsdale. *Window on Main Street*. Livonia, MI: Laughter Publication/Stabur Press. 12.

25. Lofton, Roy. Interview with Jim House. Nov. 1970.

26. Enrollment dates and course of study confirmed by Hardin-Simmons University.

27. Lofton, Roy. Interview with Jim House. Nov. 1970.

28. Lewis, Quentin. Interview with author. Jun. 30, 2007.

29. Robbins, William. "How to Build a River in the Arizona Desert to Flow Under the London Bridge." *Esquire*. Feb. 1969. 81.

30. Course of study, years attended, and degree status confirmed by University of Oklahoma by Credentials, Inc.

31. Lewis, Quentin. Interview with author. Jun. 30, 2007.

32. France. *Window on Main Street*. 12.

33. Lewis, Quentin. Interview with author. Jun. 30, 2007.

34. Ibid.

35. Ibid.

36. "Coach Concidine." Interview with Jim House. Nov. 1970.

37. Lewis, Shirley. Interview with author. Jun. 30, 2007.

38. Lewis, Quentin. Interview with author. Jun. 30, 2007.

39. Bryson, John. Interview with Jim House. Nov. 1970.

CHAPTER THREE

1. Davis, Marc. Interviewed by Richard Hubler. May 21, 1968. Quoted in Canemaker, John. *Walt Disney's Nine Old Men and the Art of Animation*. New York: Disney Editions, 2001. 271.

2. Quoted in Gabler, Neal. *Walt Disney: The Triumph of the American Imagination*. New York: Knopf, 2006. 465.

3. Broggie, Michael. *Walt Disney's Railroad Story*. Pasadena, CA: Pentex, 1997. 95–171.

4. Crowther, Bosley. "The Dream Merchant." *New York Times*. Dec. 16, 1966. 40.

5. Disney, Roy. Quoted in Hulett, Steven. "Disneyland's Beginnings Remembered." *Disney Times* 3, no. 6. Jul./Aug. 1980. 3.

6. Thomas. *Building a Company*. 179.

7. City of Burbank. Park and Recreation board minutes. Dec. 12, 1951.

8. Hale, Joe. Interviewed by Didier Ghez. Apr. 24 and 28, 2008. Unpublished.

9. Combined source: City of Burbank. Park and Recreation board minutes. Jul. 9 and Dec. 17, 1952; Hale, Joe. Interviewed by Didier Ghez. Apr. 24 and 28, 2008. Unpublished.

10. Quoted in Thomas. *Building a Company*. 179.

11. Davis, Marvin. OLC Show Awareness Interviews (interviewer unknown). Dec. 30, 1993.

12. "An Interview with Harper Goff." *E-Ticket*. Winter 1992–93. 6.

13. Luckman, Charles. *Twice in a Lifetime: From Soap to Skyscrapers*. New York: Norton, 1988. 308–310.

14. Bright, Randy. *Disneyland: Inside Story*. New York: Harry N. Abrams Publishers, 1987. 45.

15. Irvine, Richard. Interview with Bob Thomas. In Ghez, Didier, ed. *Walt's People: Volume 10*. Xlibris, 2010.

16. Davis, Marvin. Interview with Richard Hubler. In Ghez, Didier, ed. *Walt's People: Volume 6*. Xlibris, 2008.

17. Hurlbut, Bud. Quoted in Harris, Richard. "Bud Hurlbut." *Grand Scales Quarterly*, no. 29 (2009). 9–11.

18. "New Fantasyland Nostalgia." *WED-MAPO Imaginews*. Mar. 26, 1982. 1.

19. Hurlbut, Bud. Quoted in Harris. "Bud Hurlbut." 9.

20. Quoted in Gordon, Bruce, and David Mumford. *Disneyland: The Nickel Tour*. Santa Clarita, CA: Camphor Tree, 2000. 14.

21. "Harper Goff: A Disneyland Original." *WED-Way*. Jun. 10, 1977. 4.

22. Cottrell, Bill. Interviewed by Bob Thomas. Jun. 6, 1973.

23. Wallerstein, David. "Other Recollections." In Goldenson, Leonard H., with Marvin J. Wolf. *Beating the Odds*. New York: Scribner, 1991. 121–22.

24. Davis, Charles, Jr. "Disneyland Schedules Two Major Projects." *Los Angeles Times*. Mar. 1, 1965. 30.

25. Walker, Card. Interview with Bob Thomas. In Ghez. *Walt's People: Volume 10.*

26. Goff, Harper. Interview with Don Peri. In *Working with Walt: Interviews with Disney Artists*. Jackson: University Press of Mississippi, 2008. 199.

27. City of Burbank. Park and Recreation board minutes. Apr. 29, 1953.

28. "Walt Disney Plans Park for Children." *Los Angeles Times*. Mar. 28, 1952. A10.

29. Broggie. *Walt Disney's Railroad Story*. 195.

30. Goff, Harper. Interview with Don Peri. 199.

31. Disney, Roy. Quoted in Eddy, Don. "The Amazing Secret of Walt Disney." *American Magazine*. Aug. 1955. 29, 110–15.

32. Burris, Jenkins. "Snow White Disney's Biggest Moment." *Los Angeles Examiner*. May 5, 1959. 2.

33. Thomas. *Building a Company*. 182.

34. Ibid.

35. "Disney Net Profit $283,662 for 6 mos." *Film Daily*. Jun. 4, 1954. 1.

36. Quoted in Gabler. *Walt Disney*. 506.

37. The June 3 date is based on the first entry in Walt Disney's schedule book for Buzz Price, a lunch meeting attended by Nat Winecoff and Harrison (Buzz) Price. In some published works, this meeting as been repeatedly and erroneously placed on July 10, 1953, a day when Walt Disney was in London, also in April 1953, though Walt was overseas for almost the entire month.

38. Combined source: Presentation (on video) from Jun. 14, 2005, at Disneyland for cast members; Miller, Keith. "A Pioneer's Pioneer." *Funworld Magazine*. Nov. 2005; Price, Buzz. Quoted in *The Disneyland Railroad Story*. DVD. Ape Pen Publishing. 2007.

39. "Stanford Researchers Aid Southland Industry." *Los Angeles Times*. Apr. 8, 1951. 23.

40. Buzz Price, who has related this story in at least a dozen interviews, has, at times, said that Roy did attend this meeting and, other times, claimed that he could not remember if Roy attended this meeting or if he met Roy shortly thereafter. As this meeting focused on site selection and financial matters, the author feels that it is more likely that the stories in which Roy quietly attended this meeting are correct.

41. Price, Buzz. "Researching the Building of a Great Attraction." Harrison "Buzz" Price Papers, Special Collections and University Archives, University of Central Florida, Orlando, Florida. Transcript of speech delivered to the 17th Annual PATA Conference. Taipei, Taiwan. Feb. 8, 1968. 5.

42. Combined source: Price, Buzz. Presentation (taped). NFFC Convention. Jul. 15–17; Price. *Walt's Revolution!* 26.

43. Howell, Blair. "Living Treasures of Imagineering." *Storyboard Magazine* 1, no. 5. 10.

44. Nielson, Donald. *A Heritage of Innovation: SRI's First Half Century*. Menlo Park, CA: Self-published, 2004. 14–18.

45. Price, Buzz. Correspondence with author. Jul. 31, 2006.

46. Ibid.

47. Stanford Research Institute. "Land Use Report for Walt Disney." Aug. 1953.

48. Stanford Research Institute. "An Analysis of Location Factors for Disneyland" (final version). Aug. 28, 1953.

49. Price, Buzz. Public presentation. Jul. 16, 2010.

50. Stanford Research Institute. "An Analysis of Location Factors for Disneyland."

51. Presentation (on video) from Jun. 14, 2005, at Disneyland for cast members.

52. Stanford Research Institute. "An Analysis of Location Factors for Disneyland."

53. Dominguez, Ron. Interview with author. Jul. 14, 2008.

54. Johnson, Helen. "Anaheim Halloween Cauldron Bubbles as Southland's Major Frolic Nears." *Los Angeles Times*. Oct. 25, 1953. G1.

55. "Disney Designs Hallowe'en Floats." *Anaheim Bulletin*. 1953.

CHAPTER FOUR

1. Quoted in Trudell, Alan. "Could It Have Been DisneyGrove." *Orange County Daily News*. Jan. 5, 1978.

2. Tytle, Harry. *One of Walt's Boys*. Self-published, 1997. 125.

3. Irvine, Richard. Interview with Bob Thomas. In Ghez. *Walt's People: Volume 10*.

4. Price, Harrison A. "He Was Framed." Harrison "Buzz" Price Papers, Special Collections and University Archives, University of Central Florida, Orlando, Florida. Speech prepared for the Economic Round Table of Los Angeles. Mar. 22, 1990. 1–3.

5. McKim, Sam. OLC Show Awareness Interviews (interviewer unknown). Dec. 28, 1993.

6. Combined source: Ryman, Herb. Quoted in "Historical Perspectives." *Disneyland Line*. Jul. 23, 1987. 4; Allan, Robin. "Herb Ryman Interview." In Ghez, Didier, ed. *Walt's People: Volume 2*. Xlibris, 2006. 199–200; Broggie. *Walt Disney's Railroad Story*. 204–208; Ryman, Herbert Dickens. Quoted in Gordon, Bruce, and David Mumford, eds. *A Brush with Disney: An Artist's Journey*. Santa Clarita, CA: Camphor Three, 2000. 143–47.

7. Disneyland Pitchbook, prepared for Disneyland, Inc., by WED Enterprises. 1953. Magic of Disneyland exhibit. The Oakland Museum. 2006.

8. "Disney Net Profit $283,662 for 6 mos." 1.

9. Weaver, Pat. *The Best Seat in the House*. New York: Knopf, 1996. 276.

10. Hubler, Richard. Interview with Donn Tatum. In Ghez, Didier, ed. *Walt's People: Volume 8*. Xlibris, 2009.

11. Thomas. *Building a Company*. 184–85.

12. Goldenson with Wolf. *Beating the Odds*. 121–22.

13. "Walt Disney Productions, Plaintiff, v. American Broadcasting-Paramount Theatres, Inc., Defendant." United States District Court S.D. New York. Jan. 5, 1960. 114.

14. Combined source: Johnson. "Anaheim Halloween Cauldron Bubbles as Southland's Major Frolic Nears." G1; "Orange C of C Float Sweepstakes Winner." *Long Beach Independent-Press-Telegram*. Nov. 1, 1953. A11.

15. Murdoch, Keith. Public presentation. Jun. 6, 2009.

16. Combined source: Murdoch, Keith. Interview with author. Feb. 17, 2007; Murdoch, Keith. "My Recollections of Getting a Location for Disneyland and Early Contacts." Personal notes. 2007.

17. "Reveals Details of Disney Amusement Park, TV Plans." *Los Angeles Examiner*. May 11, 1954.

18. Quoted in Trudell. "Could It Have Been DisneyGrove."

19. Moeller, Earne. Introduction to *A Historical Sketch*. Earnest W. Moeller Collection. Anaheim Heritage Center, Anaheim Public Library. Anaheim, CA. Jul. 14, 1980.

20. Combined source: Murdoch, Keith. Interview with author. Feb. 17, 2007; Murdoch. "My Recollections of Getting a Location for Disneyland and Early Contacts."

21. Quoted in Bright. *Disneyland*. 48.

22. Davis, Marvin. Interview with Richard Hubler. In Ghez. *Walt's People: Volume 6*.

23. Reproduction of this artwork is included in Kurtti, Jeff, and Bruce Gordon. *The Art of Disneyland*. New York: Disney Editions, 2005. 86. Bushman discusses other design elements in: Bushman, Bruce. Interview with George Sherman. 1962. Transcript summary.

24. Linkletter, Art. Quoted in Koenig, David. *Mouse Tales: Golden Anniversary Special Edition*. Irvine, CA: Bonaventure Press, 2005. 11.

25. Price. *Walt's Revolution!* 29.

26. Wood, C. V. Interview with Gregory Brown. Jun. 14, 1977.

27. Ibid.

28. WED Enterprises. Memo. "DISNEYLAND Meeting with John Gostovich, Gen. Mgr. A. F. Gilmore Co. & Farmers Market." Nov. 6, 1953.

29. Price. "Researching the Building of a Great Attraction." 8.

30. Price, Harrison A. "The Present and Future Position of the Theme Park Business." Harrison "Buzz" Price Papers, Special Collections and University Archives, University of Central Florida, Orlando, Florida. An address to the Management Club of Knott's Berry Farm. Apr. 5, 1984. 1–2.

31. Although many later books state that WED interviewed four men from the amusement industry, the earliest accounts known to me (specifically, Buzz Price's notes housed at the University of Central Florida) state that there were seven. It is possible that four park owners attended the meeting with some being accompanied by one or two high-level administrators at his park. It is also possible that more than four parks were represented.

32. Combined source: Price. *Walt's Revolution!* 29–31; Price. "Researching the Building of a Great Attraction." 8–9.

33. Quoted in O'Brien, Tim. *Ripley's Legends: Pioneers of the Amusement Park Industry*, vol. 1. Orlando, FL: Casa Flamingo Literary Arts, 2006. 125.

34. Evans, Bill. Quoted in "The Jungle Cruise." *WD Eye*. Apr. 1990. 12.

35. Thomas, Bob. *Walt Disney: An American Original*. New York: Simon & Schuster, 1976. 250–51.

36. Gordon and Mumford. *Disneyland: The Nickel Tour*. 73.

37. "Conversation with Bill Martin." *WED-Way*. May 13, 1977. 4.

38. Combined source: Morgan, Ed. Video interview conducted by Dana Morgan with questions from the author. Nov. 10, 2006; Reynolds, Robert

R. *Roller Coasters, Flumes and Flying Saucers*. Jupiter, FL: Northern Lights Publishing, 1999. 36.

39. Wood, C. V. Letter to Earne Moeller. Earnest W. Moeller Collection. Anaheim Heritage Center, Anaheim Public Library. Anaheim, CA. Mar. 10, 1980.

40. France, Van Arsdale. *35 Years of Creating Happiness at Disneyland Park* (privately printed, comb-bound book). Santa Ana, CA: Spiral Books, a division of Van Arsdale France, Inc., 1990. 26.

41. Information taken from individual options contracts collected in the Earnest W. Moeller Collection. Anaheim Heritage Center, Anaheim Public Library. Anaheim, CA.

42. Transcript of sales meeting (notes). Mar. 14, 1954.

43. Moeller, Earne. *A Historical Sketch*. Personal notes. Earnest W. Moeller Collection. Anaheim Heritage Center, Anaheim Public Library. Anaheim, CA. Jul. 14, 1980. 1–6.

44. Ibid.

45. American Broadcasting-Paramount Theatres, Inc. Letter to Walt Disney Productions. March 24, 1954.

46. Goldenson with Wolf. *Beating the Odds*. 121–22.

47. "Disney AB-PT Sign Pact." *Film Daily*. Apr. 5, 1954. 1.

48. Pryor, Thomas M. "Disney and A.B.C. Sign TV Contract." *New York Times*. Apr. 3, 1954. 19.

49. Pryor, Thomas M. "Disney to Enter TV Field in Fall." *New York Times*. Mar. 30, 1954. 24.

50. "20th-Fox Not Ready to Give Old Pix to TV." *Film Daily*. May 19, 1954. 5.

51. Wadewitz, W. R. President's note. *Westerner*. Aug. 1955. 2.

52. Porterfield, Anita (daughter of Curtis Bellis, member of the Bombers). Interview with author. Jul. 2, 2007.

53. Ibid.

54. "Disney Chosen Chief of $9,000,000 Project." *Los Angeles Times*. May 14, 1954. 24.

55. Lemmon, Eugene "Doc." Interview with author. Jul. 26, 2006.

56. Murdoch. "My Recollections of Getting a Location for Disneyland and Early Contacts."

57. France. *Window on Main Street*. 9.

58. "The Man who Manages the Show." *New York Times*. Jun. 19, 1960. ADA18.

59. Schumacher, Fred. Interview with Jim House. Nov. 1970.

60. Lemmon, Eugene "Doc." Interview with author. Jul. 26, 2006.

61. Price, Buzz. Correspondence with author. Jan. 27, 2006.

CHAPTER FIVE

1. Justice, Bill. *Justice for Disney*. Dayton: Tomart Publications, 1992. 55.

2. Ibid.

3. Ibid., 56.

4. Hibler, Winston. Quoted in Gabler. *Walt Disney*. 523.

5. Quoted in *FantasyLine Express: The Official Publication of the NFFC*. Jun./ Jul. 2004. 23.

6. Irvine, Richard. Interview with Bob Thomas. In Ghez. *Walt's People: Volume 10*.

7. Martin, Bill. Interview with author. Jul. 19, 2006.

8. Ibid.

9. Thomas. *Building a Company*. 199.

10. Though the exact manner in which Woody profited is not clear, there are three strong possibilities: (1) the deal might have been arranged strictly to payback favors Woody owed to Vanburgh and Smithers, (2) Vanburgh and Smithers might have paid Woody a good chunk of cash on the side to close the deal, or (3) the deal might have been structured so that Woody received a percentage of American Souvenir's profits.

11. Primary details taken from court documents and transcripts concerning *American Souvenirs, Inc., vs. Disneyland, Inc.*, filed in Los Angeles Superior Court on March 26, 1956. Additional details from "Single Souvenir Jobber is Named for Disneyland." *Hollywood Reporter*. Jul. 22, 1954.

12. Miller, Ron. Interview with author. Jan. 8, 2008.

13. Combined source: Fowler, Joe. Interview with Bob Thomas. In Ghez. *Walt's People: Volume 10*; Fowler, Joe. Video presentation. Walt Disney World. Jan. 13, 1988; Becker, Elliot. "Admiral Joseph W. Fowler, The Man Who Built Disneyland." *Storyboard* 2, no. 5. 14; Fowler, Joe. Interview with Richard Hubler. In Ghez. *Walt's People: Volume 6*; Ridgway, Charles. Interview with author. Jul. 13, 2007.

14. Whitney, George K. Interview with John Martini. National Park Service, Golden Gate National Recreation Area, [606A 4009]. 2002. http://www. outsidelands.org/whitney-interview5.php.

15. Combined source: Fowler, Joe. Interview with Bob Thomas. In Ghez. *Walt's People: Volume 10*; Fowler, Joe. Video presentation. Walt Disney World. Jan. 13, 1988; Becker. "Admiral Joseph W. Fowler, The Man Who Built Disneyland." 14; Fowler, Joe. Interview with Richard Hubler. In Ghez. *Walt's People: Volume 6*.

16. Quoted in France. *Window on Main Street*. 34.

17. Combined source: Fowler, Joe. Interview with Bob Thomas. In Ghez. *Walt's People: Volume 10*; Fowler, Joe. Video presentation. Walt Disney World. Jan. 13, 1988; Becker. "Admiral Joseph W. Fowler, The Man Who Built Disneyland." 14; Fowler, Joe. Interview with Richard Hubler. In Ghez. *Walt's People: Volume 6*.

18. Goff, Harper. Interview with Don Peri. 105.

19. "An Interview with Harper Goff." 6–7.

20. WED document resulting from a June 11, 1954, visit to Long Beach Pike, later bound in a WED report titled *Amusement Parks U.S.* 28–29. Magic of Disneyland exhibit. The Oakland Museum. 2006.

21. Bushman, Bruce. Handwritten notes. 1953.

22. Irvine, Richard. Interview with Bob Thomas. In Ghez. *Walt's People: Volume 10*.

23. Korkis, Jim. "Food for Thought." *Jim Hill Media*. May 27, 2003. http://jimhillmedia.com/blogs/jim_korkis/archive/2003/05/27/1095.aspx.

24. Combined source: "Disneyland Art Director, Bill Martin." *E-Ticket*. Winter 1994–95. 10; Quoted in "Dreaming & Doing." *WD Eye*. Jul. 17, 1995. 2.

25. Disney, Walt. Letter to Joyce Hall. Jul. 2, 1954. Displayed at Walt Disney: One Man's Dream, Disney's Hollywood Studio, Walt Disney Resort, Florida.

26. Site Layout Map, Tomorrowland (presumed to have been completed in spring 1954).

27. Morgan, Ed. Interview conducted by Dana Morgan with questions from the author. Nov. 10, 2006.

28. Reynolds. *Roller Coasters, Flumes and Flying Saucers.* 26–37.

29. Combined source: France, Van Arsdale. Video interview/presentation on Disney training. Circa 1985; France. *Window on Main Street.* 9.

30. France. *Window on Main* Street. 10.

31. Ibid.

32. Combined source: France, Van A. "A Birthday Worth Remembering." *Los Angeles Times*. Feb. 24, 1985. OC A14; France. *Window on Main Street.* 10–11; France. *35 Years of Creating Happiness at Disneyland Park.* 5–7; France, Van Arsdale. Video interview/presentation on Disney training. Circa 1985.

33. Ryman. Quoted in "Historical Perspectives." 4.

34. Cline, Rebecca. "Walt Disney Studios: Disneyland's Workshop." *Disney Insider Yearbook 2005: Year in Review*. New York: Disney Editions, 2006. 49.

35. Presentation by Ken Anderson. *Persistence of Vision Tape #3*.

36. "Peter Pan, Captain Hook and . . . Frank Thomas." *E-Ticket*. Spring 1997. 27.

37. Quoted in a biographical sketch published on Disney Online: Disney Legend, Ron Dominguez. http://legends.disney.go.com/legends/detail?key=Ron+Dominguez.

38. Quoted in Bright. *Disneyland*. 92.

39. According to longtime Disney lawyer, Luther Marr, Bruce McNeil underbid on the job of land clearing to place his team first on the job site. When it came time for contractors to bid on the actual construction, no one wanted to wager what it would actually cost to build Disneyland, as the company lacked a complete site plan and full architectural blueprints. Since McNeil was already on the site, he agreed to construct Disneyland on a cost-plus basis—meaning that McNeil took on no risk and billed Disney for his costs plus a reasonable profit. This profit would be added to any jobs he also subbed out to other firms. This was, no doubt, a golden arrangement for any contractor.

40. Evans, Bill. Quoted in "Historical Perspectives." 5.

41. "Auld Acquaintance." *Disneylander*. Nov. 1957. 5.

42. Combined source: Fowler, Joe. Video presentation. Walt Disney World. Jan. 13, 1988; Becker. "Admiral Joseph W. Fowler, The Man Who Built Disneyland." 15.

43. "Excavation Firm Hired for Site of Disneyland." *Los Angeles Times*. Aug. 25, 1954. 18.

44. "A Fantasy Come to Live." *Clay Pipe News*. May–Jun. 1956. 7.

45. "An Interview with Harper Goff." 8.

46. Berg, Louis. "Walt Disney's New Ten Million Dollar Toy." *The Week Magazine*. Sept. 19, 1954. 8.

47. "An Interview with Harper Goff." 11.

48. Combined source: Fowler, Joe. Interview with Bob Thomas. In Ghez. *Walt's People: Volume 10*; Quoted in Gordon and Mumford. *Disneyland: The Nickel Tour*. 29.

49. "It Takes People (An Interview with Harper Goff)." *Disneyland Line*. Jul. 14, 1977. 2.

50. Richman, Betsy. "Harper Goff Remembers . . ." *Disney News*. Summer 1986. 15.

51. Goff, Harper. Interviewed by Robin Allan. In Ghez, Didier, ed. *Walt's People Volume 1*. Xlibris, 2005. 228–29.

52. "Disney Prods Answers Television Show Critics." *Film Daily*. Dec. 3, 1954. 1.

53. Original quote published on Apr. 14, 1955, in *Long Beach Press-Telegram*. Reprinted in "A Village Never Built." *Long Beach Press-Telegram*. Apr. 5, 2007.

54. "Fisherman's Village Planned at Long Beach." *Los Angeles Times*. Apr. 14, 1955. 24.

55. Combined source: Gurr, Bob. Correspondence with author. Dec. 31, 2006. Gurr, Bob. "Working with Walt." *Designer Times*. Dec. 26, 2006. http://www.laughingplace.com/News-ID511050.asp.

CHAPTER SIX

1. France. *Window on Main Street*. 52.

2. Fowler, Joe. Video presentation. Walt Disney World. Jan. 13, 1988.

3. Quoted in *FantasyLine Express*. 30.

4. France, Van. Video interview. Training and Traditions. 1994.

5. Delaplane, Stan. "Disneyland is Celebrating its 25th Anniversary." *Boston Globe*. May 11, 1980. 1.

6. Wood, C. V. Memo to Walt Disney. May 24, 1954.

7. Quoted in Wood, C. V. Interview with Gregory Brown. Jun. 14, 1977.

8. Schumacher, Fred. Interview with Jim House. Nov. 1970.

9. "Swift at Disneyland." *Swift News*. Jul. 1955. 3.

10. Delaplane. "Disneyland is Celebrating its 25th Anniversary." 1.

11. Albright, Milt. Interview with Didier Ghez (manuscript). Sept. 4, 2008.

12. Figures based on A-3 schedule overseeing multi-year lessees for the year beginning September 29, 1958.

13. Combined source: "Disneyland Aims at $10 Million Yearly B.O." *Variety*. Jul. 13, 1955; France. *Window on Main Street*. 37.

14. Skillman, Paul. Interview with author. Jun. 21, 2007.

15. Price, Buzz. Interview with author. Sept. 7, 2007.

16. France. *35 Years of Creating Happiness at Disneyland Park*. 79.

17. House, Jim. Interview with author. Oct. 16, 2006.

18. Marr, Luther. Interview with Bob Thomas. In Ghez, Didier, ed. *Walt's People: Special Edition on "Roy's People."* Theme Park Press. Forthcoming.

19. Thomas. *Building a Company*. 191.

20. Irvine, Dick. Inter-office correspondence to Harper Goff. Sept. 1, 1954.

21. Details for the "Flight to Mars" attraction taken from concept art (attributed to Bruce Bushman), owned by Stan Jolley.

22. Combined source: Gurr, Bob. Interview with Doobie Moseley. Sept. 10, 1999. http://www.laughingplace.com/news-pid500310-500310.asp; Gurr, Bob. Video presentation from amusements conference. Summer 1996; Gurr. "Working with Walt."

23. Shellhorn, Ruth. Apr. 27 entry. Diary of Ruth Shellhorn, 1955. Transcription (by author) of manuscript. Shellhorn Collection, UCLA Special Collections.

24. Combined source: "The Jungle Cruise." 12; "Creating the Disney Landscape: An Interview with Bill Evans." *E-Ticket*. Spring 1996. 10.

25. "An Interview with Harper Goff." 11.

26. "Dreaming & Doing." 2.

27. Koenig. *Mouse Tales*. 12.

28. Bright. *Disneyland*. 80–81.

29. *Castleview: The Disneyland Cast Magazine*. Dec. 1981. 11.

30. Wilson, Craig McNair. "Several Coats of Paint." *WD Eye*. Dec. 1989. 10.

31. Quoted in Gordon and Mumford. *Disneyland: The Nickel Tour*. 31.

32. Quoted in Cline. "Walt Disney Studios: Disneyland's Workshop." 47.

33. Presentation by Ken Anderson. *Persistence of Vision Tape #3*.

34. Marr, Luther. Interview with Bob Thomas.

35. "Field Notes." *Public Relations Journal*. May 1955. 26.

36. Combined source: "Disney Sues to Prevent Using Name." *Long Beach Press Telegram*. Mar. 23, 1955. B2; Affidavit of Moeller, Earne. Disneyland, Inc., vs. Frank J. Cimral. State of California, County of Orange. Mar. 1955.

37. Shellhorn, Ruth. May 25 entry. Diary of Ruth Shellhorn, 1955. Transcription (by author) of manuscript. Shellhorn Collection, UCLA Special Collections.

38. Sherman, Gene. "Cityside with Gene Sherman." *Los Angeles Times*. May 25, 1955. 2.

39. Thomas, Bob. "Disney Erects Vast Wonderland for Children." Associated Press article published in multiple papers, including the *Los Angeles Examiner*. May 8, 1955.

40. Heffernan, Harold. "Disney's Magic Land." *Los Angeles Examiner*. May 7, 1955.

41. Quoted in Gabler. *Walt Disney*. 529.

42. Koenig. *Mouse Tales*. 26.

43. France. *Window on Main Street*. 25.

44. Cary, Diana Serra. *The Hollywood Posse: The Story of a Gallant Brand of Horsemen Who Made Movie History*. Norman: Univiversity of Oklahoma Press, 1996. 254–55.

45. Presentation by Ken Anderson. *Persistence of Vision Tape #3*.

46. Anderson, Ken. Interview with Paul F. Anderson. *Persistence of Vision Tape #8*.

47. Quoted in Anderson, Paul F. "A Visit with Sam McKim." *Persistence of Vision*, no. 57.

48. Gordon and Mumford. *Disneyland: The Nickel Tour*. 30.

49. Thomas. *Walt Disney*. 268.

50. Fowler, Joe. Interview with Bob Thomas. In Ghez. *Walt's People: Volume 10*.

51. Ibid.

52. Figures based on A-3 schedule overseeing multi-year lessees for the year beginning September 29, 1958.

53. Shellhorn, Ruth. May 10 entry. Diary of Ruth Shellhorn, 1955. Transcription (by author) of manuscript. Shellhorn Collection, UCLA Special Collections.

54. "Peter Pan, Captain Hook and . . . Frank Thomas." 39.

55. Kurtti, Jeff. *Walt Disney's Imagineering Legends and the Genesis of the Disney Theme Park.* New York: Disney Editions, 2008. 36.

56. Disney Miller, Diane. Quoted in Taylor, John. *Storming the Magic Kingdom: Wall Street, the Raiders, and the Battle for Disney.* New York: Knopf, 1987. 18.

57. Skillman, Paul. Interview with author. Jun. 21, 2007.

58. France, Van Arsdale. *Backstage Magic: A Personal History.* Privately printed, 1980. 25.

59. Combined source: Fowler, Joe. Video presentation. Walt Disney World. Jan. 13, 1988; Becker. "Admiral Joseph W. Fowler, The Man Who Built Disneyland." 15.

60. On the Disneyland opening day telecast, Art Linkletter claims ABC used twenty-nine cameras as part of his off-the-cuff narration, but the actual number was likely closer to twenty-four.

61. "Disneyland TV Preview Will Use 24 Cameras." *Los Angeles Examiner.* Jul. 2, 1955.

62. Eisenstein, Harold. Interview with Naomi Schottenstein. Columbus Jewish Historical Society. Jul. 28, 1998. http://columbusjewishhistory. org/?post_type=oral_histories&p=111.

63. France, Van. Video interview. Training and Traditions. 1994.

64. Combined source: France. *35 Years of Creating Happiness at Disneyland Park.* 40; France, Van. Video interview. Disney Training and Traditions. Approx. 1985; France, Van. Interview. Training and Traditions. 1994.

65. Excerpt of inter-office memo from C. V. Wood to Walt Disney. Jun. 2, 1955. Reprinted in *Disneyland Line.* Jul. 12, 1984. 4.

66. Fowler, Joe. Inter-office correspondence to Walt Disney. Jun. 2, 1955.

67. Korkis, Jim. "Interview with Bill Evans (1910–2002)." Published in Ghez, Didier, ed. *Walt's People, Volume 5.* Xlibris, 2007. 323.

68. Fowler, Joe. Interview with Richard Hubler. In Ghez. *Walt's People: Volume 6.*

69. Dates of the river fill are based on construction photos housed at UCLA. By June 14, the river was roughly half full, rising to the level were it would connect to a back channel that fed the Jungle River. The upper portions of the riverbed were filled with water around July 1.

70. Combined source: Fowler, Joe. Interview with Bob Thomas. 1973; Fowler, Joe. Video presentation. Walt Disney World. Jan. 13, 1988. (The details about

the exact mixture of clay and concrete are taken from "Building the Dream." Disneyland, Inc., press release. Jul. 1955.) The early July date is based on a series of slides taken by Ruth Shellhorn which show the river being refilled (with the riverbed mostly filled sometime on Jul. 1).

71. Sklar, Martin A. *Walt Disney's Disneyland.* Walt Disney Company, 1966. 21.

72. France. *Window on Main Street.* 27.

73. "Admiral Joe: Disney's Construction Boss." *Disneyland Line.* Nov. 30, 1990. 3.

74. Bartchard, Dave. Quoted in France. *Window on Main Street.* 27.

75. Ryman, Herb. Quoted in Gordon and Mumford. *Disneyland: The Nickel Tour.* 30.

76. Bright. *Disneyland.* 92.

77. Murdoch, Keith. "Finding Disneyland." In Thie, Carlene. *Homecoming: Destination Disneyland.* Riverside, CA: Ape Pen Publishing, 2005. 12.

78. Wood, C. V. Interview with Gregory Brown. Jun. 14, 1977.

79. France. *Backstage Magic.* 47.

80. Gillette, Don Carle. "The Disneyland Story: A Unique Amusement Park Yields More Pleasure than Profit." *Barron's National Business and Financial Weekly.* Jan. 23, 1956. 9.

81. Tatum, Donn. Interview with Bob Thomas. In Ghez. *Walt's People: Volume 10.*

82. Rich, John. *Warm Up the Snake: A Hollywood Memoir.* Ann Arbor: University of Michigan Press, 2006. 39.

83. Goff, Harper. Quoted in Howell. "Living Treasures of Imagineering." 8.

84. Whitney, George K. Interview with John Martini. National Park Service, Golden Gate National Recreation Area, [606A 4009]. 2002. http://www.outsidelands.org/whitney-interview5.php.

85. Combined source: Reynolds. *Roller Coasters, Flumes and Flying Saucers.* 40–51; "Fantasyland: Looking Back . . ." *Castleview: The Disneyland Cast Magazine.* Dec. 1981. 7.

86. Broggie, Michael. Speech for window dedication on Main Street. *Machine Works: Roger Broggie, Main Street Window Dedication.* DVD. Extinct Attractions Club. 2007.

87. Combined source: Fowler, Joe. Video presentation. Walt Disney World. Jan. 13, 1988; Becker. "Admiral Joseph W. Fowler, The Man Who Built Disneyland." 15; Fowler, Joe. Interview with Richard Hubler. In Ghez. *Walt's People: Volume 6.*

88. Quoted in "Additional 'League' Facts." *E-Ticket.* Summer 1988. 29.

89. Bright. *Disneyland.* 92.

90. The name Kap was nothing more than the initials for the phrase Kaiser's Aluminum Pig, with aluminum pig being a technical term for an un-milled form of aluminum.

91. Conference presentation. Videotaped. Summer 1996.

92. "Disneyland's Rocket to the Moon." *E-Ticket*. Summer 1996. 28.

93. Combined source: Conference presentation. Videotaped. Summer 1996; Gurr, Bob. "Autopia Testing." *Designer Times*. Aug. 9, 2000. http://www.laughingplace.com/News-ID108015.asp.

94. "Kaiser Aluminum: Works its Wonders at Disneyland." Advertisement. *Wall Street Journal*. Jul. 17, 1955.

95. "Widespread Use of Natural Gas Clearly Demonstrated in Park." *Long Beach Independent-Press-Telegram*. Jul. 15, 1955. 15.

96. Earle, Eyvind. *Horizon Bound on a Bicycle*. Self-published, 1990. 236.

97. Albright, Milt. Club 55 presentation. NFFC. Jul. 12, 2005.

98. Albright, Milt. Interview with Didier Ghez (manuscript). Sept. 4, 2008.

99. Ibid.

100. Fowler, Joe. Interview with Bob Thomas. In Ghez. *Walt's People: Volume 10*.

101. Grover, John. "Disneyland Special: Tiny Horses for the Wee Folk." *Mirror News*. Jul. 5, 1955.

102. France. *Backstage Magic*. 47.

103. Taylor, Dani. Correspondence with author. Jul. 24, 2008.

104. Korkis, Jim. "The Man Behind the Mouse." *Jim Hill Media Website*. Aug. 8, 2003.

105. "Fantasyland: Looking Back . . ." 6–7.

106. Shellhorn, Ruth. Jul. 2 entry. Diary of Ruth Shellhorn, 1955. Transcription (by author) of manuscript. Shellhorn Collection, UCLA Special Collections.

107. "An Interview with Bob Penfield . . . an Original Disneylander." *E-Ticket*. Spring 2005. 26.

108. Material from a biographical sketch on Disney Online: Disney Legend, Ron Dominguez. http://legends.disney.go.com/legends/detail?key=Ron+Dominguez.

109. France. *35 Years of Creating Happiness at Disneyland Park*. 51.

110. Ettinger, Edwin D. (Ed). *A Decade with Disneyland*. Personal notes. 1965.

111. "Conversation with Bill Martin." 4.

112. France. *Backstage Magic*. 44.

113. Shelton, Earl. Interview with Jim House. Nov. 1970; Hill, Jim. "Tales from the Parking Lot."

114. Minick, Bob. Interview with author. Oct. 26, 2007.

115. Moeller. Introduction to *A Historical Sketch*.

116. Ettinger. *A Decade with Disneyland*.

117. France. *Backstage Magic*. 44.

118. Roth, Rolf. Interview with author. Aug. 24, 2007.

119. Wood, C. V. Letter to Earne Moeller. Earnest W. Moeller Collection. Anaheim Heritage Center, Anaheim Public Library. Anaheim, CA. Mar. 10, 1980.

120. Caots, Alan. Interview with author. Mar. 12, 2011.

121. Shellhorn, Ruth. Jul. 6 entry. Diary of Ruth Shellhorn, 1955. Transcription (by author) of manuscript. Shellhorn Collection, UCLA Special Collections.

122. Shellhorn, Ruth. Jul. 8 entry. Diary of Ruth Shellhorn, 1955. Transcription (by author) of manuscript. Shellhorn Collection, UCLA Special Collections.

123. Shellhorn, Ruth. Jul. 9 entry. Diary of Ruth Shellhorn, 1955. Transcription (by author) of manuscript. Shellhorn Collection, UCLA Special Collections.

124. Shellhorn, Ruth. Jul. 11 entry. Diary of Ruth Shellhorn, 1955. Transcription (by author) of manuscript. Shellhorn Collection, UCLA Special Collections.

125. Rich. *Warm Up the Snake*. 38.

126. Nelson, Miriam. Interview with author. Mar. 28, 2010.

127. Sklar. *Walt Disney's Disneyland*. 21.

128. Rich, John. Interview with author. Mar. 27, 2010.

129. France. *35 Years of Creating Happiness at Disneyland Park*. 53.

130. Ettinger. *A Decade with Disneyland*.

131. "Harper Goff: A Disneyland Original." 5.

132. "An Interview with Art Linkletter." *E-Ticket*. Fall 2003. 10.

133. Quoted in Broggie. *Walt Disney's Railroad Story*. 121.

134. Johnson, Gene. Interview with author. Nov. 15, 2005.

135. Skillman, Paul. Interview with author. Jun. 21, 2007.

136. Though I did not have access to Walt's personal financial documents to verify this final life insurance loan, Walt appears to talk about it on Jul. 16, 1955, while at the park. Furthermore, it appears to be suggested in an interview Bill Davidson (of the *Saturday Evening Post*) conducted with Walt in 1964.

137. Branham, Patricia. Interview with author. Aug. 24, 2010.

138. "Opening Day Blues." *Los Angeles Times*. Jan. 20, 1980. R10.

139. Goff, Harper. Interview with Don Peri.

140. Nelson, Miriam. Interview with author. Mar. 28, 2010.

141. Combined source: Williams, Pat, with Jim Deney. *How to be like Walt*. Deerfield Beach, FL: HCI, 2004. 208; Koenig. *Mouse Tales*. 58.

142. "Dreaming & Doing." 3.

143. Combined source: Bosquet, Jean. "$17,000,000 Disney Dream Comes True." *Los Angeles Examiner*. Jul. 18, 1955. A2; Bright. *Disneyland*. 72.

144. "It Takes People: 30 Years of Catching the Spirit." *Disneyland Line*. Jul. 17, 1995. 5.

145. Schartz, Ray. Quoted in France. *Window on Main Street*. 30.

146. Johnson, Jimmy. *Inside the Whimsy Works: My Life with Walt Disney*. Jackson: University Press of Mississippi, 2014. 99.

147. Combined source: Anderson, Ken. Interview with Ken Anderson on *POV Tape #8*; Williams with Deney. *How to be like Walt*. 208.

148. In a presentation for the Oakland opening of the "Behind the Magic" museum exhibit, Diane Disney Miller relayed that her father, Walt Disney, had told his family that he "didn't want any of you women out there. It's going to be a mess and I don't want to have to worry about you, too!" (May 5, 2006).

149. Thompson, Bette. "All Around The Town." *Amarillo Globe-Times*. Feb. 3, 1956. 15.

CHAPTER SEVEN

1. "The Man who Manages the Show." ADA18.

2. France. *Window on Main Street*. 30.

3. Sargent, Cora Lee. Quoted in *Club 55—The Pioneers*. Privately published, 1975.

4. "The Last of the 'Club 55'ers." *Disneyland Line*. Jul. 25, 1997.

5. "An Interview with Bob Penfield . . . an Original Disneylander." 24.

6. Dreager, Bud. Interview with author. Mar. 31, 2007.

7. Nunis, Dick. Video interview. Training and Traditions. 1994.

8. "Walt's Happy Place, an Interview with Michael Broggie." *E-Ticket*. Spring 2003. 8.

9. Sklar, Marty. "Disneyland: Opening Day Stories." *WD Eye*. Summer 1990. 20.

10. France. *Window on Main Street*. 30.

11. Gregory, John. "Disneyland: It's Here in All Its Glory—Now What?" *Los Angeles Times*. Dec. 5, 1971. OC1.

12. Green, Amy Boothe Green, and Howard E. Green. *Remembering Walt*. New York: Disney Editions, 1999. 153.

13. Thomas. *Building a Company*. 195.

14. Bright. *Disneyland*. 96.

15. Murdoch, Keith. "Finding Disneyland." 37.

16. Nunis, Dick. Video interview. Training and Traditions. 1994.

17. Koltnow, Barry. "*Recall* Mixes the Old and the New: Palmer Relives Stories of His 30-Year Career on Show." *Orange County Register*. Nov. 22, 1990. K1.

18. Koenig. *Mouse Tales*. 23.

19. Wood, C. V. Interview with Gregory Brown. Jun. 14, 1977.

20. Korkis, Jim. Interview with Tom Nabbe. Jun. 2003.

21. Quoted from the backside of the press preview ticket.

22. Tytle. *One of Walt's Boys*. 129.

23. Combined source: Ridgway, Charles. *Spinning Disney's World*. Branford, CT: The Intrepid Traveler, 2007. 4; Ridgway, Charles. Presentation to NFFC. Jul. 13, 2007.

24. Wood, C. V. Interviewed by Gregory Brown. Jun. 14, 1977.

25. "Happy Birthday to an Original." *Disneyland Line*. Jul. 14, 1983. 2.

26. Ames, Walter. "Train Failure Reddens Disney's Face; Network Inks Pediatrician for TV." *Los Angeles Times*. Jul. 22, 1955. 24.

27. "500 Local Sunday School Children to Play Role in Disneyland Opening." *Anaheim Bulletin*. Jul. 14, 1955. 3.

28. "Happy Birthday to an Original." 3.

29. Disney company memo distributed to studio employees in July 1955. (Gift of Florence Rosenthan, a Disney employee, to the Margaret Herrick Library.)

30. Kinney, Jack. *Walt Disney and Assorted Other Characters: An Unauthorized Account of the Early Years at Disney's*. New York: Harmony Books, 1988. 176.

31. *Dateline: Disneyland*. ABC. Jul. 17 1955.

32. Gibson, Blaine. Interview with author. Feb. 25, 2008.

33. McKim, Sam. Video interview. Training and Traditions. Dec. 28, 1993.

34. Combined source: Morgan, Ed. Interview conducted by Dana Morgan with questions from the author. Nov. 10, 2006; Reynolds. *Roller Coasters, Flumes and Flying Saucers*. 47.

35. Broggie, Michael. Interview with author. Feb. 18, 2010.

36. Combined source: Morgan, Ed. Interview conducted by Dana Morgan with questions from the author. Nov. 10, 2006; Reynolds. *Roller Coasters, Flumes and Flying Saucers*. 47.

37. Nielson. *A Heritage of Innovation*. 14–20.

38. Nunis, Dick. Video interview. Training and Traditions. 1994.

39. In home movies from July 17, the Dumbo attraction is clearly seen arranged in this stationary position—with individual elephants at varying heights.

40. Lindquist, Jack. Interview with author. Jul. 17, 2007.

41. On the TV show *Dateline: Disneyland*, park guests can clearly be seen on the balcony of the castle.

42. France. *35 Years of Creating Happiness at Disneyland Park*. 65.

43. Combined source: Nehamkin, Lester. "Disneyland's Autopia." *Rod & Custom*. Nov. 1955. 62; Gurr, Bob. "Disneyland: Opening Day Stories." *WD Eye*. Summer 1990. 22; Gurr, Bob. "Opening Day." *Designer Times*. Sept. 13, 2000. www.laughingplace.com/News-ID108020.asp.

44. Goff, Harper. Quoted in Janzen, Jack E. "Main Street: Walt's Perfect Introduction to Disneyland." *E-Ticket*. Winter 1992. 33.

45. The story has been both presented as happening on opening day and as happening a few days later. The majority of people who have discussed this event, including Disneyland executive Dick Nunis, have placed it on opening day.

46. Combined source: O'Brien. Interview with author. Jan. 3, 2010; Wadley, Carma. "Man Who Sank the Mark Twain." *Desert News*. Oct. 21, 2005.

47. Quoted in Thomas. *Building a Company*. 197.

48. Ridgway. *Spinning Disney's World*. 4.

49. VanDeWarker, Ray. "30 Years of Catching the Spirit." *Disneyland Line*. Jul. 17, 1985. 5.

50. Quoted in Bright. *Disneyland*. 100.

51. Nabbe, Tom. Interview with author. Aug. 21, 2014.

52. "Walt's Happy Place, an Interview with Michael Broggie." 8.

53. France. *Backstage Magic*. 55.

54. Sargent, Cora Lee. Quoted in *Club 55—The Pioneers*.

55. Nunis, Dick. Quoted in McGrath, Bob. "Through the Looking Glass: An Incidental History." *Disneyland Line*. Jul. 17, 1980. 5.

56. Nabbe, Tom. Interview with Jim Korkis. Jun. 2003.

57. Goff, Harper. Interview with Don Peri. 207.

58. Gurr, Bob. Quoted in Thomas, Bob. "It Wasn't So Magical on Day 1." *Torrance Daily Breeze*. Jul. 17, 2005. A17.

59. Combined source: May, Patrick. "Two Magic-Makers Celebrate Life after Disneyland." *San Jose Mercury*. Jun. 14, 2005; Morgan, Ed. Interview conducted by Dana Morgan with questions from the author. Nov. 10, 2006.

60. Hulett. "Disneyland's Beginnings Remembered." 3.

61. Quoted in Boettner, Jack. "Disney's 'Magical Little Park' After Two Decades." *Los Angeles Times*. Jul. 6, 1975. OC–C1.

62. Bosquet. "$17,000,000 Disney Dream Comes True." A2.

63. Quoted in Gabler. *Walt Disney*. 532.

64. "Thousands Jam Disneyland at Preview Opening." *Orange County Plain Dealer*. Jul. 18, 1955.

65. Irvine, Richard. Interview with Bob Thomas. In Ghez. *Walt's People: Volume 10*.

66. Ettinger. *A Decade with Disneyland*.

67. May. "Two Magic-Makers Celebrate Life after Disneyland."

68. Price. *Walt's Revolution!* 129–39.

69. Quoted in Thomas. *Building a Company*. 199.

70. Sherman. "Cityside with Gene Sherman." 2.

71. "Chaos in Disneyland." *Fortnight*. Aug. 1955. 39.

72. Ibid.

73. Ibid.

74. Dains, Hank. Quoted in Sampson, Wade. "A Salute to Club 55." *Mouse Planet*. Jul. 17, 2007. http://www.mouseplanet.com/articles. php?art=ww070717ws.

75. Martin, Bill. Interviewed by Dave Smith. Apr. 21, 1977. In Ghez, Didier, ed. *Walt's People: Volume 15*. Theme Park Press, 2016.

76. Wood, C. V. Interviewed by Gregory Brown. Jun. 14, 1977.

77. Martin, Bill. Interviewed by Dave Smith. Apr. 21, 1977. In Ghez, Didier, ed. *Walt's People: Volume 15*. Theme Park Press, 2016.

78. Wood, C. V. Interviewed by Gregory Brown. Jun. 14, 1977.

79. Bright. *Disneyland*. 105.

80. Wood, C. V. Interviewed by Gregory Brown. Jun. 14, 1977.

81. "Disneyland Opens Gates to Thousands." *Los Angeles Times*. Jul. 19, 1955. 2.

CHAPTER EIGHT

1. "Disneyland Opens Gates to Thousands." 2.

2. Attendance figures taken from Disneyland, Inc., Ride Summary, 1955, presumably completed by Milt Albright.

3. Ettinger. *A Decade with Disneyland*.

4. Boettner. "Disney's 'Magical Little Park' After Two Decades." OC–C1.

5. Disney, Walt. Interview with Pete Martin. 1956.

6. Herubin, Danielle. "Walt Disney: 100 Years of Dreams Come True." *Orange County Register*. Dec. 2, 2001.

7. Combined source: Morgan, Ed. Interview conducted by Dana Morgan with questions from the author. Nov. 10, 2006; Reynolds. *Roller Coasters, Flumes and Flying Saucers*. 42–44, 48.

8. Martin, Bill. Interview with author. Jul. 19, 2006.

9. According to Jack Lindquist, Roy Disney once explained the origins of Tom Sawyer Island: "When we were kids, out on the Mississippi, there was a

little sandbar about thirty or forty yards offshore . . . we built a raft, we went over there, and then we'd get cardboard boxes, we'd get old pieces of wood. We built a fort on this little island. . . . When he grew up and had the opportunity, he just reproduced what we'd played on as kids."

10. Lindquist, Jack. Interview with Bob Thomas. Aug. 26, 1995.

11. Harpman, Fred. Interview with Chris Merritt.

12. Whitney, George, Jr. Disneyland, Inc., inter-office communication. "Proposed Modifications to Amusements and Rides." Aug. 3, 1955.

13. "Nixon Takes Time Out for Disneyland." *Los Angeles Times*. Aug. 12, 1955. 2.

14. "Carrier Boys" (photo and caption). *Los Angeles Times*. Oct. 11, 1955. A1.

15. Wong, Herman. "Can Disneyland Top 15 Years of Success?" *Los Angeles Times*. Jul. 12, 1970. B5.

16. Wood, C. V., III. Correspondence with author. Sept. 20, 2005.

17. Price. *Walt's Revolution!* 65.

18. Skillman, Paul. Interview with author. Jun. 21, 2007.

19. Minick, Bob. Interview with author. Oct. 26, 2007.

20. "Ron Dominguez . . . at home in Disneyland" (interview). *E-Ticket*. Fall 2005. 9.

21. Lewis, Quentin. Interview with author. Jun. 30, 2007.

22. Parsons, Marijess. Interview with author. Jun. 29, 2007.

23. "Bombers from Amarillo Patrol New Disneyland. *Amarillo Globe News*. Aug. 5, 1955. 1.

24. Wood, C. V. Interview with Gregory Brown. Jun. 14, 1977.

25. Price, Harrison "Buzz." Interview with author. Aug. 11, 2005.

26. Wood, C. V. Interview with Gregory Brown. Jun. 14, 1977.

27. Quoted in Thomas. *Building a Company*. 199.

28. France. *Window on Main Street*. 50.

29. Ibid.

30. Albright, Milt. Interview with Michael Mallory. In Ghez, Didier, ed. *Walt's People: Volume 12*. Xlibris, 2012.

31. Irvine, Richard. Interview with Bob Thomas. In Ghez. *Walt's People: Volume 10*.

32. Quoted in Thomas. *Building a Company*. 199.

33. Ibid.

34. Price, Buzz. Interview with author. Sept. 7, 2007.

35. Broggie, Michael. Interview with author. Apr. 20, 2008.

36. Porterfield, Anita. Interview with author. Jul. 2, 2007.

37. Walker, Cliff. Interview with author. Nov. 17, 2005.

38. Skillman, Paul. Interview with author by phone. Jun. 21, 2007.

39. Martin, Bill. Interview with author. Jul. 19, 2006.

40. Miller, Ron. Interview with author. Jan. 8, 2008.

41. Dominguez, Ron. Interview with author. Jul. 14, 2008.

42. "Wood Resigns at Disneyland." *Billboard*. Feb. 4, 1956. 71.

43. Sullivan, Bill "Sully." Interview with author. Nov. 7, 2007.

44. Disney, Walt. Interview with Pete Martin. 1956. Disneyland Exhibit, Walt Disney Family Museum.

45. Minutes of the meeting of the Disneyland Merchant's Association. Jan. 25, 1956. Posted by *Desert Sun*. http://voices.mydesert.com/wp-content/uploads/2013/12/2244_001.pdf.

46. Goldenson with Wolf. *Beating the Odds*. 124

47. France. *Window on Main Street*. 50.

48. France. *Backstage Magic*.

49. Smith, Dave. Correspondence with author. 2006.

50. Minutes of the meeting of the Disneyland Merchant's Association. Jan. 25, 1956.

51. "Wood Resigns at Disneyland." 71.

52. "Disneyland's Visitors Pass 2,000,000 Mark." *Los Angeles Times*. Jan. 29, 1956. D2.

53. France. *Window on Main Street*. 50.

54. "Disneyland Suit Asks Curbs on Ex-Manager." *Los Angeles Times*. May 18, 1960. 28.

55. France. *Window on Main Street*. 50.

Index